Marginal Writings in English

Bengali and Other Regional Literature

Marginal Writings in English

Bengali and Other Regional Literature

Jaydeep Sarangi
&
Champa Ghosal

AUTHORSPRESS

Worldwide Circulation through Authorspress Global Network
First Published 2013
by
Authorspress

Editorial
Q-2A Hauz Khas Enclave
New Delhi-110 016

Marketing
E-35/103, Jawahar Park
Laxmi Nagar, Delhi-110 092

e-mails: authorspress@rediffmail.com; authorspress@hotmail.com
Website: www.authorspressbooks.com

Marginal Writings in English:
Bengali and Other Regional Literature
ISBN 978-81-7273-717-7

Printed in India at Krishna Offset, Shahdara.

Dedicated to
All those voiceless creative souls....

Dedicated to

All those nameless [illegible]

Preface

'Dalits'—the word has different sets of meanings to the socially marginalized compared to what is popularly understood. It was popularised by the "Dalit Panther Movement" when they adopted this term as an act of confident assertion, rejecting Mahatma Gandhi's nomenclature—'Harijan', or children of God. *Dalit Panthers* defined this word in their 1972 manifesto as: "A member of Scheduled Castes and Tribes, neo-Buddhist, the working-people, the land-less and poor peasants, women, and all those who are being exploited politically, economically, and in the name of religion". Mahatma Jotirao Phule used the word 'Dalit' in connection with lower caste in a socially stratified society.

'Dalit' means oppressed or exploited on the basis of caste. It describes the people who have been traditionally considered untouchables and oppressed by the mainstream culture. *Chaturtha Duniya, Adhikar, Nikhil Bharat* and *Dalit Mirror* are the four leading magazines from West Bengal where the focus is on dalit aesthetics and dalit writings; these magazines are the platform for the rhetorics of resistance and the polyphony of voices from the marginal community *Dalit Mirror* is a literary endeavour of editorial board consisting of a group of dalit writers from Kolkata and Agartala. Manohar Mouli Biswas, the editor of *Dalit Mirror,* writes "FORGET NOT that the Dalit Literature are in their first generation writing." According to Manohar Mouli Biswas (2004), "Physical violence on dalits in West Bengal is definitely less than the states like Bihar, Tamil Nadu and Rajasthan because of the fact that they remain silent in case of their deprivation in employment, education etc. But day-to-day social oppression and harassment and exploitation of the dalits are still common in West Bengal like many other parts of rural India. In Bengali there is a very nice proverb to tell: *Bell pakley kaker kee.* It says that a crow cannot get at the food of a hard shell ripe apple. The dalits were marginal and remain marginal."

The Department of English, Jogesh Chandra Chaudhuri College (Kolkata) in collaboration with the Bangla Dalit Sahitya Sanstha, Kolkata organised a two day UGC-sponsored National Seminar on Writing as Resistance: Bengali and Other Dalit Writings in English on November 29 and 30, 2011. It was historical in many ways. The inaugural session kicked off with the inaugural song by the students of the Department of English followed by lighting the lamp and *Stotra path* and *Mantrocharana* by Dr. Sunanda Roy Chaudhury. Professor Sanjukta Dasgupta, the renowned poet-critic, and Dean, Faculty of Arts, Calcutta University, the Chief Guest of the seminar explained the so-called position of the marginal literature in Bengal. She read out two poems and the audience was overwhelmed by her verbose and expressive presentation. Dr. Prioyosh Khan,the Principal of the college, welcomed the participants and distinguished guests in his welcome address. He rightly pointed out the objective of the seminar. Mrs. Champa Ghosal, Head, English department, said, "Dalit writings have been neglected for long in academics. Our aim is to focus on dalit writing, which should be an integral part of literature in our state." She clearly expressed the objective of the seminar and the follow-up course. Dr Jaydeep Sarangi, a faculty member of the organizing committee, explains the theme of the seminar in an emphatic manner: "Sudying Dalit literature is a sociological engagement. Dalit literature in India is structurally alternative to models prescribed by traditional Hindu aesthetics precisely because it is the literature of sociological oppression and economic exploitation. Dalit literature is essentially a shock to the so-called traditional senses. It is an assault on the anthropomorphic practice of casteism in India. A sound piece of dalit literature is that which is militant in texture." He further stressed on the need to translation of Bangla (and Santali) dalit writings into English. Publication of translated texts in reputed journals and anthologies is a must, if we really look forward to an all-inclusive canon. Dr. Sarangi quoted the translated work by Professor Meenakshi Mukherjee on Manoranjan Byapari. He defined dalit literature as literature written by dalits who have the experience of dalit life (oppressed and subjugated under the hammer of caste startification). "Dalits have never got a platform to speak of their experiences or voice their anger," says Manohar Mouli Biswas, writer and editor of *Dalit Mirror*, a bi-monthly English magazine. The recent issue of "Dalit Mirror" was launched. Dr. Jaydeep Sarangi was asked to launch the same on the dais. Mr Amar Biswas, President, Dalit Sahitya Sanstha, Kolkata expressed that the seminar would help take dalit writings to more people. Professor Suhrid K. Bhowmik, the Resource Person on Santali language and literature, made a comparative analysis of Tagore's sons and Santali songs available. Harish Mangalam (Akademi- winning Gujarati writer) called the moment "historical". He further said, "In Gujarat, not less than hundred writers have started the dalit literature movement by writing in various forms of literature, likewise, poetry, short story, novel, essay and portray etc. We have formed the organization *Guarati Dalit Sahitya Academy* and started its magazine named *'Hayati'* And since the last 15 years have been publishing regularly. We also publish books of dalit literature. And till today 55 books have been published of dalit literature, i.e., in English, Hindi, Gujarati, etc."

Twenty-seven distinguished scholars from different parts of the country read out their works and the sincere audience took part in lively discussions. Professor Bajrang Korde (Professor of English, University of Pune, Pune) delivered the keynote address which was enthusiatically received by the learned audience. In his address he said, "Literature of resistance or dalit literature comes under internationally-recognized literary/social category called subaltern studies. One of the notable characteristics of the subaltern studies is that the roots of these studies are in the lives of those social groups/individuals who are covered by a specific subaltern study. In short, dalit literature is a child of a peculiar Indian social system. And therefore, for proper understanding of the writings related to Indian subaltern groups such as dalits, women and tribals, some knowledge of the lives of these subaltern groups is necessary." Dr M.B. Gaijan, the noted Gujarati dalit critic, elaborately analysed the subject through his paper, "Gujarati Dalit Poetry in twenty-first Century". He further said, Gujarati dalits have the vast oral literary treasure as a heritage. From the early eleventh century till today it was enriched by the known and unknown dalit literary genius which remained the great source for dalits to survive in all adversities. Earlier it was in a poetic form, In folk literature, it was in the form of folksongs/tales and spiritual songs. Still it exists in Gujarat".

Ms. Brati Biswas's paper entitled 'Silence to Speech: Reading Bangla Dalit Literary Expression as Resistance' was extremely thought-provoking. Dr Arpita Chattaraj (Mukhopadhyay) of Presidency University read out a brilliant paper packed with rare information on the subject entitled, "Dalit Life Narratives: From Silence to Articulation". Dr. Sayantan Dasgupta of Jadavpur University critically explored isues related to Bangla dalit writings with special reference to Provas Ray, Manoranjan Bapari and Manohar Mouli Biswas in his research article, "Writing Resistance, Righting Repression: A Reading of Three Stories by Provas Ray, Manoranjan Bapari and Manohar Mouli Biswas".

Dr. Dipesh Lahiri, senior eminent scholar, chaired the final session of the first day of the session. He briefed the papers elegantly. There were two papers on Mahasweta Devi's works. Other important speeches include Dr. Amrit Sen's "Translating Dalit Literature: Texts and Problems" and Mousumi Sen

Bhattacharya's "Poetry and Resistance: The Literature of Manipur." Dr. Sen read out Mrs. Sen's paper in absentia. The paper explored the metaphors and strategies of resistance in the poetry of Rajkumar Bhubansana, Robin S. Ngangom, Yumlembam Iboucha, Saratchand Thiyam and Gambhini Devi to interrogate how the sense of Manipuri identity is expressed through poetry. In doing so, this paper will explore how social and economic exploitation as themes in dalit literature may be welded with the question of political identity. Dr. Shipra Mukherjee, Associate Professor of English and Head, West Bengal State University, Barasat said it was time dalit writings found space in grand narratives. "Civic society can't move forward if the marginalized sections are ignored,"she added. She explained the position of Bangla dalit literature in the existent canon explicitly and clarified many misconceptions regarding dalit corpus in Bengal when she chaired the last session: Bangla Dalit Writings. Mr. Manohar Mouli Biswas, Secretary, Bangla Dalit Sahitya Sanstha, had a very emphatic paper, "Writing as Resistance: Bengali Dalit Literature and Culture." He claimed, "Aesthetics of resistivity disowns the triadic of *Satyam-Shivam-Sundaram*—replaced by 'reality' and 'beauty'—a binomial aesthetic.— Beauty of 'nothing' or 'zero'—everything to understand—to the people outside the domain as well as within the domain. —A 'zero' shares the half of an integer—as found in computer philosophy. —They who grow fodder food—now with pen in hand—write on themselves—identity is glorified—inner strength is magnified—literature and culture to the enrooting in new soil."

Parimal (Marshal) Hembram, Kalyani Thakur Charal, Jatin Bala, Manju Bala and Sukanta Mandal read out (along with translation) two poems each in the poetry reading session. Leading Bengali dalit writers were Manoranjan Bapari, Lakhi Mandal, Dhurjoti Naskar, Sunil Kr. Das, Lily Haldar, Shritikana Hawladar, S. Pramanick, Nakul Mallick, Debasish Mandal and Prasad Mandal. Adivasi writer Pashupati Prasad Mahato was also present and contributed to the seminar to a great extent.

The collaborator of the seminar, Bangla Dalit Sahitya Sanstha, is an organisation of movement of dalit literature and culture of Bengal. People who believe in cultural and literary identity of dalits as one different from the mainstream are generally associated with this apolitical organization having been working throughout West Bengal for the last one and a half decade. There was a wonderful atmosphere during the final session of the seminar and at no stage did the discussions and poetry reading give rise to boredom. Prof. Champa Ghosal, Head of the English Department, briefed the recommendations from the seminar and she thanked everyone, who helped the organizers to host the same, in a very significant manner during her valedictory address. Students' volunteers worked like skilled professionals. Ms. Suchetana Roy, the convener of students' volunteers, marshalled her troop with authority. Ankit, Saptarshi, Swagata and other students' volunteeers worked day and night to make the seminar a grand success. Colleagues of various departments, all learned partiocipants, and the college administration deserve credit for this intellectual extravaganza! We also put on record the contribution of our ex-students and students' union of the college for the grand success of the seminar. We are grateful to University Grants Commission for their support. Last but not least, we express our 'thanks' to Sudarshan Kcherry for this elegant publication of the seminar volume. The seminar humbly attempted to provide a much deserved platform to this rich symphony of egalitarianism.

March 2012 **Jaydeep Sarangi & Champa Ghosal**

Contributors

Abhinandan Malas. Substitute Lecturer (UGC XIth Plan, FDP), Department of English at Ramananda College, Bishnupur, Bankura, West Bengal, India. *abhinandan_4712@rediffmail.com*

Abin Chakraborty. Currently working as a Senior Research Fellow at the Department of English, University of Calcutta. Also, Teaching as a Guest Lecturer at Presidency University, Department of English. BC 24/6 Saltlake, Kolkata-700064. *abin_chakraborty@yahoo.co.in*

Amrit Sen. Department of English & OMEL, Visva-Bharati, Santiniketan, Birbhum, West Bengal. *amritsen@gmail.com*

Anirban Guha Thakurta. Assistant Professor, Serampore College *guhathakurta2008@gmail.com*

Arpita Chattaraj (Mukhopadhyay). Assistant Professor of English. Presidency University, College Street Kolkata-700073. *chattarajarpitac@rediffmail.com*

Baisali Hui. Department of English, University of Kalyani, Kalyani-741235, Nadia (Dist.), W.B.:*baisalihui@gmail.com*

Bajrang S. Korde. Professor of English, University of Pune, Pune, MS. *korde@unipune.ac.in*

Bisweswar Chakraborty. Assistant Professor, English, Jhargram Raj College Jhargram-721507, Paschim Medinipur. *parijat2007@rediffmail.com*

Debasri Basu. Department of English, Jhargram Raj College (Govt.), Jhagram, Paschim Medinipur. *diibii@gmail.com*

Gouri Das. Assistant Professor in English, Department of Applied Sciences & Humanities, Haldia Institute of Technology, Haldia, Purba Medinipur, West Bengal. *gourienglish@gmail.com*

Harish Mangalam, Additional Collector (Rtd.), 7 Durgakrupa Society, Nr. Kirtidham Tirth, Chandkheda, Ahmedabad-382424. He is a noted Gujarati writer.

Jaydeep Sarangi. Department of English, Jogesh Chandra Chaudhuri College, Kolkata: 700033, West Bengal. *jaydeepsarangi@gmail.com*

Joyjit Ghosh. Department of English, Vidyasagar University, Medinipur-721102. West Bengal. *pathu_ghosh@yahoo.co.in*

M.B. Gaijan, Head, Department of English, Samaldas Arts College, Bhavnagar University, Bhavnagar, Fessor 364002, Gujarat. *gaijanmb@yahoo.co.in*

Manohar Biswas. Secretary, Dalit Sahitya Sanstha. 651 V.I.P Nagar. Gouranga Palli. Kolkata-700100. *manoharbiswas@yahoo.co.in*

Mausumi Sen Bhattacharjee. Assistant Professor of English, Bolpur College, Bolepur- 731204, Birbhum, W.B. *mausumisen@gmail.com*

Meenakshi Dey, Assistant Professor (English), School of Applied Sciences and Humanities. Haldia Institute of Technology, ICARE Complex, P.O. HIT Campus, Hatiberia, Midnapore East. West Bengal- 721657.*mdey99@gmail.com*

Oindrila Ghosh. Assistant Professor, Head, Department of English, Naba Ballygunge Mahavidyalaya, Kolkata. *oindrila_24@yahoo.com*

Sarottama Majumdar. HOD, Assisstant Professor Department of English, Sarsuna College, Kolkata-700061. West Bengal *sarottama@yahoo.com*

Sayantan Dasgupta, Assistant Professor, Comparative Literature, Jadavpur University. *dasgupta.sayantan@gmail.com*

Sibasis Jana. Assistant Professor in English, Department of B.Ed, Panskura Banamali College. Panskura, Purba Medinipur-721152. *sibasis.om@gmail.com*

Sipra Mukherjee.: Associate Professor and Head, Department of English, West Bengal State University, Barasat, fessor, 700126, 24 Parganas (North). *mukherjeesipra@gmail.com*

Soumitra Chakraborty, Assistant Professor in English, Department of Humanities, Mallabhum Institute of Technology, Bishnupur, Bankura, West Bengal. *soumitra.chk@gmail.com*

Sravasti Guha Thakurta. Department of English, Jogesh Chandra Chaudhuri College, Kolkata. *sravasti.guha@gmail.com*

Srideep Mukherjee, Assistant Professor in English, School of Humanities & Social Sciences, Netaji Subhas Open University, *srideep.nsoueng@gmail.com*

Contents

1

Keynote Address on Literature of Resistance or Dalit Literature

Bajrang Korde

Literature of resistance or dalit literature comes under internationally-recognized literary / social category called subaltern studies. One of the notable characteristics of the subaltern studies is that the roots of these studies are in the lives of those social groups / individuals who are covered by a specific subaltern study. In short, dalit literature is a child of a peculiar Indian social system. And therefore, for proper understanding of the writings related to Indian subaltern groups such as dalits, women and tribals, some knowledge of the lives of these subaltern groups is necessary.

As we all know, some of the major features of Hindu social system were phenomena like *Varna* and caste systems. *Varna*, in one sense, means a category. Hindu society was divided into four *Varnas* such as brahmin, kshatriya, vaishya and shudra. Those who were beneficiaries of *Varna* system put forward a theory about the creation of *Varnas*. As a part of propagating this theory, they said that the *Varnas* came from different parts of Brahma's body. Brahma is supposed by the religious-minded Hindus as God- the-Creator. So, it was further said that brahmins came from the head (upper) part of Brahma's body, kshatriyas came from his shoulders, vaishyas from stomach and shudras from legs. Because the head is the upper part of the body of a being whose physique/

anatomy is like a human being and because the head has the human brain, which controls the body, people born in brahmin *Varna*, who were supposed to have been originated from the upper part of Brahma's body, were treated as superior to all other *Varnas* since rest of the three *Varnas*, it was said, were created from the lower parts of Brahma's body compared to the part out of which brahmins were said to have been created.

In this whole hierarchy, the shudras – out of which fold the present-day dalits came – were given the lowest status / value since. It was said that, they were created from the lowest part (i.e., legs) of Brahma's body. By using this so-called logic and justification for the creation and existence of the dalits, the upper castes like brahmins gave the dalits the lowest possible position on the rung of the social-status ladder in Hindu social structure. Further, due to their so-called lower status, they were exploited at various levels. In the pre-independence Hindu system, the dalits were given almost an animal-status. Resultantly, their life ultimately turned out to be a really horrible life.

It is said that the caste system was born was out of the *Varna* system and one of the most exploitative, unbearable, and torturous aspccts of Hindu social system for dalits was untouchability. Further, it was a matter of great shock and surprise that the system of untouchability was supported and justified by some Hindu "religious" scriptures such as *Manusmriti*. In regard to caste system, at one point, Dr. Babasaheb Ambedkar said:

> .... The problem of untouchability is really a class-struggle between caste Hindus and untouchables and this seems to be a never-ending conflict.

Greatly offended at the unbearably and indescribably adverse effects of untouchability on the lives of the dalits for thousands of years, Dr. Ambedkar said:

> Nowhere in the history of mankind can one notice inequality which is more intense and pernicious than the practice of untouchability.

And hence:

> Untouchability was such an abominable stain that it would not matter even if some lives were sacrified to wash it out.

One of the historical periods during which Maharashtrian dalits were tortured to the utmost degree on the basis of the notion of untouchability was the period of the Peshwas, the brahmin rulers, who operated from Shaniwarwada of Pune in Maharashtra. About this totally oppressive period for the dalits, Dr. Ambedkar stated:

> Under the rule of the Peshwas, in the Maratha country, the untouchable was not allowed to use the public streets if an upper-caste Hindu was coming along lest he should pollute the upper caste Hindu by his shadow. The untouchable was required to have a black thread either on his wrist or in his neck as a sign or mark to prevent the upper caste Hindus from getting themselves polluted by his touch through his mistake. In Poona, the capital of the Peshwas, the untouchable was required to carry strung from his waist a broom to sweep away from behind the dust he treaded on lest a Hindu walking on the same should be polluted. In Poona, the untouchable was required to carry an earthen pot, hung in his neck wherever he went, for holding his spit lest his spit falling on the earth should pollute a Hindu who might unknowingly happen to go that way.

It has been pointed out that Kautilya's *Arthashastra* also suggests that the disadvantaged be kept disadvantaged. In his *Arthashatra*, at one point, he is reported to be suggesting to the upper caste Hindus that

> ... the untouchables should not be allowed to inhabit a certain place for a long time. In case they stay for a long time at one place, they should be immediately driven away.

The necessity to write a literature like dalit literature arises because, we have seen that very few writers from the so-called upper castes have written about the miserable plight / lot of the dalits. Not only did the upper caste writers neglect the dalits, but some of the writers who originally hailed from lower castes were also so much haunted and mentally-conditioned by the *varna* system that they also toed the line of the upper caste writers, i.e., the line of not taking cognizance of the lower classes and their pains and pangs and the line of recording the lives and affairs only of higher classes and highly-placed individuals like kings, queens, princes, princesses, army generals and so on and so forth. This is precisely what Daya Pawar, a Marathi poet, states while he assesses Valmiki's literary contribution made by him through his writing of the epic *Ramayana*.

> Oh! Valmiki.
> Should you sing the praises of Ramrajaya
> Because you're the poet of poets?
>
> ---
>
> You were born outside the village
> In a shunned neighbourhood — where misery itself was born,
> never festooned with fruit or flower ...
> The dejected faces ... furrowed with care ...
> Is it true never heard
> their lament as they cried for liberation?
> One Shambuk of your own blood
> Caught fire, rose in anger.
> Oh Great poet,
> Singing the praises of Ramarajya,
> even there the icy cliff of inhumanity towered up
> Oh great poet,
> How then should we call you a great poet?
> Had you written just one single verse
> Exposing this injustice, this outrage –
> then would your name have been carved on our hearts.
>
> (Mulk Raj Anand & Eleanor Zelliot 132)

And the so-called mainstream also upheld texts like *Ramayana* because it upheld the superiority of the higher classes. By implication, this means that the texts which did not fall into the line of the so-called mainstream writing were swept under the carpet.

Of course, some sensitive people tried to record the lives of and issues related to the downtrodden. In this connection, works such as Gautam Buddha's *Jataks Kathas,* his philosophical tracts, Mahanubhava's *Leelacharitra*, Kabir's Dohas, S.M. Mate's *Upekshitanche Antarang*, a Marathi text first published in 1941, Mahatma Phuley's writings, can be cited.

At social level, brahminism and its so-called philosophical/religious documentary foundation entitled *Manusmriti* were playing havoc with the lives of the dalits – suppressing, oppressing, subjugating them in all possible ways and thereby making life so intolerably difficult for them that they felt death was the only liberation from the tortures they were made to experience.

Of course, intermittently, voices were raised against this kind of oppressive system and they advocated a fundamental change in this exploitative system. Some of these social reformers who raised their voices were against this kind of oppressive system were: Gautams Buddha, Charvaka, Kabir, Varakaris, Mahanubhavas, Sant Basaveshwara, Mahatma Phuley, Narasi Mehta, Rajarshi Shahu, Chaitanya Prabhu, Mahatma Gandhi, Dr. Babasaheb Ambedkar, Ramaswami Periyar Naikar, Vitthal Ramaji Shinde and others.

It is this practice of subjugating the dalits to inhuman tortures which made Dr. Ambedkar feel that he had no motherland – a land that takes care of him like a mother does of her child. This was the feeling which he expressed during one of his dialogues with Mahatma Gandhi in Yerawada prison in Pune during Mahatma Gandhi's historic fast against Dr. Ambedkar's demand for separate constituencies for dalits.

This notion expressed by Dr. Ambedkar is shared by almost all the dalits, and hence a poet like Baburao Bagul in his poem "You who have made the mistake" states that dalits have made a mistake by taking birth in this country:

Those who leave for foreign lands,
Embrace other tongues, dress in alien garb
— them I salute.
And those who don't forget,
And don't change even after being beaten up for centuries
— such hypocrites I ask:

What's an untouchable like? What does he look like?
Does he look like the very image of leprosy?
Or like a heretic, a sinner, a profligate, or an atheist?
Tell me,
What will your answer be?
Will you reply without hesitation:
'Untouchable – that's me?'
That's why I say —
You who have made the mistake of being born in this country
must now rectify it: either leave the country,
Or make war!

I feel the extreme pole of this notion is reached in Tryambak Sapakale's poem entitled "Then what shall I do?" from his collection of poems titeld *Surung* (Dynamite) wherein he says:

Oh mother India! When did you
Shower affection on me?
Hence, in the passage of time
Instead of being a Karna
If I enter your bed by being an Oedipus
How can you blame me?

In another poem of his entitled "I will be neutral", Sapakale says:

You wanted to be a Kunti
Should I necessarily be a Karna?
You never had affinity for me
You never fed me from your breast
Still how can you have
The claim of motherhood on me?

The tortures of the dalits, based on *Manusmriti*, at least officially on paper came to an end on 26 January 1950 when the Indians adopted the Constitution chiefly drafted by Dr. Babasaheb Ambedkar. Some people feel that Indian Constitution replaced *Manusmriti* and hence they call Dr. Ambedkar the 'Modern Manu'. But I think it would be an insult to Dr. Ambedkar to connect him to Manu in any way, in any form, in any context because, in a way, Dr. Ambedkar spent almost whole of his lifetime fighting against Manu's hangover spread over this country. As we all know by now, dalit literature, as we know it today, first came out in the late 60s and early 70s, and the main inspiration behind it was Dr. Ambedkar's philosophy and social, cultural, political activities for the liberation of the dalits which he began from 1924 onwards. Dr. Ambedkar's philosophy and activities include the phiolosophies and activities of social reformers such as Bhagavan Gautama Buddha, Sant Kabir and Mahatma Phuley.

> It will have to be noted that, of all the Indian languages, it was in Marathi that Dalit literature was written first. So, Dalit literature in Marathi initially functioned as some sort of a lighthouse for Dalit writers in other Indian languages.

Dalit writers have handled a number of literary genres such as poetry, autonaratives, short story, dramas, novels, philosophical, critical, theoretical writings etc. to project their experiences, sensibility etc. Of all these genres, the most prominent one is poetry. Some of the major writers in various Indian languages are as follows:

A . Dalit Literature in Marahti

1. Poetry

a) Major Poets

Pandit Kondiram (Mahatma Phuley's contemporary), Kisan Fagu Bandsode (18. 02. 1879 – 12. 10. 1946), Kerubaba Gaikwad, Poet Dinbandhu, Narayan Gangaram Surve, Namdeo Dhasal, Keshav Meshram, Waman Nimbalkar, daya pawar, Tryambak

Sapakale, Pralhad Chendavankar, Ja. Vi. Pawar, Arjun Dangle, Yashwant Manohar, Raja Dhale, Madhav Kondavilkar, B. Rangrao, Prakash Jadhav, Damodar More, Ram Dotonde, Baban Chahande, Bhimsen Dethe, Shiva Ingole, Yuvaraj Sonatakke, Uttam Ambhore, Mangesh Bandsod, Keshav Ba. Vasekar, Chokha Kamble, Nareshkumar Ingale, Sukhram Hivarale, Umakant Randhir, Arun Kamble, Neelkant Chavan, Ramakant Jadhav, Dharmaraj Nimsarkar, W. Kapoor, Bhai Panchabhai, E. Mo. Naaranaware, Kaa. Raa. Waladekar, Dhanraj Dahat, Damodar More, Amitabh,

b) Folk Poets

Dalit folk poets also contributed quite notably to the process of creating awareness among the downtrodden masses. Some of the prominent names of dalit folk poets are: Bhimrao Kardak, Shahir Ghegade, Wamandada Kardak, Devanand Gadapayale, Vitthal Umap, Sambhaji Bhagat.

B. Autonarratives

After poetry, the other most notable and most effective genre which dalit writes handled is autonarratives. Some of the representative practitioners of this genre are: Pra. Ee. Sonakamble, Madhav Kondwilkar, Daya Pawar, Shankarrao Kharat, Laxman Mane, Laxman Gaikwad, Uttam Bandu Tupe, Dr. Narendra Jadhav, Sharankumar Limbale, Kishor Shantabai Kale, Partha Polake, Rustum Achalkhamb, Dadasaheb More, Bhimrao Gasti, K. O. Girhe, Gulab Waghmode.

C. Dramas

Dalit writers have also handled drama as a form of literature. Some of the prominent dalit dramatists are: Kisan Fagoji Bansode, Ma. Bhi. Chitnis, Gangardhar Panatawane, Datta Bhagat, Bhi. Shi. Shinde, Ramnath Chavan.

D. Novels and Short Stories

Some of the dalit writers who contributed in these genres are: Anna Bhau Sathe, Baburao Bagul, Shankarrao Kharat, Naa. Raa.Shende et al.

E. Women Writers

Quite a few dalit women have have contributed to the corpus of dalit literature in their own ways. Some of the most prominent ones are: Baby Kamble, Shantabai Kamble, Kumud Pawade, Shantabai Dani, Mukta Sarvagaod, Urmila Pawar, Janabai Girhe, Jyoti Lanjewar, Hira Bansode, Cicilia Carvalo, Sugandha Shende, Leela Patil, Asha Thorat, Surekha Bhagat, Pradnya Lokhande, Nirmala Londhe, Pratibha Ahire, Maya Vasanik, Usha Hingonekar, Jyotsana Chandgude, Sandhya Rangari, Nilambari Shirke, Dhammajyoti Kamble, Usha Ambhore, Meena Gajabhiye.

Bama is a very well-known dalit woman writer who writes in Tamil.

Dalit Literature: Some Salient Features

A reading of some of the major literary texts of dalit literature shows that some of the notable features of dalit literature are:

1. Representative expression of a vast number of people from dalit community about whom the writer writes.
2. Expression of anger about, irritation towards and challenge to the oppressive system.
3. Occasional helplessness.
4. Hope / zeal for conquest, optimism.
5. Protest against /resistance to exploitative social, cultural, religious order created and implemented within the framework of *Varna* and caste systems in India.
6. Scientific temperament.
7. Universality, advocacy of human rights.

Gujarati Dalit Writers

Chandubhai Ramajibhai Mehariya, Pravin Gadhavi, Mangal Rathod, Pathik Parmar, Dalpat Chavan, Sahil Parmar, Shankar Painter, Neerav Patel, Nilesh Kathad, Yoseph Macwan, Harish Mangalam, Jayant Parmar, Mohammed Ishaq Sheikh, Narsingh Ujamba, Yashwant Waghela.

Other notable writers, journalists, editors, publishers from Gujarati who handled different genres and contributed to the furtherance of dalit writings in Gujarati are: Joseph Macwan, Jethalal Jadhav, Bhanubhai Adhvaryu, Raju Solanki, Anup Singh, Kisan Sosa, Mohan Parmar, Hiralal Parmar, Walajibhai Patel, Rameshchandra Parmar, Laxmanbhai Chauvan, Narendra Nakum, Anil Vaghela, Sidhdaraj Solanki, Bhin Vankar, Shankar Bhu Patel, Anup Singh, Naikal Gangera, Bipin Gohil, Madhukant Kapil (Madhukant Vaghela), Raghavji Madhad, Dasarath Parmar.

Kannada Dalit Writers

Prominent Kannada dalit writers are: Chennanna Walikar, Siddalingaiah, Dr. Buddanna Hingamire, Chandrashekhar Patil, Devanooru Mahadeva.

Other notable dalit writers or writers with dalit sensibility in Kannada are: Dr. Somashekhar Imrapur, Baraguru Ramchandrappa, Gangadhar Mudaliyar, Givindayya, Indudhar Honnapur, Saraju Katkar, Bal Raju, Ramjan Darga, Tejaswi Kattimani, V. T. Rajashekhar Shetty, Siddhaling Desai, Jagadish Mangalurmath, Allamprabhu Betadur, Vijay Patil, Vijay Mangalur, Harave et al.

Hindi Dalit Writers

Historically speaking, some scholars opine that dalit writings in Hindi started from the times of saints like Kabir and Ravidas (or Raidas). Some people feel that modern dalit writings in Hindi can be said to have started from Swami Acchutanand who was born on 8 May 1879. Acchutanand's foresightedness is evident from the fact that he had harshly criticized *Manusmriti* through his poem entitled "Burning due to *Manusmriti*" written in 1925 whereas Dr. Ambedkar burnt it down on 25 December 1927.

Some of the prominent dalit writers in Hindi are: Hira Dome, Mohandas Naimisharay, Dr. Kusum Viyogi, Omprakash Valmiki, Satyaprakash, Ratnakum Sambhariya, Bipin Bihar, Dr. Dharmaveer, Mataprasad, Rajpalsingh 'Raj', D. R. Jaatav, Jayprakash Kardam, Surajpal Chauhan, Tejpalsingh 'Tej', Ajay Yatish, Daal Chand Gautam, Prabhakar Gajabhiye, Shatrughna Kumar, Prem Kapadia, Sushil Takabhare, Rameshchandra Jalauniya, Karmasheel Bharati, Laxminarayan Sudhakar, Dr. Purushottam 'Satyapremi', Mansaram 'Vidrohi', Dr. Shyauraj Singh, 'Bechain', Vijay Chakravarti, Devendra Pathak et al.

Telugu Dalit Writers

Some of the notable Telugu dalit writers are: Yendluri Sudhakar, Satish Chander, Madhuri Nagesh Babu, Pydi Teresbabu, Vemula Ellaiah, Venkat, Khaza, Joolur Gowri Sankar, Durga Prasad, Khader Mohiyuddin, Prasada Murthy, Sky Baba, Kalekuri Prasad, Kopra, Sikhamani, G. V. Ratnakar, Challapalli Swaroopa Rani, Vinodini, Darise Sasi Nirmala, Vijayasree, Vijaya Lakshmi, Denchanala Sreenivas.

Telugu dalit poetry written by Joshua and his successors like Jala Rangakavi, Nakka Chinavenkaiah, Nuthakki Abraham, Johnson, Kusuma Dharmanna was mostly Gandhian in its tenor.

The issue of who can write dalit literature is generally discussed when people talk about dalit literature. I feel a couple of definitions of dalit literature would be helpful in throwing some light on the issue. Keshav Meshram defines dalit literature as follows:

> We should call those untouchables Dalits who were subjected to injustice for thousands of years. And we should call Dalit literature to that literature which is created by the writers from the erstwhile untouchable class.
>
> (*Prabuddha Bharat*, 04/03/1958).

As is clear from the above-mentioned text, this definition seems to be assuming that dalit literature can be and should be written only by those who come from the erstwhile untouchable class.

Then the question is: Can't a non-dalit write literature about dalits? In this regard, one can mention a definition of Dalit literature by a dalit leader-thinker-writer, namely, Raja Dhale from Maharashtra who states as below:

> Whoever will create literature by adopting a stance of opposition to cultural conspiracy and oppressive social system and whoever will try to bring on the right track a misguided society could be called a practitioner of Dalit literature.
>
> (*Jaatak*, 01/03/1977)

As can be seen, the definition by Raja Dhale does not emphasize on the caste / class of the writer who writes dalit literature. Raja Dhale's definition requires only the progressive mindset of the writer.

In this regard, there is one more trend which opines that an upper caste person can also write dalit literature if he develops a genuine anger against the oppressions to which the dalits were subjected by his ancestors. In other words, if a non-dalit genuinely rebels against his historical past,then he should be able to write dalit literature.

Moreover, it can be seen that a number of progressive-minded non-dalits have greatly contributed to the movements aimed at the upliftment of the downtrodden. Some of such well-meaning non-dalits are people like Gautama Buddha, Kabir, Mahatma Phuley, Rajarshi Shahu Maharaj, Ramaswami Periyar Naikar, Vi. Raa.Shinde, Chaitanya Prabhu and the like.

Although the above-mentioned great souls were not hard-core dalits, they very sincerely did their best to ameliorate the miserable conditions of the dalits, and people like Dr. Babasaheb Ambedkar have also acknowledged the social debt of the three among them by calling them his gurus in social work. They are Gautama Buddha, Kabir and Mahatma Phuley. So, if the above-mentioned non-dalit social reformers were totally genuine in their efforts to uplift the dalits and if, therefore, they are accepted as a part of dalit movement, then, can't we accept non-dalit writers as a part of dalit literature if they genuinely rebel against their historical past, and if they write honestly, genuinely, committedly and authentically about dalit life? Of course, I leave it open for all to discuss it further.

Aesthetics of Dalit Literature

One of the frequently-mentioned issues in relation to dalit literature is the issue of aesthetics of dalit literature. There is need for an independent aesthetics of dalit literature because dalit literature cannot properly be evaluated within the framework of traditional aesthetics, i.e., the aesthetics of the so-called mainstream literature. Doing this is necessary because the traditional aesthetics is hugely influenced by brahminical-feudal-paternal phenomena, and the Western aesthetics is influenced by imperial-colonial-postmodern phenomena. Both these streams of aesthetics are unsuitable for the appropriate understanding of dalit literature. Hence, for the proper evaluation of a literature like dalit literature, we have to reject the hegemony of the so-called mainstream aesthetics and develop an alternative aesthetics of resistance/protest which, in other words, would be developing new aesthetics for humanity as a whole because the so-called mainstream aesthetics is the aesthetics of the elites who are few in number in any of part of the world. The new aesthetics will be born out of an understanding of the excruciating nature of pain, and out of a conflict that will occur for changing for the better.

Traditional Indian aesthetics evaluated both the arts as well as literature. Some of the key concepts in the traditional Indian aesthetics are *alankar, reeti, dhvani, vakrokti, rasa* etc. A number of Indian aesthetes from Bharat (in 1st B. C.) to Jagannath Pandit (in 17th century) contributed to the development of Indian aesthetics. A consolidated list of some of the major names of these contributors is as below: Bharat, Bhamah, Dandi, Ubhdat, Vaman, Rudrata, Anandvardhan, Rajashekhar, Kuntak, Bhoj, Abhinavgupta, Kshemendra, Mammat, Ruyyak, Hemachandra, Jaydev, Vagbhat, Vishwanath, Roopgoswami, Appaya Dixit and Jagannath Pandit.

All these aesthetes accepted the authority of the *Vedas*. That is, since Indian aesthetics is fundamentally based on vedic tradition, it does not recognize the aesthetics of Bauddha and Jain religions as well as of *Darshanas*. Indian aesthetics evaluates literary and artistic creations through the points of view inherent in the so-called classical Indian tradition and in Sanskrit language and literature. That is, the general Indian writers', scholars', critics' literary and critical sensibilities end near the border of Sanskrit; they don't go beyond that. And, now, with our realization that Sanskrit is not the be-all and end-all of everything and that a number of vistas of knowledge lie beyond Sanskrit also, we can say that the parochialism and hegemony of Sanskrit point of view-perception cannot be upheld or justified in the present context as the only dominant / appropriate discourse / perception.

Brahminical aesthetics was based on the slavery of *varna*-caste-women as well as on the hegemony of Sanskrit literature and criticism whereas the present Marathi aesthetics is a combination of brahmincal aesthetics and Western aesthetics, and I think that what is applicable to Marathi aesthetics is more or less applicable to the aesthetics of most of the Indian languages. Both these streams of aesthetics, i.e., brahminical and Marathi – almost totally neglect dalit sensibility from their domain / jurisdiction / purview. This means that vedic system deleted from its consciousness social groups such as shudras, women and tribals. The horizon of Vedic system did not reach these social groups. In other words, whatever kind of world the Vedic system structured, that world almost completely denied and, at times, opposed a major social, cultural, religious tradition like Buddhism which encompassed shudras, women and tribals, and by doing so, the Vedic system snapped all possibilities of a mass-dialogue. Hence, the Vedic structure of the world turns out to be parochial, partial and biased. Moreover, the Vedic / Sanskrit authority opines that the man-made world does not exist at all which means that whatever exists in this world is God-made (made by God) only. But on the other hand, they create a whole philosophy of human existence, knowledge, thought-processes, ethics, beauty etc which are related to human action. This is the contradiction in the Vedic structure of the world.

Exactly contrary to the Vedic view of the world, dalit as well as progressive-minded writers, thinkers believe that man himself is the real creator of the human world. In this regard, a non-dalit, but progressive-minded Marathi poet, Keshavsoot writes:

> Let it be known
> to the people that
> deities and devils
> are of man's making only.

A dalit writer, namely, Baburao Bagul says:

> Oh man, you called a planet
> the sun and that planet
> became the sun.
> You called a planet
> the moon and that planet
> became the moon.

Another dalit, Marxist, a progressive-minded Marathi writer, namely, Anna Bhau Sathe says:

> This earth does not rest on the hood of the mythological snake namely shesha, but it rests on the palms of dalits and toilers.

In short, the basics of Vedic / Sanskrit / brahminical consciousness and that of the dalit consciousness are poles apart. If this is the reality, then how can brahminical aesthetics appropriately evaluate the literature written out of dalit consciousness? This is almost an impossible feat because their points of inspiration/are almost diametrically opposed to each other.

Aesthetics of dalit literature will be a new horizon encompassing new compositions, new challenges, new appeals, new sensibilities, new changes, liberation of the exploited and the exploiters. It will be a critical discipline aimed at creating exploitation-free, equality-oriented, humanitarian literary / critical environment. It will also be an attempt in the direction of understanding and experiencing real life and happiness. It will try to remove the blot on aesthetics as a weapon to be used against somebody. It would be an experience of guilt-free, pure aesthetic pleasure. It would also be breaking taboos imposed on people by the traditional aesthetics. With such favourable developments in the fields of literature, arts and criticism, we can expect that the undue influence and dominance of brahminical aesthetics will wither away due to the humanitarian dalit aesthetics. In this connection, Sharad Patil opines: "Brahminical aesthetics is not true aesthetics. Brahminical criticism could create only theory of literature and not aesthetics of literature". In addition to all other related points stated before, dalit aesthetes will also have to give a serious thought to the opinions of people like Sharad Patil while formulating dalit aesthetics.

Present Condition of the Dalits

As has been stated before, a literature like dalit literature is a product of specific social situations and movements. Therefore, for knowing the present condition of dalit literature, it would be necessary to know the present condition of social situations and movements of the dalits. One of the most disadvantageous things for the future progress of the dalits is that the castes and sub-castes which are covered by that umbrella term "dalit", unfortunately, are not always united. Some of them are seen to be joining hands with those social and/or political groups whom they called casteists and fundamentalists till recently. If this is the actual scenario, the question is: how convincingly can the present-day as well as future dalit writers write about the injustices done to them? I have myself been thinking on these issues for some time now and I put forth these issues for your consideration also.

Future of Dalit Literature

As we know, the roots of dalit literature are in the discrimination against and exploitation, marginalization of dalits inherent in Indian caste and *varna* systems. Hence, so long as dalits are overtly or covertly exploited, humiliated, discriminated against, sometimes physically assaulted and even killed on the basis of their caste, a literature like dalit literature will be continued to be written. In our country, we still experience periodical massacres of dalits as we saw them in recent past in Jazzar in Haryana or in Khairalanji in Maharashtra. Some people have erected Manu's statue in front of the Rajasthan High Court. In hushed up tones some people seem not to be respecting the Constitution of India in the spirit in which they should be doing it. Sometime back, some people talked of reviewing / revising / reformulating / restructuring Indian Constitution. They don't talk of amending; it has been amended many times; no one can have an objection to amendment. But they want to revise / reformulate it. And as we all know, the Indian Constitution is the only ultimate safeguard of the rights of the dalits which were snatched away from them by Manu and his *Manusmriti* for thousands of years. It seems that some people have been, indirectly, trying to bypass the authority of the Indian Constitution because they probably feel uneasy and suffocated under the rule of the Indian Constitution. This shows their anti-dalit bent of mind. In short, so long casteism – either openly expressed and surreptitiously practised – exists in our country, Dalit literature, unfortunately, will not lose its relevance. So, to put it humourously, we can say that so long casteism exists in India, the future of dalit literature is very bright.

Of course, dalit writers will be the happiest lot the day the relevance of dalit literature comes to an end because, the end of the relevance of dalit literature would mean the end of exploitation, subjugation and discrimination against the dalits. And that is precisely what the dalit writers wish to happen.

In short, if we closely analyse what dalit writers basically want to achieve through their writings, we find that they wish to bring about in our country an environment of freedom, equality, fraternity and justice which are the values stated in the "Preamble" of the Indian Constitution.

Dalit writers have so far rightly depicted the neglect of, injustice towards and atrocities against the dalits. In addition to these issues, they should also write about current issues such as increasing population, inflation, corruption, unemployment, terrorism etc. since exploitation, suffering, sorrow and loss are inherent in these current issues too, since common man is the worst victim of these phenomena and since majority of the dalits are a part of the common masses.

Works Cited

Dangle, Arjun ed. *Poisoned Bread.* Bombay: Orient Longman, 1994 rpt.

Hemade, Shreenivas. "Dalit Sahityache Saundaryashastra: Nirmitivishayak Kahi Prashna" (Aesthetics of Dalit Literature: Some Issues about its Formulation). *Vidrohi,* May-June-July-August, 2006, pp. 32-50.

Kattimani, Tejaswi. *Bharatiya Dalit Sahitya: Ek Parichay* (Hindi). New Delhi: Valmik Publishers, 2002.

Limbale, Sharankumar. *Towards an Aesthetic of Dalit Literature.* New Delhi: Orient BlackSwan, 2007. Trans. from Marathi into English by Alok Mukherjee.

Masure, Jeevan & Sanjay Kulkarni. *Voices from Marginality in Literatures in English*. Nanded (M. S.): Harnai Prakashan, 2011.

Meshram, Yogendra. *Dalit Sahitya: Udgam aani Vikas* (Dalit Literature: Origin and Development). Nagpur: Shri Mangesh Prakashan, 1998.

Narasaiah, G. Lakshmi. *The Essence of Dalit Poetry: A Socio-Philosophical Study of Telugu Dalit Poetry*. Hyderabad: Dalit Sana Publications, 1999.

Nimbalkar, Waman. *Dalit Literature: Nature and Role*. Nagpur: Prabodhan Prakashan, 2006. Trans. from Marathi into English by Prof. Vandana Pathak & Dr. P. D. Nimsarkar.

Prasad, Amar Nath & M.B. Gaijan. *Dalit Literature: A Critical Exploration*. New Delhi: Sarup & Sons, 2007.

Sarangi, Jaydeep ed. *Writing as Resistance: Literature of Emancipation*. New Delhi: GNOSIS (An Imprint of Authorpress), 2011.

Sherrif, K. M., Trans & ed. *Ekalavyas with Thumbs: Selections from Gujarati Dalit Literature*. (1999).

2

Building a Movement of Faith: The Matuas of Bengal

Sipra Mukherjee

This essay will focus on the making of the Matua dharma, a religious sect of the Namasudras, an outcaste community outside the four-tiered Hindu *varna* system. This religious sect, begun in early nineteenth century Bengal, was initiated by Sri Harichand Thakur and was then ably continued by his son, Sri Guruchand Thakur, through the nineteenth century. By the early twentieth century, the followers of the Matua dharma had multiplied manifold, attracting several among the lower castes with its simple message of love and worship.

Constituting the second largest Hindu caste group in colonial Bengal, the establishment and spread of the Matua dharma among the Namasudras had significant consequences outside the religious sphere. The numerical strength of the community added a political dimension to the faith with the Namasudras finding, as James C. Scott would have termed it, a 'discourse of dignity' made accessible by the new faith. They organized themselves around this faith, drawing strength and sustenance from the religious literature created over time by the faithful. It is this religious as well as its political aspect that the essay will attempt to explore the literature authored by the community. Through this literature, the 'individual' Matua subject is redefined in relation to caste, gender, linguistic, regional and national identities as it engages with issues in and beyond the sacred. Examining the relations of power, cultural practices and literary production, the paper will read some of their literature with reference to the new religious identity created. Among the religious narratives that this essay will refer to are Matua hymns and the hagiography of Sri Harichand Thakur, the founder of the Matua faith.

To begin with a very brief introduction to the Matua faith. Harichand Thakur was born into the Namasudra community in 1811-12 in the Orakandi village of Gopalgunj in the Faridpur district. He was born into a family which, like many lower caste families of Bengal, were followers of the Vaishnava faith. Ramakanta Chakravarti provides a list of 16 such castes and tribes whose main religion was Vaishnavism. This list includes the Baiti, Bhuimali, Dhoba, Doai, Dom, Gonhri, Jalia Kaibarta, Malo, Kandura, Pod, Rajwar, Sunri, Tiwar and tribes like Kora, Mahali and Oraons; to this may be further added the Namasudras. The high caste GaudiyaVaishnavas did not maintain any social relations with them and people like Bipin Chandra Pal described them as 'out-caste Vaishnavas' (Chakravarti 330-333).

Harichand Thakur, born Harichand Biswas, founded the Matua faith which was unlike the other Nadia-based minor religious sects of the nineteenth century in that the faith "developed from and remained integrally connected to the organised social movement among the Namasudras, one of the most politically articulate dalit groups in colonial Bengal" (Bandyopadhyay 2004: 95). The Matua dharma rejected all brahminical hegemony and rituals, believing in egalitarianism of both caste and gender, and preaching a simple message of devotion and honesty. Its emphasis on bhakti reveals the legacy of the bhakti tradition, but significantly rejects Gurubaad. It was under Harichand's son Guruchand Thakur (b. 1846) that the Matua sect achieved a certain cohesion and organisation, when it came to be associated with the Namasudra social protest movement that began in the year 1872.

This association of the faith with the social movement of the community is explicit in Harichand's Thakur's hagiography, *Shri Shri Harililamrita*. Authored by Tarakchandra Sarkar, the book traces Harichand's life from his birth, the 'Abirbhab Khando' to his death, 'Tirobhah Khando'. The reason for the 'abirbhab' of Harichand is stated very clearly. Having failed to spread eternal purity and love among the mortals through His many avatars, God promises to send his avatar to earth once again during the Kaliyug:

> 'Will come as humanity, will connect with humanity,
> Will complete Lila as humankind.
> That is when you will know me,
> When I am born again as humanity.'
>
> (*SSH* 2010, 20)[1]

Harichand's birth into the lowliest of the communities is interpreted as the Lord's desire to "bend low to liberate the lowly" (*SSH* 39) because the avatar's greatness lies in his ability stoop to the lowliest:

> I will bend low to liberate the lowly,
> In stooping lower than the lowliest is the avatar's worth.
> The purity of Krishna's love is not at an unreachable high
> Like water it searches out the lowliest plane.
>
> (*SSH* 39)

While the use of words like 'avatar' and 'lila', with their Hindu associations, may be seen as attempts at appropriation by the Matua dharma of the mainstream Hindu concepts, some difficulties arise, as can only be expected, in the epistemology of the terms. The concept of *maya*, closely associated with the concept of divine *Lila* is one that is strongly rejected within the Matua philosophy. Both Harichand and his son Guruchand very deeliberately opposed Sankarite Vedantism or the monistic

1. All references to Shri Shri Harililamrita (SSH) are from Tarakchandra Sarkar, *Shri Shri Harililamrita*. Sridham Thakurnagar: Modern Press. 2010.

philosophy of spiritual salvation: transcending the illusory sensory world to attain the supreme truth or Brahma, who defied embodiment. Belief in this other-worldliness was for Guruchand a trick used by the brahminical elite to keep the marginalised shudra in a state of perpetual subjection, keeping the Sudra in hope and therefore consoled, by promises of salvation in the next life. The importance given to this life is in fact an element that distinguishes the Matua faith from other religious sects in Bengal. Harichand's dictum of 'Hate kaam, mukhe naam' ('Work in hand, His Name on lips') offered a way out of the philosophy which justified worldly degradation by preaching a work ethic and encouraging social mobility. Instead of preaching the ascetic and celibate path of devotion, he preached the *grahasthya* dharma, saying that the life of the dutiful and responsible *grihi* was superior to that of the ascetic who took up *vanaprastha*. By combining devotion with action (*bhakti* with *karma)*, Guruchand's teachings encourage and justify the desire for upward social mobility, while eluding its more materialistic dimensions of profit and greed.

Named and structured like the hagiography of the greatest of the Hindu sages, the book *Shri Shri Harililamrita* articulates what Roger Chartier has called the "both the acculturated and the acculturating" features of all religions, popular as well as the religion of the clerics (Chartier 1995: 88). This is evident in the myths of origin regarding the Namasudras. At least three of these myths including the one in *Shri Shri Harililamrita* which gives details of Harichand's brahminical genealogy, place the Namasudras within the caste principles of purity and pollution. These myths trace the descent of the Namasudras from brahmin ancestors who lost their caste due to various reasons. Sekhar Bandyopadhyay surmises that this genealogy was felt necessary by the Namasudra community when, in the late nineteenth century, their earlier "almost amphibious existence" in the boats and on the marshy lands began to change and they began to emerge as a settled peasant community (Bandyopadhyay 2004: 154). These myths historicize the fall of the Namasudras from their actual brahminical status, In the process of being acculturated, the smaller faiths accept the hegemonic community's rules and conventions, and do not challenge the caste hierarchy or the concepts of purity and pollution. On the face of it, by accepting these origin-myths the Matua faith appears to accept the dictates of what constitutes the marks of servitude. Like other idioms of domination, this too works through contradiction and arbitrary selection. It raises the Namasudras to a position above that of the Sudras, but at the same time encourages them to internalize their devalued status.

The narrative of Harichand Thakur's life exemplifies the very different concept of popular memory, with the different significations that emerge without the elite community's manipulation of folk sense and common sense. What emerges is an ideology very different from that usually found in mainstream Hindu hagiographies. Aspects like the equality of the genders being repeatedly emphasized, early marriage discouraged and widow remarriage allowed, distinguishes the sect from brahminical Hinduism. Their religious leaders are called Gosains and both men and women can become Gosains. The privileging of the other-worldly and the transcendental usually found in hagiographies is often absent here. To take the example of one simple incident narrated in the book: Harichand is called by the Magistrate for a meeting and realises he has nothing decent to wear. The problem is discussed in real terms with no reference being made to the usual philosophizing about the superficiality of clothes and the authenticity of the person. Harichand's son is sent to get appropriate clothes for the princely sum of Rs 500, and the episode ends with a happy description by the writer of the gorgeously attired Hari Thakur. The narrative is interspersed with a few songs and sections in the oral rhythm, obviously meant to be read or sung aloud. One such song of the Matua as narrated in the hagiography is like this:

My Gourango has come dressed, come Qazi, come.

> Last night you broke the khol and the kartal, now where will you go? …
> What do we care for Brahma-Vishnu-Maheswar, We know only you!
>
> (*SSH* 311)

The words echo Harichand's bold instruction to his followers:

> Do not call on Hari, for Hari will call on you.
>
> (*Mullick* 2010: 17)

The songs and hymns played an important role in keeping the community together. They became a ritual to assert their political will, as the songs often contained messages for boosting self-confidence and the collective ego of a depressed community, whose members otherwise felt powerless to face the obstacles of life. The songs frequently articulate the difference of the Marua beliefs from that of brahminical Hinduism, as in this one:

> You've put the noose of Guru's blessings upon my neck, and the shackles of dharma upon my feet.
> Now with the scriptures-sooty come stand before me,
> So I can break the bondage of Mukti.
> Pleasures and salvation, are both servants.
> They try to bind me with the chains
> of delight and satisfaction….
> Oh help me evade the prison-house of that Heaven..
>
> (Sarkar, 98)

An aspect that returns in the lines of the narrative and of the songs is the emphasis on education. Among the rhymes made popular among the Matuas by Harichand and his son Guruchand, such as "Work on your hands, God on your lips," are also the lines:

> Of no matter whether I live or I die,
> A school in every village is what I want, O *bhai*.

This prominence given to education through the Matua faith has made it almost obligatory for all Namasudras to seek some form of education. Since there is a relatively wide range of levels of income and social standing within the large Namasudra community, this drive towards education has encouraged many among the very poor who may otherwise not have felt impelled to educate their children. This is reflected in the 2001 literacy rate of the Namasudras, a high 71.93 per cent, compared to the lower 68.46 per cent of the state of West Bengal (Bandyopadhyay 2011: 262). This is quite an achievement considering the devastating consequences of the Partition that the Namasudra community faced. As the Dalit writer Manoranjan Byapari writes:

> Prior to 1947 almost 90 per cent of them (Namasudras) lived in East Bengal in the districts of Khulna, Faridpur, Jessore and Barishal. ... The fear of communal violence drove them away from their villages. In the darkness of night they crossed the border, leaving behind their land, houses and all material possessions. Year after year they lived under trees, on pavements, on railway platforms, in refugee camps – existing at a subsistence level. In the name of rehabilitation, some were sent to uninhabited islands in the Andaman region, some were packed off to the forests and the unproductive terrain of Dandakaranya in Madhya Pradesh and other barren pockets of the country. Thus an organised and cohesive community got fragmented and lost its strength.
>
> (Mukherjee 2007: 4117)

This was followed by the dark chapter of the Marichjhaapi Massacre, which may have been erased from public memory and documented history unless Amitav Ghosh had recreated it in vivid detail in his novel, *The Hungry Tide.* Despite these tremendous setbacks, Bandyopadhyay notes that "those who have remained in West Bengal have surged ahead since the 1980s. Instead of business and enterprise, they chose the parh of education and profession, a path that had been prescribed by Guruchand" (Bandyopadhyay 2011: 262).

The political implications of the movement were visible as early as the 1920s, and has since been amply made visible in the last elections by the rush of political parties to woo the Matuas.

Much like the movement of the African Americans, the Matuas have drawn strength from their faith andreligious beliefs. The organization of the Matua community itself has been essential in motivating them to act individually and collectively to both challenge their given situation and improve their worldly lot. A tracing of the Matua faith would reveal how it has gradually become more than a religious sect: it is now a movement of faith, with an ideology that inspires and unites often disparate individuals into a community. It is this message of garnering and capitalizing on their strength that finds articulation through their poetry:

> Send this message to every door
> We want no plough, no land.
> First we want a king. Let your roar be
> 'With *our* votes, *our* King.'
>
> (Kalyani Thakur Chanral, *They Who have no King*)

Books Cited

Bandyopadhay, Sekhar. 2004. *Caste, Culture and Hegemony*. New Delgi: Sage Publications.

_______. 2011. *Caste, Protest and Identity in Colonial India: the Namasudras of Bengal, 1872 –1947*. New Delhi: Oxfor University Press.

Chakravarti, Ramakanta. 1985. *Vaishnavism in Bengal, 1486 -1900*. Calcutta: Sanskrit Pustak Bhandar.

Chartier, Roger. 1995. *Forms and Meanings: Texts, Performances and Audiences, From Codex to Computer*. Pennsylvania: University of Pennsylvania Press.

Mukherjee, Meenakshi, Manoranjan Byapari. 2007. 'Is there Dalit Writing in Bangla?' Perspectives, *Economic and Political Weekly*, 13 October, 4116-4120.

Mullick Nakul. 2010 'Thakur Harichand Gruchand O Babasaheb Ambedkar', in Kalyani Thakur Chanral ed. *Matua Dhrama Prasange*. Kolkata: Bangla Dalit Sahitya Sangstha.

Sarkar, Ashwini Kumar. 2010. *Shri Shri Hari Sangeet*. Sridham Thakurnagar: Sushila Printers.

Tarakchandra Sarkar. 2010. *Shri Shri Harililamrita*. Sridham Thakurnagar: Modern Press.

3

Gujarati Dalit Poetry in Twenty-first Century

M.B. Gaijan

As I start to write, something happen to them,
I write on my misery, and something happens to them.
Who are the dirty? Whose minds are full of vices?
As I raise the basic quest, something happens to them.
There is no monopoly of any on virtues,
See, I am ashamed and something happens to them.[1]

The land, since last thousand years known as Gujarat, has remained very significant place in Indian since the time immemorial. Lothal, Dholaveera and other historical places in Gujarat indicate that thousands of years back there dwelled highly civilized human race. Hindu God Lord Krishna's arrival in Dwaraka and Mohammad Gazanavi's attack on the Somnath Temple indicate prosperity of the land and the people of the land. This is the land where Mahatma Gandhi was born and worked for the nation, even in the twenty-first century the state is emerging as one of the fast developing states in India.

But since a ancient times till today one section of humanity was/ is not wholeheartedly accepted as human beings by the mainstream society. They were/are segregated from the mainstream society on different grounds. They frequently became/ become the victims of man-made injustice, cruelty and were condemned to suffer for long without their fault. Earlier they were known as *untouchables*, now they are known as dalits, the citizens of this Democratic Republic India.

Gujarati dalits could survive in all adversity because of their cardinal support of their literature. They have the vast oral literary treasure as a heritage. From the early eleventh century to till today it was enriched by the known and unknown dalit literary genius. Earlier it was in poetic form and in folk literature. It was in the form of folksongs/tales and spiritual songs. It still exists in Gujarat. The spiritual songs composed by the dalit saint poets have the great humanitarian values so even today these songs are highly popular and accepted by all, mainstream and the marginalized people of Gujarat.

But after independence, from the mid-70s of the twentieth century, Gujarati dalit literature has gradually become secular. It represents dalits' socio-cultural, educational, political issues and the issues that challenge to their existence as human beings in the democratic India. Poetry becomes the most favourite literary form to express feelings for the dalit genius. It has become the expression of their identity, existence, culture and their struggle to survive and struggle to get human identity in India. Twentieth century Gujarati dalit poetry remained remarkable with anger, fury, struggle for identity and other aspects.

But Gujarati dalit poetry of the twenty-first century becomes more profound. In spite of advancement in Gujarat, still in the twenty-first century Gujarat, injustice and cruelty on dalits are going on. So the Dalit poets have composed poems on various aspects of their suffering. Their struggle for existence, identity, fight against injustice and cruelty, dalit culture and other aspects still remain at the centre of their creativity.

Untouchablility-based social evils are not totally removed from Gujarat, still it is existing. Though they have taken different forms, they are the rejection of dalits, unacceptability of dalits, nausea for dalits and inhuman dealings with dalits. These social evil practices have directly or indirectly created injustice to many them. So the dalit poets have composed poems on untouchability or untouchability-based evils. They composed poems with a view to remove these evils forever. Their protest is highly rational.

Harish Mangalam in his poem *Oncology* writes about untouchablity. It is compared with the deadly disease cancer:

> Truly, I too have had a melting taste (experience) of this cancer,
> Balakdas Gokaldas, my first teacher would,
> To appear a religious man, place the *Gita* on the table.
> Then eyeing me sternly through
> The spectacles resting on the tip of his nose
> He would fling the cane at me (For fear of being polluted)
> And it would hit my untouchable being.
> The untouchable swelling arisen from
> The wound is still intact with the name plate of B.G.
> ....
> B. G. is no more but he has left behind
> An inheritance of innumerable cancroids bacteria.
> Truly cancer is a fatal disease and it has no cure.[2]

The poet has metaphorically presented the issue of untouchability. It spread very fast and before it could be identified it controlled the whole Indian society. Now untouchability has taken different forms and are more dreadful. Caste-based social division was/is the mother of many social evils in India. And it is also a fact the caste-ism is the killer factor of Indian society to create hurdles in forming an egalitarian society even in the twenty-first century. It is the mother of segregating humanity in India on irrational base. The poet wants emancipation from this disease.

Vinod Gandhi, a dalit poet, has presented social reality of Gujarat in his poem "*Still Today*":

> Still today, a cup with broken handle,
> Laying in the corner of verandah of Kana Patel.
> Still toady, in the drawer of barber's wooden shop,
> Separately kept scissors and razors laying with rust.
> ....
> Still today, a stout spouse of village-merchant,
> After cleaning the toilet by the Sweeper's,
> On the steps pours the clean water.
> ....

> Still today, Dudhojee, the milk man after asking;
> "Which is your milk?"
> then pour it into the bowl by keeping distance.
> Still today, a school teacher with big moustache,
> in the school general register,
> with the name of the newly admitted student's caste column,
> by mistake writes "*Dhe....*" disgustingly then erase it.[3]

Further, in the poem the poet writes that, when the upper-caste identifies a dalit as a fellow travel then as a fellow bus traveller the he keeps his distance. At the end of the poem the poet says, "Oh! God, if *You*, to be born in 2007, then tell me where are you to be born in the 'family', untouchablity and unacceptability of dalits still exist in society. The poet has pictured the unpleasant truth. Upper castes' disgust towards dalits doesn't disappear. Still it is there in remote rural areas.

Mukesh Boricha, a young dalit poet, writes with extreme worry and anger when he is identified as a dalit and treated with prejudice. In his poem, "Since how Long"? he expresseshis feelings that he has left his birthplace a Bagsara, a small town, his parents, his dalit colony, and settled down 172 km in Bhavnagar, away from his home-town, for his earning and future for the next generation. But here, as earlier in his home-town, he also becomes a victim of untouchability;

> Since our forefathers' times stuck untouchability has not gone at all, It has stuck to us since generations, then tell us still how long it will remain stick to us.[4]

Untouchability and untouchability-based social attitudes have killed social harmony and harmed unity among the citizens of the land. So the dalit poets collectively protest to remove untouchability-based inequality.

In rural areas dalits are still in more miserable conditions due to their economic dependence. Mainly they are farm labourers and living away from the village in their huts in their ghetto. The poet has symbolized them as their home huts. Mukesh Boricha writes in his poem *A Hut*:

> A hut in the Dalit ghetto of a village,
> desires to breathe (life) for surviving.
> ....
> Dark-shadow of untouchability is spread everywhere,
> The desire of unity and integrity wants the hut.
> ....
> Homeless remained at the outskirt of village,
> The hut desires to emancipate from that misery.
> It is the desire that Ambedkar Baba gets rebirth,
> Keeping that desire the hut is waiting.[5]

In this poem the poet has metaphorically presented dalits and their wretched condition in the huts in rural areas. House is important for shelter and to live but hunger is more important than shelter. Sources for their livelihood are unorganized and uncertain. For earning sometimes they have to remain as labourers. In their wretched condition they want equality and human acceptance.

Dr. Vinod Shrimali in his poem *How Strange This Religion is!* writes about how religion has paralyzed dalits' human liberty:

> Feelings of Dalits, how religion has interwoven in it.
> "We will accept Dalits today to bring the human equality."
> But something is told and practiced something differently,
> Then how the human equality can be established?[6]

It is as true as the sunrises that the Hindu spirituality does not teach or preach to divide human beings, oppress and exploit them. It has preached to have compassion, love and acceptance of all animals, birds, even trees. But the message of Hindu spirituality was/ is not practised by the shallow interpretations. It is a politics of the shallow-minded orthodox to enslave and so get their goals. In Gujarat there are many religious places and organizations but the poet's feeling shows that still a homogeneous society needs to be created.

Dalit women's condition too doesn't improve. They become victims of injustice, in their homes and out of their houses. Naishedh Makwana in his poem "Pains" writes about dalit women's misery:

> They put on white clothes and put marks on their foreheads, and then talk too high, they are known as saints, millionaires and leaders, but they do not look at their own loincloths!
>
> When I go in their streets with broom in hand they keep their necks straight and eyes fox on me.
>
> The burning fire like tale of the pains, how unbearable the (God) *You* have given?
>
> While giving water in cupped hands of mine, the spouse of the millionaire keeps the distance of her water metal-pot.
>
> When the gutter at the back of their house overflowed,
>
> From that emerges bones and meat.[7]

The poem is satirical and exposes the pain of a dalit woman. It is highly symbolical. Most of the illiterate dalit women have to do cleaning job for livelihood. When they are out of their houses/ huts or ghettoes they have to face many problems. And they have to bear them all silently. In this poem the poet has presented a dalit woman's helpless misery. As while doing cleaning work, that when she needs water to drink, the lady of the house pours water from a height in the cupped hands of the dalit woman. The last lines of the poem are satirical. When their gutter overflows and she is called to make it clean, while cleaning the gutter pipe the dalit woman finds bones and meat as a blockade. In Gujarat due to *Vaishanavism*, Gandhiji's Jainism and Swaminarayana Sect's influence, eating meat is considered as sin, inferior. It is believed that non-vegetarians are bad. But secretly the upper-caste people take it. In this poem the poet has exposed this hypocrisy of the so-called vegetarians.

Jesangbhai Solanki's "*Ever I Have the Hot Summer*" presents the struggle of a dalit woman in her wretched condition:

Ever I have the hot summer.
In the early morning the hungry kids cry for food,
And T. B. patient husband demands bunch of *biries*.
Ever I have the hot summer.
By struggle I try to meet the need but I fail ever,
Ever something is lacking to pacify the fire of bellies,
To live or to die, the dilemma, creates confusion,
Ever I have the hot summer.[8]

In the poem, the poet presents how the woman is harassed by her supervisor when she is at a cleaning job. She has to protect herself in all adversities, to satisfy her family's needs and thus she has to live her life. It is a microscopic presentation of the tragedy of dalit women. Many suffer thus.

Purushotam Jadava's poem *Do Something of These Legs* is very interesting. It is composed in the North Gujarati dialect by selecting the term *Legs* instead of *Shudras.* In the Hindu scriptures shudras are considered as the feet of God's body. Dalits, ati-shudras were considered untouchables by the all four *varnas* as presented in the scriptures. Ati-shudras had descended from the shudras. So the poet has used *Legs,* not Shudras. The poem begins with the typical north Gujarati slang:

These brothers-in-law!have started abusing us, do something of these legs!

We become greater that's why, and so tried be hypocrite as possible as, but,

These brothers-in-law! have started abusing us, do something of these legs!

That's why we have segregated, one is high another is low,

And it was not enough so created wall in between them, but

These brothers-in-law! have started abusing us, do something of these legs![9]

In this poem the poet has satirically presented the worry of the shallow-minded orthodox upper castes, the upper castes that remained dominant since long. But now there is a change in society. Due to this change none can be high, none can be low. The dalits have now challenged injustice if committed to them. The charm of the poem is in the use of dialect.

Humanity, mutual faith, brotherhood, love and compassion are the basic needs for human beings to create a civilized human society and prosper in it. But contemporary social reality is something different. As a result dalits suffer a lot. Arvind Vegda's poem "Human Mask" presents this truth:

> Wearing a human mask silence waiting in deserted streets
> Like lepers trudge their way and merge into someone.
>
> Then something grows grotesquely, bloodshot eyes, bulbous biceps,
> Sword shimmering in hand and mask noisily peeling off.
> A violence wolf comes into being and tears to shreds humanity
> bending to gather existence scattered in lanes.[10]

In this poem the poet has exposed the hypocrisy in the name of humanity. As a matter of fact, a democratic republic state governing system is that sort of governing system where the welfare and prosperity of all, including the last, is envisaged. But reality is something different. Here only those who have higher caste, class, and money prosper. It is a remarkable aspect of dalit poetry to expose reality by using satire. Vegda's poem has a unique importance in that way.

To get human dignity and human rights for the dalits, non-dalit poets in Gujarat have also extended their hands on humanitarian ground. They too have created dalit-centred literature with the spirit as we find in dalit poets. In their poems the dalits' struggle for human dignity and human rights is at the centre. Among these writers Pravin Gadhavi, Silas Pateliya, Pritam Lakhalani, Manilal Patel's contributions are praiseworthy. Manilal Patel's "Get up, You Get" the poem presents the orthodox upper castes' exploitation, and advises the dalits:

> Beware always of these *Black English,*
> As their work is done,

> Then accept that immediately your thumb will be cut off!
> Your condition would be like the condition of the weavers of Dhaka,
> Before that, you get up.[11]

The poet presents the true picture of the selfish mentality of the orthodox upper castes, not all. When their work is done they kick the dalits out of their circles. The poet has considered the native exploiter as the Black English. As their work is done they forget every bond of humanity connected to dalits. By using the tragic episode of cutting Ekalavya's thumb and cutting the hands of the expert weavers of Dhaka, the poet has warned the dalits to beware before it happens to them.

Pravin Gadhavi in his poem "Tragedy" writes about the remarkable aspect of dalits' literary creation. He writes about the mainstream literature, that whether it is a comedy or a tragedy delight is the centre of their creativity. From tragedy catharsis is the ultimate conclusion. But dalit writings are different. He writes:

> But, Our Dalit tragedy doesn't mean for your delight.
> Our pains are not for giving you delight,
> but for giving you pains.
> Our tragedies are our pains, our anger.
> We have not held the pens in hands to please you.
> We hold the pens to fight against you.
> Our pens are not merely pens, but are the swards.[12]

The poet has well presented the truth about the mainstream literature of upper castes. The mainstream writings can be evaluated on the base of "how much delight it serves to the readers". Delight is the centre of the literature. But the dalit writing is different. It is not created for delight of the dominant castes/classes. It is created for empowering the powerless, powerless they remain due to religious and state-supported politics in the past.

Pritam Lakhalani in his poem "Education" writes about the new identity of dalits. Earlier dalits were feeble and submissive but after getting education they have become stronger. They raise their voices against injustice:

> Friends, time has taught us,
> by begging nothing can be achieved!
> We are, now, not simple like pet pigeons,
> But we are the vultures
> born on the acacias
> in the deep jungle!
> Does it necessary to teach them
> What is Right? And How to get Rights?[13]

The poem indicates the importance of education for the dalits' advancement. Now in the twenty-first century the third generation of dalits is getting education. They are not as submissive and simple as their forefathers. After being educated they now know how to get their constitutional rights.

Gujarati dalit poems published in the first decade of the twenty-first century indicate clearly that still there are plenty of social issues for dalits in society. Still the untouchability-based social evils are spoiling the minds of the orthodox, and as a result human equality cannot be established. In rural areas as also their condition is still more pitiable. Their ghettoes are still awaiting basic facilities, their acceptance as fellow human beings with dignity. In this their struggle for human dignity, the enlightened non-dalits' contribution is a remarkable aspect of Gujarati dalit poetry of the twenty-first century. Right from the first decade of the twenty-first century, the dalits and non-dalits are active in creating an egalitarian ideal human society in Gandhi's Gujarat.

References

1. Parmar Pathik, "Something Happens to Them", in *Skylark India* 96, ed. Harish Mangalam, Aligarh, 2005, p. 62.
2. Mangalam Harish, *Oncology* in *Pristine Land: Gujarati Dalit Literature*, ed. Harish Mangalam & M. B. Gaijan, Yash Publication, New Delhi, 2009, pp. 206-207.

3. Gandhi Vinod, *Still Today,* in *Hayati* (Journal of Gujarati Dalit Literature), Gujarat Dalit Sahitya Akademi, Ahmadabad, March 2007, pp. 3-4.
4. Boricha Mukesh, "Since How Long?" In *Since How Long?* Published by the author and financially aided by the Deptt. of Social Justice & Empowerment, Govt. of Gujarat, 2009, pp. 78-79.
5. Boricha Mukesh, "The Hut", op. cit. p. 14
6. Shrimali Vinod, "How Strange This Religion is!" *Hayati*, op.cit., March 2007, p.8.
7. Makwana Naishedh, *Pains*, in *Hayati*, Gujarat Dalit Sahitya Akademi, Ahmadabad, June 2010.
8. Solanki Jesangbhai "Ever I Have the Hot Summer", in *Dalit Geet–Gazal*, ed. Pathik Parmar & Harish Mangalam, Kum Kum Publication, Ahmadabad, 2006, p. 40.
9. Jadava Purushotam, "Do Something of These Legs" in *Dalit Geet–Gazal*, ed. Pathik Parmar & Harish Mangalam, op. cit., p. 46.
10. Vegda Arvind "Human Mask", in *Pristine Land: Gujarati Dalit literature* op cit. p. 229.
11. Patel Manilal "Get up, You Get", in *Hayati*, Gujarat Dalit Sahitya Akademi, Ahmadabad, March 2006, p. 9.
12. Gadhavi Pravin, "Tragedy", in *Hayati*, op.cit., September 2010, p. 4.
13. Lakhalani Pritam, "Education", in *Hayati*, op.cit., p. 5.

4

Writing Resistance, Righting Repression: A Reading of Three Stories by Provas Ray, Manoranjan Bapari and Manohar Mouli Biswas

Sayantan Dasgupta

Dalit literature in Bangla has remained a largely neglected archive.[1] It is only relatively recently that we have begun to see a sustained academic recognition of this body of literature.

Dalit literature in Bangla, as indeed in most other languages, possesses a political edge[2] and is often concerned with highlighting the workings of caste discrimination in 'modern' Indian society.[3] Yet it is important to reiterate that it is not just a grammar of victimhood that this body of literature textualises; more often than not, dalit literature concerns itself with tracing trajectories of resistance as well. In some cases, the act of writing itself may constitute an act of resistance as dalit literature often borders on the *testimonio*[4] and draws from life experiences. And this act of writing often employs various different, at times sophisticated, strategies—irony, satire, sarcasm and the use of an apparently naïve, child-like narratorial voice to imply the opposite of what is actually said.

My paper tries to read tropes of repression and resistance in three Bangla short stories—Provas Ray's "Shol Machh," Manoranjan Bapari's "Ribaj" and Manohar Mouli Biswas's "Jougin." I shall try to present how traditional discourses and repressive structures are interrogated in these stories. All three stories deal, in some way or another, with the spiritual economy of caste; each foregrounds the body as both site of repression and site of resistance; it is on the body that brahminism-centric knowledge system seeks to exercise power, and it is indeed, through the body that the subaltern is seen to strike back in these stories, albeit in very different ways.

Bapari's "Ribaj" is set in the remote *Vanrajya*. It is ruled by the *Babhans* (brahmins); to the 'low-caste' Chamrahas and Charbahas who inhabit the region, they are representatives of Linganathan, the god who created *Vanrajya* and left them in charge. The *Babhans* invent and enforce various rites that keep the 'low caste' villagers marginalised—materially, financially, sexually and psychologically. This very powerful story is about the transition from helpless acquiescence to resistance and revenge; it is about the complex dialogue between a brahminical knowledge system and a from-below atttempt to interrogate its truth claim.

Every male of *Vanrajya* has to first offer his bride to the *Babhandeotas* for the first few nights—only then is he allowed to take her home. It is common knowledge—and I use this term consciously to highlight the politics of the production of knowledge itself (all knowledge, all history, after all, is written by whoever is in power, and therefore is open to being interrogated from below)—that Linganathan, the god, had warned the *Babhans* about Matangi, the evil goddess—

> Make sure no spy of Matangi dares set foot on this land. That bitch sets up her den in the impenetrable darkness of the female genitalia. Only a man who possesses *Brahmatej*, a *Babhan*,can conquer her.

That is why every woman who enters *Vanrajya* must go through a *shuddhi* at the hands of the *Babhans*. This knowledge that is so ubiquitous is of course 'revealed knowledge', it is the brahmins, mediators between the gods and other human beings, to whom it was apparently revealed. The hegemony of this knowledge system is what Maniram challenges when he asks, "Says who...? How do you know that's true, chief? Who said that...? Who was witness to these events?" Maniram recognises that this custom is little more than a construct meant to legitimize gangrape and sexual and psychological repression of the *Chamrahas* and *Charbahas* by the brahmins.

Maniram's rebellion also throws into relief the discourse of guilt, which is so often used to silence resistance. A potential rebel is often sought to be brought in line by trying to convince him that his transgression will spell doom not only for himself but for his entire community—thus is the status quo of power sought to be maintained. This is portrayed as such in Manju Bala's short story, "Dain," and in Manoranjan Bapari's "Ribaj" as well. Thus, in "Ribaj," the village chief, urges Maniram:

> If there's a drought, will your crops be the only ones affected? If the Kotri swells up, will your hut be the only one to be washed away? If lightning strikes, will you be the only one who will die? Don't be such a fool! I'm telling you—reach your wife there and everything will be fine.

Significantly, it is not a brahmin saying this; it is the village chief, Dongaram, who himself had to give up his wife to the brahmins before he could have sexual relations with her. Clearly, he plays the role of the proverbial collaborator here, as indeed does Dholku.

Yet, even Dongaram's attempts to coax Maniram into falling in line go beyond a naïve acceptance of the brahmin knowledge system; this is evident in the telling lines used by the author: "The village chief feels angry. He is the oldest person in the village, and the most respected. If his family could not escape the *Babhans*, why should Maniram?" The dialogue between repression, acquiescence and resistance is thus shown to be replete with complexities and far from one-dimensional.

All three stories interrogate the discourse of guilt that would construct the dalit subject as one who would/ should readily succumb to oppressive traditions and practices for an imagined greater common good. Thus, in Manohar Mouli Biswas's story, "Yogin," we learn:

> Fifty years ago. In the Valmiki neighbourhood, KunoValmiki's daughter had become a yogin... The village was saved... The epidemic couldn't touch their village that time.

Official history would of course remain silent on uncomfortable questions such as how willingly Kuno Valmiki's daughter became a yogin and what became of her later. It is this silence that Manohar Mouli Biswas's story powerfully critiques by mirroring Kuni Valmiki's daughter in Venna, who shares a similar fate.

The strategy of putting the onus of communal/ familial good in the hands of the potential rebel to wean him away from rebellion is in evidence in "Shol Machh" as well. The story begins with an act of rebellion when Moti Mondal refuses to heed the warnings of Chhotthakur Keshab Chakraborty who wants him to give up the huge *shol* fish he has just caught. Yet, his rebellion seems destined to failure. For, his wife, on hearing how the Brahmin had tried to wrest control of the fish, warning him of divine punishment, refuses to let him keep the fish; she makes it clear she would blame him if anything were to happen to the children for consuming a fish *eyed* by a brahmin. Very interestingly, it is almost an inversion of untouchability that the author seems to use here; just as the Mishras ("Ribaj")and the Thakurs apparently steer clear of the prospect of being 'polluted' by the Dalit's touch, here, it is the 'lower caste' woman who displays an almost tactile aversion to the gaze of a brahmin: " 'My children won't be able to digest a fish eyed by a brahmin,' Chapala muttered and walked off towards the kitchen."

The use of inversionas a strategy seems common to all three writers. Thus, Bapari's "Ribaj", too, ends with a similar inversion, with Maniram saying as he is about to leave the village, "I'll just go do the *shuddhi*." The meaning of *shuddhi* undergoes a transformation here as the story ends with Maniram going and chopping Deonandan Mishra down.

In "Shol Machh," the calculus of dalit-brahmin relationship is highlighted right at the beginning. The story begins with an interaction between Chhotthakur, the scion of the brahmin family, and Moti Mondal, a poor peasant whose family had been *yajamans*of the former for generations. I read a small passage from the story: "Moti Mandal was walking briskly past the Thakurs' drawing room. Hearing Chhotthakur's call, he stopped in his tracks. He tried to guess why he was being called. He scrutinised his circumstances mentally. How did matters relating to land and monetary transactions stand? Was there any loan that was yet to be repaid? Did he owe anything as Chhotthakur's client?"

These three questions the omniscient narrator identifies as passing through Moti Mondal's mind immediately throw into relief the hierarchical relationship between Moti and the 'Thakurs'.

It is important to note that soon after refusing to heed Chhotthakur's 'advice', Moti starts having second thoughts:

> Moti suddenly remembered that his mother was on her deathbed... They would have no option but to call *Chhotthakur* in then. He would have to touch his feet and pray, *Thakurmashai*, please see that my mother attains salvation. Again, when his younger daughter got married, he would have to implore him, *Thakurmashai*, please bless them so that they live happily ever after. At the time of the ceremony to mark the commencement of his grandson's education, he would have to depend on the *thakur* again. In other words, you simply could not do without a *purohit*.

Chhotthakur, on his part, has no compunctions about using the spiritual to monopolise the material. Thus, when he sees Moti Mondal with the huge fish, he advises him to give him the fish: "You will enter your house with a *shol* fish on a Saturday evening?

What about the great sin you will be committing? Do you know what havoc it can wreak in your life?"

He even calls for his almanac and cites from it to prove his point. We learn later he was actually on a page that carried the schedule of marriages as he pretended to read out the strictures on consuming fish. Even though Moticarries on with the fish, he soon suffers from niggling doubts: "Who knows, there may be some truth in Thakurmashai's words. His heart missed a beat in anticipation of some unknown catastrophe that might befall his children."

Dalit writing in Bangla thus goes far beyond depicting a simplistic conflict between repression and resistance. As in Bapari's story and Manohar Biswas's story, so too in "Shol Machh", the dialogue between orthodox Brahminical hegemonic discourse and an alternative discourse that dissects the former is quite complex. We note, thus, how different, even contradictory sentiments seem to echo in Moti's mind: "It's just our fate—who else can be blamed for it?", "He himself knew not why he was doing this—was it because of the deep-rooted, traditional beliefs, or did he aspire to accumulating *punya*?," and finally, "The Thakurs have reached the pinnacle of wealth and prosperity, yet they remain recipients of charity, while we, poor hapless peasants continue to revel in the role of the donor."

It is by assuming the role of the donor that Moti manages to turn the scales; he puts himself ina position of power from where he can afford to be benevolent towards the petty brahmin. Yet, the author has another twist in the tale reserved for us. As he gifts the Thakurs the huge *shol* fish and other presents, he is asked to stay and share the meal. He is caught in a quandary—having the fish which his children have been deprived of will break his heart, yet, refusing would be to defy the brahmins. This is where things begin to unravel. In some of the most hard-hitting passages of the story, the author writes:

> As he sat down to eat, Moti found himself tormented by a thought—
>
> The *arum* nourished by the tender care of Gopal's Mother and the *shol* fish caught by me are welcome in the kitchen of the Thakurbari, yet I am not allowed to sit even on the verandah. Could there be a greater insult than this? Yet we are happy enough to depend on them blindly for our well-being in this life as well as in the afterlife. Moti could think no more.

Finally, Moti tears free of the shackles of tradition and rejects the meal he is served: "A *yajman* had rejected the prasad of the Thakurs. It was a great insult for the purohit brothers."

Like "Ribaj" and "SholMachh", Manohar Mouli Biswas's "Yogin" is a powerful critique of traditional brahminical hypocrisy. It is Labhamkrishna, the rich brahmin and aspiring politician, who nudges Venna's father towards making her a yogin, once again for the greater common good. As floods bring epidemics to the unhygienic Mala-Madiga-Valmiki neighbourhoods, Labhamkrishna revels in his role as conduit to the gods and as repository of revealed knowledge: "Labhambabu sent a reminder—the law of the Shastra decreed only one way to escape incessant rain, drought, epidemics and floods. One of the villagers would have to be sanctified as a yogin." This is, like the contentions of the *Babhans* in "Ribaj", revealed knowledge and is therefore unverifiable o the non-brahmin. It is again this very Labhamkrishna who, once Venna becomes a yogin, fathers her daughter, and continues abusing Venna for seven more years until Venna runs away with the daughter whom Labhamkrishna would never recognise. Finally, it is the same Labhamkrishna who comes to the neighbourhood where Venna has now settled and gives a pre-election speechcriticising the evils of the yogin system and promising to root it out if he came to power.

We also note that "Yogin," like the other two stories discussed in this paper, depicts repression, collaboration and resistance not as watertight categories, but as entities that co-exist and cohabit, if in a condition of perennial tussle. This is so evident in the conversation between Labhamkrishna and Venna's father. When Labhamkrishna asks him to make his daughter a yogin, he says: "We are poor, illiterate people, babu. Low caste. I've always heard it's the girls from low caste families who become yogins." This may sound at first like an internalisation of caste hierarchies but it is clear from the second part of the response that this is no passive acquiescence. There is a searing question, a simmering consciousness of the oppression his kind is subjected to in the apparently innocent reference he makes to the fact that it is always girls from lower-caste families who becomeyogins.He stakes his claim here to the status of the articulate dalit subject who sees through the myths perpetuated by the brahmin oppressor. Yet, if this is resistance from Venna's father, it is immediately followed up by: "If god so wishes, I'll make my Venna a yogin... . Will you give me a *pali* of rice today, babu? Or a *kunika* of wheat? Otherwise the little ones will have to fast tonight," which translates into a cryof acute helplessness, desperation and submission.

The story winds its way to a powerful climax when Venna hears Labhamkrishna's speech declaiming the evils of the yogin system, which he himself had so mercilessly used against Venna. Venna can do little more than to walk out of range of Labhamkrishna's voice with her young daughter, but before she does so, she spits in disgust in the direction of the voice—this is the ultimate act of revenge, an expression of extreme disgust, and again an inversion of great significance where the brahminical obsession with pollution is mimicked, mirrored, critiqued and used against itself to reiterate and reinscribe its hollowness and utter hypocrisy.

Notes

1. The term 'Dalit literature' was first used all the way back in 1958, at the first Dalit Literature Conference, held in Bombay. Yet, most discussions on dalit literature focus on Marathi, Kannada, Gujarati, Tamil, Telugu and Hindi; not many have spoken of a dalit literary 'movement' in Bangla.

2. In fact, as Arun Prabha Mukherjee writes, the very signifier 'Dalit' itself is "a political identity, as opposed to a caste name. It expresses Dalits' knowledge of themselves as oppressed people and signifies their resolve to demand liberation through a revolutionary transformation of the system that oppresses them." ("Introduction", Omprakash Valmiki, *Joothan*, tr. Arun Prabha Mukherjee. New York and Chichester: Columbia University Press, 2003, p.xix)
3. In this, Bangla is, of course, no exception; "caste and caste-based oppression are the most important themes of Dalit writing," writes ArunPrabha Mukherjee ("Introduction", OmprakashValmiki, op.cit., p. xx). One may, however, problematize this a little further by thinking of writers like Manoranjan Bapari in Bangla, whose works seem to focus more on class conflict than on the workings of caste (though questions of caste do come up very powerfully in stories where he does focus on caste), but the contention seems to hold good for the larger section of the body of dalit literature in Bangla and other languages as well.
4. For a more detailed analysis of this question, please see Sayantan Dasgupta, "Dalit Writing in Bangla: Repression and Resistance in ManoranjanByapari and ManjuBala's Narratives" in Kavita Panjabi ed., *Jadavpur Journal of Comparative Literature 46*. Kolkata: Jadavpur University, 2008, pp.125-138.

Works Cited

Bapari, Manoranjan, "Custom."Tr. Sayantan Dasgupta. Accepted for publication in Tutun Mukherjee et al eds., *The Oxford Anthology of Dalit Writing from Eastern India*. Original Bangla "Ribaj."

Biswas, Manohar Mouli, "Yogin."Tr. Smita Basu. Accepted for publication in Tutun Mukherjee et al eds., *The Oxford Anthology of Dalit Writing from Eastern India*. Original Bangla "Jogin."

Dasgupta, Dr Sayantan, is Coordinator, Centre for Translation of Indian Literatures, Jadavpur University, and teaches Comparative Literature there. He has edited *A South Asian Nationalism Reader* and is author of *Indian English Literature: A Study in Historiography* and *Shyam Selvadurai: Texts and Contexts*. He is currently Secretary of the Comparative Literature Association of India.

Ray, Provas, "The Fish."Tr. Urmi Sengupta. Accepted for publication in Tutun Mukherjee et al eds., *The Oxford Anthology of Dalit Writing from Eastern India*. Original Bangla "Shol Machh."

5

Translating Dalit Literature: Texts and Problems

Amrit Sen

While the role of the translator has been a vexed critical issue, the case of dalit translation has provided significantly dense critical challenges in this context. Why does one translate dalit literature? Who are its readers and how does their perspective condition their translation? How is the identity of the translator and target audience related to the accuracy of the translation? What is the relationship between the aesthetics of translation and the agenda of the source dalit text? This paper seeks to raise a few of these questions in the context of my attempt to translate the Bengali dalit story *Ekhono Aadim* by Shymal Kr. Pramanik and the responses to my effort in a workshop in Vidyasagar University. The question of why one should translate dalit Literature is seminal because dalit literature is generally available in regional local languages, each with their dialects, nuances and cultural inflections. In the absence of a critical body of texts that can communicate with each other, the extent and the range of dalit consciousness cannot be adequately mapped. Thus, translation assumes a vital role in making the range of dalit literature available to audiences who are ignorant of the similarities of the cultural contexts.

As Arun Mukherjee points out:

> With the so-called "cultural turn" in translation studies, translators have come to be perceived as mediators working in the contact

> zone to shape cultures. Depending on their translation practice, they may introduce the radically new and previously unthought into a culture or work to shore up established values. (Mukherjee, "Translating Minoritized Cultures")

Unfortunately dalit texts have hardly been translated across other Indian languages and in most cases, these translations have been made into English where the translators have limited access to dalit consciousness. Yet this remains a decision of strategic importance as Arun Prabha Banerjee points out:

> English in India today is not the colonizer's language recalling a colonial past, but the language of power, culture and global access—emblematic of the ultimate in privilege. It is officially constructed both as a "link language" within the country and as a "window" on, or a "pipeline" to, the rest of the world. It is the language through which aesthetic and cultural standards are mediated. I would suggest that to choose this language to offend, educate and engage society, to present a mirror, as it were, is both audacious and pragmatic. (Mukherjee, "Translating Minoritized Cultures")

Very often the language of such translation is English and the readership is dispersed, thereby forcing the translator to homogenise and simplify many of the inflections and resonances of the particular language for his target audience. The syntactical and rhetorical strategies of dalit literature are often not adequately communicated in the target language, thereby diluting the sense of anger and suffering and intense emotional response of the dalit writer. As Sharan Kumar Limbale points out:

> Are human beings only beauty-mad? Do they only want pleasure? The answer to both questions is no, because hundreds of thousands of people appear to be passionate about freedom, love, justice and equality. They have sacrificed themselves for these ideals. This implies that for them social values are at least as dear to their lives as, if not dearer than, values of art. Equality, freedom, justice and love are the basic sentiments of people and society. They are many times more important than pleasure and beauty.

There has never been a revolution in the world for the sake of pleasure and beauty. Many governments have been overturned for equality, freedom and justice. This is history. The literature that glorifies pleasure gives central place to the pleasure-seeking aesthete. The literature that promotes equality, freedom and justice is revolutionary, and it emphasizes the centrality of the human being and society. If pleasure-giving literature arouses joy and sympathy in people, revolutionary literature awakens consciousness of self-respect. (Limbale 119)

Given these limitations, how does the translator approach the dalit text?

Another significant issue deals with the accuracy and aesthetics of the translated text, given that the primary aim is in communicating the angst or suffering of the dalit, especially of communities that have been bypassed by education. Dalit texts often use rhetoric and a language that can pose a challenge through its awkwardness. As Limbale points out:

> The reality of Dalit literature is distinct and so is the language of this reality. It is the uncouth-impolite language of Dalits. It is the spoken language of Dalits. This language does not recognize cultivated gestures and grammar.
>
> For their writing, Dalit writers have used the language of the quarters rather than the standard language. Standard language has a class. Dalit writers have rejected the class of this standard language. Cultured people in society consider standard language to be the proper language for writing. Dalit writers have rejected this validation of standard language by the cultured classes, because it is arrogant. To Dalit writers, the language of the basti [that is, settlement] seems more familiar than standard language. In fact, standard language does not include all the words of Dalit dialects. Besides, the ability to voice one's experience in one's mother tongue gives greater sharpness to the expression.
>
> (Limbale 33-34)

Does the translator retain this awkwardness and aesthetic lack in the translated text? Or does he use Nabokov's post-structuralist idea that the author dies in translation to breathe a different aesthetic and revise the text for his readership? These are some of the important theoretical considerations that I faced while engaging with my translating Pramanik's story.

Given that dalit literature is primarily considered with identity, it was my responsibility to remain vigilant that I could remain faithful to the dalit consciousness in this short story. Pramanik's story is about a family of dalits that depend upon gathering grains accumulated by mice in holes after the reaping of the corn. This particular short story narrates the encounter of Raju Rajwan with a coiled poisonous snake in his effort to extract some corn from a similar hole. While his sickly son and wife watched traumatized, the desperate Raju, challenging the snake clasps it and risks his life for the handful of grain. The short story also narrates the hostility of the different farmers against these vagrant tribes. How accurately could I, a translator located in my cocoon of middle class comfort, be able to do justice to the raw intensity of such a text?

The first thing that struck me about the text was the staccato quality of the prose punctuated by short passages of narration. The language was marked by a relative lack of dialect which made my job somewhat easier. I decided consequently, to use a similar staccato like simple prose that would do justice to the source text, while using the original Bengali expressions to communicate the precise degree of emotion. For example, I decided to retain the guttural 'Nah' instead of the more mundane 'no' to communicate Raju's sense of desperation. Words like *shala* provided a different problem altogether which could not communicate the sense of frustration to a wider audience. I decided therefore to change it to the more English "damn". The ferocity of the snake expressed through the images of the *Nagraj* and the *Rudramurti* had to be unfortunately diluted to the 'King of Snakes' and 'ferocity'. The word *badjat* that Raju uses to protest against the upper class farmers was translated by me to 'swine' and participants in the workshop suggested 'scoundrels'. But the play of the *jat* or 'caste' was lost in this process. A fresh problem arose when Matiya refers to the snake as *Ma Manashar jib*. While my initial impulse was to use the term 'snake goddess', I decided to use only *Manasha* with an appended note explaining Manasha's significance to the indigenous population. However,it piques me whether such annotations take away or interrupt the process of reading.

There were several other problems that cropped up. Raju Rajwari's father, initially a resident of Bihar, had migrated to Bengal due to sheer economic necessity. The words thus frequently used are rudimentary Bengali punctuated by a significant Bihari words. The contrast or hybridity of this language communicates the sense of non-belonging and liminality that operates here. Unfortunately, in the English translation, the sense of liminality was largely homogenized in the absence of any alternative. The narration proved to be largely unproblematic. Incidentally, the largely syntactic narration alternated with an awkward and ungrammatical dialogue in Bengali, which sought to accentuate the identities of the characters. Thus, *bhagaban nebey na bhalo* could be translated into a more colloquial version of English as 'God will not take it lightly'. The staccato quality of the prose was retained in the translation of the emotions of despair and fright within the translated text. Thus 'look at this damned snake', 'why can't it', 'lets get our grain', 'Babu lets go elsewhere', 'I won't retreat' could be used to create that sense of dramatic tension both externally and internally within the story and characters. The phrase *sapta baroi badmash* was translated as 'the snake in wicked'. But even here 'wicked' was a rather inadequate word since Raju's tone was not merely of hostility towards the snake but a subterranean agony at his own fate.

The climactic moment where Raju clasps the snake and tames it, aware that any lapse would lead to death, was suddenly conveyed in terms of the image of the *jamdyut* (the agent of hell) which could hardly be communicated in the English translation.

Two major problem areas for me were in the use of the narrative tense for short story. The original Bengali used the immediate present tense to narrate the incident often alternating it with past tense to refer to Raju's history. However, for an English translation, the use of the immediate present tense posed a problem of readability, and therefore I decided to switch to a more readable past tense. Was I violating the sanctity of the source text here? The immediacy of the experience lost in the change of tense. But to what extent was my liberty justified? I examined this critically and surmised that no major thematic inadequacies were observed. It made sense to switch to the convenience in the target language.

More extensively debated and critiqued was the change of title that I had provided for the story. The initial Bengali title *Ekhono Adim* provided me with a challenge. I had toyed with the title 'Primitive, Still/ Primitives' but had settled for 'Survival'. Aware from my post-colonial perspective that the word primitive had a certain baggage and that the story was about the conflict for survival between marginalized man and cornered beast, I had felt 'survival' would be a better index of the story's theme. Scholars at the workshop saw this as a case of over-translation and a case of my identity and its discomfort with the term *Adim*. They felt that the deliberate play on 'primitive' was an ironic reminder was a dalit title was still considered a primitive in a farming community controlled by the higher castes and consequently the subject of violence. It thus conformed to Limbale's markers of Dalit consciousness; "Rejection and 'revolt' in dalit literature have been birthed from the womb of dalits' pain. They are directed against an inhuman system that was imposed on them. Just as the anguish expressed in dalit literature is in the nature of a collective social voice, similarly, the rejection and revolt are social and collective (Limbale 31). It is in this context that the snake and the man share an empathetic bond. Was I more concerned with the target audience largely a readership of English literature students when I was distilling my own version of the theme for them? Or was it a sub-conscious desire to elide over the caste overtones of the story?

Ironically the editors of the volume decided to retain my original title 'Survival' despite my offer to revise it and this is the title of the entire volume (*Survival and Other Stories*). Apart from identity then, the question of readership and print convenience could often dilute the resonances of a dalit text in translation. A peculiar problem cropped up with the last time when Matiya and Sonu stand beside Raju in whose eyes there is *ujjwal ananda*. The final words are *tader du chokey jaler phonta*. In my translated version I had used the line "Matiya and Sonu stood by the side, their tears glistening in the sunlight." It was pointed out that this too was a case of over translation where I had added the element of sunlight to the tears of Matiya and Sonu and I had no business taking liberty with the text. Granting the validity of this objection, I surmised that my objective in adding an aesthetic dimension to the text. Can the translator of dalit literature take this liberty or is such an addition or qualification a deliberate or an undermining of the aim of dalit literature and its relative awkwardness of style? Or did I as a critical translator have the responsibility to transcreate this text so that it could be better received while retaining its theme?

There is no debate about the fact that the translation of Dalit literature is an integral part of documenting and disseminating the range of dalit responses and dialogues across regional parameters. However the fact remains that this process is a deeply problematic act both in terms of its politics and aesthetics. Who translates dalit literature and for whom? What are the sensitivities and self consciousness that he brings to the act of translation? How does he approach the form and the language of a dalit text so that the theme of protest and suffering do not get obscured? Translators are often accused of being traitors, in this case the vigilance of a translator is even more necessary.

Works Cited

Limbale, Sharankumar. *Towards an Aesthetic of Dalit Literature: Histories, Controversies and Considerations*. Trans. Alok Mukherjee. Delhi: Orient Longman, 2004.

Mukherjee, Arun. "'You Don't Even Want to Go There': Race, Text, and Identities in the Classroom."*Home-work: Postcolonialism, Pedagogy and Canadian Literature*. Ed. Cynthia Sugars. Ottawa: University of Ottawa Press, 2004. 189-212.

— Alok Mukherjee and Barbara Godard. "Translating Minoritized Cultures: Issues of Caste, Class and Gender". *Postcolonial Text*, Vol 2, No 3 (2006) *http://postcolonial.org/index.php/pct/article/view/501/309*.Accessed on 15 January 2012.

Pramanik, Shyamal, "Ekhono Aadim" translated as "Survival", trans. Amrit Sen in Sankar Prasad Singha and Indranil Acharya eds. *Survival and Other Stories: Bangla Dalit Fiction in Translation*. New Delhi: Orient Blackswan, 2012. 154-59.

6

"A Poetry of Resistance": The Literature of Manipur

Mausumi Sen Bhattacharjee

Sharankumar Limbale in his attempt to define 'Who is Dalit?' broadens its categorical premise:

> All the untouchable communities living outside the boundary of the village as well as Adivasis, landless farm labourers, workers, the suffering masses and nomadic criminal tribes. In explaining the word, it will not do to refer only to the untouchable castes. People who are lagging behind economically will also need to be included.
>
> (Limbale 11)

The notion of the dalit has played upon the notion of the identity of an 'other' segregated from the mainstream based on categories like caste. Manipur with its assorted scheduled tribes has also witnessed this sense of denial of identity and its poetry has been one of isolation and denial. What is interesting is the demand for modernity that had initiated much of the dalit project vis-à-vis the European Enlightenment project has also been a major factor in modern Manipuri poetry.

The literature of the north-east states of India is a ventilation of the economic oppression suffered by these people long marginalized by the mainstream Indians. In this paper through my analysis of the poetry of Rajkumar Bhubosana, Robin

S. Ngangom and Thangjam Ibopishak, I intend to explore how their protest and resistance against state oppression has been a major factor in their identity formation that inevitably is the paradigm of the dalit.

The struggle waged by the people of Manipur since Independence is in reality their resistance to state repression and deprivation through the brutal AFSPA 1959 act that is totally detrimental to the United Nation Human Rights Charter by the United Nations in 1991. Such legislations have subjugated and maimed their very identity and capacity to undertake protest movement. In this context we may cite the case of the rape of a Manipuri student Irom Sharmila on 11 July, 2004 whose 'fast unto death' demanding the withdrawal of the Armed Forces Act was answered by her brutal rape and murder – one of the most sadistic murders committed by Indian Paramilitary troops. On 15 July Manipuri women staged an unusual form of protest by appearing nude with banners such as 'Indian Army Rape Us' to shame the Indian State. Such instances show how Manipur although part of the country have been long oppressed and relegated to the darkness of brutality, molestation and torture. This oppression quite naturally is replicated in their literature. In Bhubosana's poem "Should Light be Put Out or Mind Kept in Dark" we observe the poet's desperation to seek modernity and its advantages. Despite repetitive promises however, the state apparatus to provide its people a better mode of existence has always been phlegmatic. Here unavailability of electricity to Manipuri homes is foregrounded to highlight the crisis and lack of resources in their daily existence. The darkness of mind alternates with the darkness of their homes:

> The place is kept in darkness
> Loadshedding is imposed regularly Because of the government's inefficiency.
>
> (Bhubosana 36)

Electricity is a metaphor for modern amenity in Manipuri life. The poet uses this opportunity to list the various governmental schemes apparently aimed for economic growth of these marginalized spaces. The Loktak Hydropower Project is one such project:

> ...there was no light in Manipur
> Even after the commissioning of Loktak Project
> There is no light
> On the other hand
> Loktak Project wastes paddy fields and fishes
> Causes submergence under water
> Spoils man
> Takes away homesteads ...
> Causes resentment.
>
> (Bhubosana38)

The promotion of hydropower project has thus, as the poet expiates not only failed to generate sufficient power but also led to severe threats to ecological processes and functions of the wetland, inundation of agricultural lands and displacement of people from flooded lands, loss of fish population and diversity. Thus, the denial of modernity is coupled with a cognate theme in dalit poetry—the denial of the very environment that they sustain upon.

On the other hand, unavailability of electricity metaphorically underscores the darkness of mind in the sense when they will be deprieved not only of modern facilities but also the enlightenment of education. The poet is caustically cynical in pointing out that this place deters development because

> If mind is developed, one becomes aware of the wrongs...
> If the wrongs are made public in our place
> One gets bashed up, hip broken.
> So its better to keep mind in dark.
>
> (Bhubosana 39)

The poet sums up the state's inhuman oppression to any form of protest with

> Front teeth are bashed out
> In Manipur, the land of jewels.
>
> (Bhubosana 39)

This remains the grotesque reality before these deprieved people. Thus, ironically the question of identity in the Foucauldian sense vis-à-vis the people of Manipur perpetuates the binary opposition between the strong state and the weak hill people. Hill valley, tribal, non-tribal, Meiei-Mayang all irrespective of their ethnicity are subjected to equal fate and hence comes within the purview of the dalit. The poet cannot detach his poetry from this reality. As Ngangom writes:

> Whatever our personal weaknesses may be, the nobility of our craft will always be rooted in two commitments, difficult to maintain: the refusal to lie about what one knows and the resistance to oppression. In contemporary Manipuri poetry, there is a predominance of images of 'bullets', 'blood', 'mother', the colour 'red' and, paradoxically, 'flowers' too.
>
> (Ngangom *Contemporary Manipuri Poetry: An Overview* 299)

Thangjam Ibopishak in his poem "I Want to be Killed by an Indian Bullet" tries to view his protesting persona as 'a seer with oracular powers' and deliberately undercuts it with the alternative 'are you a madman' (Ibopishak 57). In this fictitious altercation with protesting rebels raising their voice against the Indian State machinery, the poet persona is a coward with his hollow patriotism. The anti-state feeling is very obvious when the poet persona pleads: " 'I don't want to die from a foreign bullet'...'Your wish cannot be granted. Don't ever mention Bharat to us'" (Ibopishak 57). This poem incidentally articulates the sense of the bind of the Manipuri people caught between the two extremes – the brutality of the Indian state and army on the one hand and the sweeping monolithic violence of the insurgents on the other. Robin S. Ngangom talks about this "darker more somber and questioning mood" that releases "a skeptical post-Independence poetics in which satire, irony and detachment or confrontation became the prime means of self discovery" (Ngangom, *Contemporary Manipuri Poetry: An Overview*, 298).

In another poem called "Gandhi and Robot" the poet sardonically critiques the hollow promises made from time to time by the political leaders of India including Nehru and Vikram Sarabhai. The ridicule rises to a climactic apex with his deliberate play with the term 'Harijan' – Gandhi preached their betterment with the freedom of the country. But the reality of the Harijan factor in the post- modern context is delineated with parodic images here:

> In Delhi's Red Fort donkeys bray
> On empty stomachs and parched throats;
> The dhobis who rear them
> feed them Old copies of the newspaper 'Harijan'
> By tearing them up into pieces.
>
> (Ibopishak 58)

The redundance of the 'Harijan' project vis-à-vis the deprivation of the Manipuri people even after sixty-four years of independence justifies their repetitive unrest and protest. I would like to linger on this poem because the ironies latent within it draw close associations between the casteism of Hindu society and the Manipuri experience. The derision for Gandhi as "Ballabhaiji possessed a Gandhi borrowed from Birla" (Ibopishak 57) is reminiscent of the mistrust of Gandhi in the early Dalit consciousness. The perceived hollowness of Gandhi's rhetoric in *saVarna* Hindu society is highlighted in the fact that that it is fodder for donkeys. In the background is a celebration of the new 'pagoda at Pokhran/ To keep the 'New Buddha'" when "empty stomachs and parched throats exist" (Ibopishak 58). At the heart of this poem there is a double poetics of exclusion of the Dalit from the cosmoloy of *savarna* consciousness, the very exclusion of India's modernity excludes 'ahimsa' too in the new Bharat. The sense of exclusion and identity thus brings the Manipuri poetry within the broader ambit of Dalit poetry.

Robin S. Ngangom's poem "Everywhere I Go" graphically lists the brutality. He ridicules the irrational interference of the army in deciding their future – "...retired generals analyze the fate of my people and their misery" (Ngangom 46). He further didactically asserts how he intends to "tell my poet friends/ Of the twelve mothers who stripped themselves and asked soldiers to rape them" (Ngangom 47). Here entities representing power, progress, modernity are diametrically opposed to the suffering lot:

> Those who speak the language of progress
> call my homeland a mendicant state
> not knowing its landlocked misery,
> its odd splendor,
> and no one knows who picks up its bodies.
>
> (Ngangom 47)

But the poem ultimately winds up on a positive note when the poet opts out to 'save' the 'tunes of my homeland' instead of brooding. The 'tunes' here brings in the notion of asserting one's identity while preserving its ethnicity. His poetry becomes a mouthpiece for the politically discriminated against and historically overlooked people of Manipur.

The question of extending the frontiers of dalit poetry as it stands on crossroads is an urgent one. If casteism has initiated a voice of identity and protest, the politics of exclusion demands that the indigenous voices of the north-east be recognized, examined thereby creating an opportunity to examine the heterogeneity of possible dalit experiences within the poetics of pain, suffering and anger.

Works Cited

Sharankumar Limbale, *Towards an Aesthetic of Dalit Literature: Histories, Controversies and Considerations.* Trans. Alok Mukherjee .New Delhi: Orient Blackswan, 2010

Tilottama Misra ed. *The Oxford Anthology of Writings from North-East India: Poetry and Essays.* New Delhi: Oxford University Press, 2011.

7

Repression and Resilience: Exploring Indigenous Women's Representations in Mahasweta Devi's *Imaginary Maps*

Meenakshi Dey

Mahasweta Devi, a widely acclaimed spokesperson of the indigenous people of India, is one of the few Indian writers whose works are most sought after for translation, and consequently for a better comprehension of the life and culture of the subalterns in India. She has observed that the non-productive practices of the brahminic culture has found some space in the British and Indian archives, but the life of the tribal women of India have been for centuries erased from narratives written before and after India gained freedom from colonial oppression. Lack of education of the tribal women, combined with sexual, economic, social and political exploitation by higher castes men and the violence and abuses faced within the family had found lesser or no space in the elite pages of history. In addition, the representation of indigenous women as hard working, strong in mind and body, as a thinking individual, as an individual who can protest against injustice has also not found proper delineation in the elite narratives of our country.

This paper aims at exploring the representations of indigenous women in Mahasweta Devi's *Imaginary Maps.* The stories that will be specifically explored are 'Douloti the Bountiful' and 'The Hunt'. The protagonists in both the stories are character-wise poles apart. While Douloti represents the helplessness of the bonded labourers in the face of economic and sexual exploitation by the privileged in the society, Mary Oraon in 'The Hunt' represents the Third World feminists who are conscious of their right to lead a life of honour and strive hard to attain it. The former is a symbol of repression and the latter is a symbol of resilience.

In the story 'Douloti, the Bountiful', Douloti is a female representative of the bonded slavery. Her father, Ganori Nagesia, a dalit, is also a slave but his exploitation is restricted to excessive hard labour which at one point due to an accident makes him invalid for life. To repay Ganori's debt of three hundred rupees and the multiple interests accrued on it, Douloti is handed over to Paramanand Misra, a brahmin, who promises to marry Douloti and also pays off Ganori's Debt. From here Douloti treads on a path from where there is no return. The yoke of slavery passes from the parent to the child and Douloti is caught in the vicious cycle of enslavement. Paramanand turns out to be a brothel owner who offers Douloti at first to a government contractor named Latia Sahib and then to Singh Sahib.

When Douloti is discarded by Singh Sahib, she returns to Paramanand's brothel which is now run by his son, Baijnath Misra because of Paramanand's sudden demise. Unlike his father who was considerate regarding the number of customers a kamiya whore should serve every day, Baijnath believes in making fast money by sending dozens of customers to every girl at a cheap price. He considers the kamiya whores as trucks which are to be always kept loaded and plying on the road. He does not worry about the effect of such overloading on the whores as he knows a good drought would easily replenish his depleting whore resources. Consequently, many whores including Douloti become sick, emaciated and die due to not only continuous sexual oppression but also lack of medical attention.

Here lies the difference between the exploitation of a subaltern man and a subaltern woman. Douloti being a woman kamiya is not exploited by excessive hard labour jobs. Her job is to gratify the sexual desires of her dozens of customers on a daily basis and that too without sufficient amount of rest to rejuvenate her body. This job is not only an excruciating physical job (she is left bloodied by most of her customers) but also a humiliating and dehumanizing experience which shatters her initial innocence about the big, bad world and the greedy wolf-like creatures like Paramanand, Latia Sahab, Munavar, Baijnath Mishra waiting to prey on girls like her.

The title of the story is also ironic. Douloti means wealth. But in the story Douloti remains forever in the grip of poverty and her owner reaps huge monetary benefits by forcing her into prostitution. Douloti's gruesome death and that too at the age of twenty seven is Mahasweta Devi's means of portraying to the readers that just as excessive ravaging of a woman's body can turn it from a beautiful to a wasted and diseased one in the same way excessive exploitation of natural resources can turn a fertile land into a barren, wasted and abandoned land. Both land and a woman's body can remain fertile and productive till the time they are taken care of properly. So Douloti's body stretched out inside the map of India is a symbol of not only the miserable plight of all the bonded slaves, particularly women, spread all over India but also it serves as a warning against continuous exploitation of natural and human resources.

After Douloti's death, her body will be removed from the place that has been tainted with her diseased blood and body. This will be done to facilitate the flag hoisting and celebrate the nation's independence from colonial rule. But the terrible end of this subaltern signifies that the nation's independence had been founded on continuous exploitation of the masses belonging to the caste and gender synonymous to Douloti.

Previously there was external colonization with the colonizers being the British and after independence the colonizers are the government officials, landlords, contractors, zamindars etc. who occupy a dominant position in the societal hierarchy. In both the situations the tribals and their common property resources are the source of rich mineral resources as well as cheap labour whose benefits reach the richer class, urban middle class and the rural upper classes and leave the tribals impoverished and displaced. Thus Douloti's contaminated dead body is a text which questions the profitability of the so called development projects such as coal mines and dams introduced by the government at the expense of the tribal's well being and existence.

Though the government tries to show its concern for the displaced tribals by providing compensation and promising jobs, the ones to actually benefit from such promises are very few. If the tribals are not displaced from their forest homes, if their natural resources are not exploited beyond limits, if there are no external encroachers on their lands, then they would live a life of self sufficiency as earlier times and not face continuous social, economic, physical and sexual exploitation as they are doing today. The tribal/dalit women like Douloti would then live a life of dignity and happiness instead of being sold off by their parents into the profession of prostitution to escape the intolerable burden of bonded slavery. The tribals would not then consider independence of the nation as a myth because they would be truly free from external and internal colonizers and living their simple and happy lives.

In contrast to Douloti is the character of Mary Oraon in the story 'The Hunt'. Mary is a strong half-tribal woman with a white planter as a father and a tribal woman as her mother. Mary's father deserted her mother soon after impregnating her. As Mary does not possess a pure tribal blood, she is considered as an outcaste by the Oraon community. She is also not bound by the laws imposed on women of the Oraon community and lives an independent life and according to her own dictums. She is even engaged to a Muslim boy named Jalim. She works hard and is appreciated by everyone for her business making qualities. Even the owner's wife admires Mary as she says, "You have to take words from a girl who works like an animal, carries a forty pound bag on her back, and boards the train, cleans the whole house in half an hour." Mary is courageous, confident, outspoken and intelligent. All these qualities set her apart from the other tribal women of her community and also Douloti.

Mary's life becomes miserable when the developer Tehsildar Singh sets his lustful eyes on her. He makes amorous advances towards Mary, who refuses to buckle down under pressure. As the Tehsildar becomes impatient, he attempts to grab Mary one day while returning from market. Mary somehow manages to escape the sexual violation of her body by saying that she is "unclean" and he must wait till the following day to gratify his amorous desires. That very day she decides to avenge her insult and secure her dignity by killing the Tehsildar. She invites the Tehsildar to a forest rendezvous on the day of the annual spring festival. The unsuspecting developer then comes to the forest only to die at the hands of Mary Oraon.

In the tribal society, women are respected and committing rapes is considered a sin. Mary by killing the Tehsildar not only avenges her insult as a woman but also avenges the colonizer, Tehsildar's attempt to take advantage of her community's dalit position in the society through violence and injustice. Mary kills him with her machete and at a time when the tribal women instead of men become hunters on the twelfth year of the annual spring festival. As per ritual, the ones who have committed any crime are given punishment by the tribal women during this occasion. Every year this role of imparting justice is performed by the tribal patriarchy. But in the twelfth year there is gender-reversal ritual. So through the character of Mary, Mahasweta Devi has tried to ventilate that in this patriarchal society women can alter their subaltern position only by recognizing that they are individuals who deserve equal status as men and that they should protest against the injustices committed on them not only individually but also collectively.

The story is a revolt against gender oppression and the colonial system both internal and external which exploits the aboriginals and their natural resources under the pretext of development. By killing the lumber contractor, who comes to the remote village of Kuruda to acquire sal trees, Mary eliminates not only the threat to her body but also the threat to the Oraon community of losing their natural resources which provide them food and cultural continuity.

The findings of this paper thus indicate two aspects of the tribal women's lives...one – a life of constant subjugation, sexual and economic exploitation and the other – a life of resilience, rebellion and honour. Douloti is representative of the life of myriad oppressed tribal women, and Mary is representative of the tribal women who have revolted against different kinds of exploitations. In both the stories, Mahasweta Devi makes the subaltern speak in different ways. In case of Douloti, she attempts to speak about the miserable plight of women of her caste and bond slavery through her tragic death. Her corpse sprawled across the map of India becomes an instrument of voicing out the atrocities and subjugation faced by a subaltern in a world of gendered and political hegemony. On the other hand Mary Oraon speaks not only through verbal threats to the Tehsildar against harassing her but also through her action of killing the Tehsildar, she sends the message that excessive repression will only result in resilience and repercussion of a violent and catastrophic form.

Works Cited

Devi, Mahasweta, *An Anthology of Recent Criticism*, ed. by Nivedita Sen and Nikhil Yadav, Pencraft International, 2008.

_______, *Imaginary Maps*, tr. and ed. by Gayatri Chakravorty Spivak, 1995.

Chakravorty Gayatri Spivak, Women in Difference: Mahasweta Devi's Douloti the Bountiful, in *Nationalisms and Sexualities*, et al, eds. London: Routledge, 1992.

8

Dalit "Draupadi": Violation of Women and the Subversion of Epic Tradition

Baisali Hui

> Mahasveta Devi is firmly ensconced in tradition alongwith the parallel thread of enlightening modernity. However, she yet firmly stands by the energy imparted by fables, folklore, riddles, rituals, death rites. It is a treasure trove of wisdom for her, and this has been effectively communicated. Relatedly, once exhausted on a walk with tribals, thinking she would die, the tribals promised to get "big boulders" for her grave – the ultimate tribute.
>
> *The Hindustan Times*, April 1997

The centre of dalit writing is located in the perceived necessity of sounding a protest and building a resistance against class and caste-based discriminations. The beginning of resistance is, naturally, located in the source and extent of pain and suffering and of enforced silence. Justifiably enough, anger, hatred and mistrust are at the core of all such experience that thrive on assumed mainstream-marginal or central-peripheral relationship. Mahasweta Devi's short story "Draupadi", likewise, has its beginning in the untold recesses of mute suffering, scathing injustice and discrimination that are inherent in the corrupt class and caste-ridden social structure led by the so-called urbanized, educated elite. The choice of the name Draupadi itself can be seen as an act of subversion as Spivak points out in her discussion on the tale:

> Draupadi is the name of the central character. She is introduced to the reader between two uniforms and between two versions of her name: Dopdi and Draupadi. It is either that as a tribal she cannot pronounce her own name (Draupadi), or the tribalised form, Dopdi, is the proper name of the ancient Draupadi. She is on a list of wanted persons, yet her name is not on the list of appropriate names for the tribal women. (387)

Thus, circumscribed and straitjacketed by the standards and norms of a partial society (that even looks askance at a tribal woman having an elitist Sanskrit name or rebelling against the dictum of the corrupt landowner of the locality), Dopdi and her husband Dulna Majhi decide to revolt. And, thus they become, like hundreds and thousands of poverty-stricken, uneducated common peasants of the forests, meadows and plateaus of Bengal, Bihar or Uttar Pradesh, sympathizers of the Naxalite movement raging through the country during the 1970s.

The story of the other Draupadi from the epic, thus, becomes linked to the tale of the hapless Dopdi here. The daughter of a king and the wife of five most illustrious men of their times, Krishna Draupadi is, if we look at her careergraph in *The Mahabharata*, an unfortunate woman, after all. She is tricked out of her home and lawful possessions by the cunning Kauravas, is destined for twelve long years to be hunted through dangerous forests and inaccessible mountain ranges, her dignity compromised as the hand maiden of a lesser queen during her year of secret exile, her modesty being outraged at the public court more than once in silent presence of her powerless husbands, her sons killed treacherously and the integrity of her character put to question again and yet again.

Unlike Sita of *The Ramayana*, Draupadi is difficult to define, her characteristics failing to satisfy or be comprehended by the patriarchal order that the epics represent. She does not, in the patronizing sense of the term, possess the archetypal feminine "virtues" of mute suffering, silent tolerance, uncomplaining self-sacrifice or unconditional subjugation to authority. She is the one who speaks her mind. She is the one who asks for justice, who rants and fumes, curses and seeks vengeance on her opponents; she is the one who does not leave her life to destiny but, in a world dominated by fatalism, seeks to change her fate. She is called Draupadi (the daughter of King Drupad) and Panchali (the princess of the kingdom of Panchal) in lieu of a proper name for herself. But she appears to outgrow both these epithets in her ability to move out of the shadow of her parentage and royal ancestry. She remains, perhaps, only Krishna, the dark-complexioned one, emerging out of the golden sacrificial fire, resplendent in her own dark beauty. Like Lord Krishna who is considered to be the friend of her soul, her complexion as well as her nature, both are subversive of the existing Aryan standards of acceptability.

She is hailed as sharp-witted, intelligent, conversant in court politics of the times and far-sighted. In a man these would have been acclaimed as rare virtues; in a woman, sadly enough, they spelt self-disaster. She is a wronged woman in the narrative, not because she is more sinned against than sinning but because of the flawed representation of her character. The epic poet's male gaze fails to interpret her differently, fails to decipher the anguish behind her anger, the claustrophobic environment of court politics, of power struggle, of eternal calculations of loss and gain, triumph and defeat smothering the soft and the creative in her nature. In a primitive civilization where polygamy is rampant and victory is celebrated with the possession of the female body (the victor, almost as a norm, marrying the beautiful princess at the end of a war, a contest or a sport), Draupadi provides the only example of polyandry. The epic relates how often she broke the court decorum but is silent on how she must have felt when the Pandavas decided and rationalized over what to do with her at different stages of her life. She is married to all five brothers, though Arjun alone had won her hand and on their last journey heavenwards when she falls, Yudhisthira complacently comments that her sin has been to love Arjun most, though by duty she was bound to love all five equally. She is the one who had listened more to her heart than her head, relied more on her female instincts to take a decision. Naturally, therefore, she is not invoked as a self-effacing mother like Kunti nor a devoted wife like Gandhari. She stands tall amidst her peers in solitary resolution and silent sympathy.

These evocative aspects of Draupadi's character open up possibilities for the modern day author dealing with the complexities of contemporary life and the dalit question. It is striking to note that the epic tradition, as upholding the ethos of the dominant civilization, had often been effective in subduing the voice of the disadvantaged, the marginal and the defeated. But when Draupadi being central to the mainstream narrative and a representative of the dominant ethos, questions the validity of its moral set-up, the epic itself becomes the resource for subverting tradition and for rewriting history. And dalit literature, side by side relying upon folk culture and tribal languages draws its material from the existing mainstream tradition, too, as Charles C. Davis says about black Amarican writing appropriating history:

> For every black work, there is a double history of another sort as well. We have, of course the tradition of American letters, that continuity in form and ideas that contributed much...But beyond this there is the hidden tradition, the rich and changing store of folkforms and folk materials, the advantages of a dialectical tongue, with a separate music of its own, and the background of rituals, learned responses and wisdom that grew from a community given an amount of homogeneity through isolation and oppression. (51)

For the conceptualization and narration of the dalit experience there is a latent double history at work, likewise. Dopdi Mejhen in Mahasweta Devi's story is not a high- born princess but an impoverished tribal farmhand, a dark Santal girl of twenty seven who is wanted by the army as an accomplice in the Naxalite atrocities on grain brokers, landlords and moneylenders. Dopdi's past is narrated as a long combat against poverty, injustice and victimization. Along with her husband Dulna Majhi, Dopdi worked as farm labourer though the districts of Birbhum, Burdwan, Murshidabad and Bankura at harvest time. They were closely connected with the murder of landowners "occupying upper-caste wells and tubewells during the draught" and gave shelter to the Naxalite young men the police were after. At the much-publicized Operation Bakuli led by Arjan Singh, in which hundreds of tribal people were mercilessly gunned down, the couple miraculously escaped and went underground at the impenetrable forest of Jharkhani. An arduous battle between the state power armed with guns, ammunition and advanced war technology on the one hand and the primitive tribes defending themselves with bow and arrow ensues. Innocent Santals are killed during the search for Dulna and Dopdi. The flaunting of law and power by the state agencies to subdue a peasant-aided revolt is depicted ironically here:

> Senanayak knows the activities and capacities of the opposition better than they themselves do. First, therefore, he presents an encomium on the military genius of the Sikhs. Then he explains further... Without a gun even the "five K's" come to nothing in this day and age. These speeches he delivers to all and sundry. As a result, the fighting forces regain their confidence in the *Army Handbook*. It is not a book for everyone. It says that the most despicable and repulsive style of fighting is guerrilla warfare with primitive weapons. Annihilation at sight of any and all practitioners of such warfare is the sacred duty of every soldier. Dopdi and Dulna belong to the category of such fighters, for they too kill by means of hatchet and scythe, bow and arrow, etc. (137-38)

The involvement of Dulna and Dopdi in the extreme-Left politics of the young intellectuals rebelling against the injustice and ill distribution of wealth in society leads us back to the origin of the ill-fated Naxalite movement, originating as a peasant revolt in the Naxalbari area of West Bengal in 1967 and spreading to Orissa, Bihar, Uttar Pradesh and other parts of the country. Years of suppression, oppression and hunger led to an outburst of the economically weak and low class tribal people in the form of bloody violence. Whatever the outcome of the rebellion, whatever the reasons for its failure—in directionless mayhem or internal sabotage—the cause for the uprising remains significant because of the dreams of hundreds of Dulnas and Draupadis who dared challenge the powers-that-be.

The armed forces in the leadership of Senanayak close in on the forest of Jharkhani. The end of the desperate tale of the couple is predictable enough. Dulna is killed as he came to drink water from a spring that was the only source of drinking water in the dense forest and Dopdi, walking back to the hide-out where her comrades from Calcutta are waiting for information from her, is "apprehended" by the army. She is taken in for questioning which predictably lasts through the night and the next morning the sun rises to bathe the naked body of the woman, crushed and gangraped by the soldiers, bloody through tortures all night long. It is not this end that surprises us, but Dopdi, the woman who will survive yet. The wonder is not in the army's procedure to inflict pain and humiliation, it is at the individual's ability to tolerate and surmount it. So after her *Vastraharan* when the next morning the sentries come to take her to the Officer's camp, she walks straight to him, upright but stark naked. The Senanayak is scandalized:

> Draupadi comes closer. Stands with her hand on her hip, laughs and says, The object of your search, Dopdi Mejhen. You asked them to make me up, don't you want to see how they made me?
>
> Where are her clothes?
>
> Won't put them on, *sir*. Tearing them.
>
> Draupadi's black body comes even closer. Draupadi shakes with an indomitable laughter that Senanayak simply cannot understand. Her ravaged lips bleed as she begins laughing. Draupadi wipes the blood on her palm and says in a voice that is as terrifying, sky splitting, and sharp as her ululation, What's the use of clothes? You can strip me, but how can you clothe me again? Are you a man? (146)

She has no Lord Krishna to save her from physical violence and public humiliation, but her voice rings out clear like that of the epic heroine who, forgetting the modesty of her station had asked Bhishma and the other senior courtiers whether her husband had the right to put a bet on his wife in a game of dice. Does the king who has lost his kingdom, all his possessions and even himself (metaphorically as well as actually) in a silly game of dice, still own his wife to lose her now? As Draupadi's question ages ago had shamed and silenced the wisest men of Hastinapur, it does the same to the army officer who stands dumbstruck and terrified. Dopdi Mejhen rejects the clothes that they had stripped off her in the darkness of night and hypocritically gave her back in the morning to cover her wounded body, to hide her marks of shame.

In rejecting her clothes she rejects the possessive imposition of 'honour' and 'shame' on the female body, a patriarchal construct to keep women subdued and silent. In a different context Kamla Bhasin and Ritu Menon (1998), and then again, Urvashi Butalia (1998) have talked about the imposition of silence on women, the worst victims of Partition atrocities in the Indian subcontinent, in the post-Partition era in the name of family honour and forgiveness. But even out of such impositions emerges those voices that break the silence and help in reviewing the established status quo and rewriting history. Dopdi, an illiterate low caste woman, gains enormous strength and active agency by consciously discarding her clothes. Now it is the turn of the well-dressed Senanayak to be ashamed and to lower his eyes in fear and shame at the sight of the blood-stained exposed body of the dark woman, her mangled breasts, bruised skin. His unjustified 'making up' of this poor, unfed tribal woman and the feeling of elation at being able to reinstate the strongly moral and unmistakably patriarchal structure of law and order in the forest areas are razed to dust. Suddenly he realizes that he stands, after all, in front of the unfathomable mystery of the dark forests, the starving children of generations of poor untouchables and outcastes, their courage evolving out of desperation and hope. Long back Dulna had assured Dopdi about the choice of their vocation, "Dear, this is best! We won't get family and children this way. But who knows? Landowner and moneylender and policemen might one day be wiped out!" The story, after all, remains a fictionalized representation of history in a different way, as Carolyn M. Eliott remarks, talking about women reconstructing their personal histories vis-à-vis the changing times:

> Can these narratives be considered the social history of previous generations? They are not eyewitness accounts of the past, and are clearly mediated by each author's contemporary effort to explain herself. Yet al history is mediated by its teller. I would argue that these narratives contain the stuff of history, materials to be taken along with others, to help construct a portrait of the past. (14)

An interesting comparison may be drawn between the government/state apparatus functioning with male authority and the guerilla warfare of the dalit peasants and fugitive Naxalites being invested with the qualities of the female. The firearms are fearsome and wield enormous power of destruction exploding "out of the male organ of a gun." The primitive bow and arrow and axe, on the contrary, seem to represent the instinctive dexterity of the forest people at self-preservation and cunning ambush. The knowledge of war from the *Army Handbook* falls far short of the knowledge of combat that runs in tribal blood through generations. The male force of artillery fire is countered appropriately by the female hide-and-seek of intelligent guerilla warfare. The dense and mysterious forests as battlefields for such combats scare the outsiders away, but once the army succeeds in penetrating the green cover, they launch a direct attack. Thus Dopdi, a tribal woman becomes the proper symbol for this war between state-aided organized military forces and the instinctive local tribes fighting for their cause. Dopdi, walking through the forest with a little rice in her west band, picking lice from her hair and thinking of her fugitive life is tracked down and easily caught. The situation that led to the killing of Surja Sahu, a rich landowner at Bakuli which unleashed a torrent of military action on the tribal populace comes back to her mind. It had very little to do with politics, but more with the insolence of a greedy, rich landowner who wanted more when the poor were dying of thirst:

> That was a troubled time. Dopdi is confused when she thinks about it. *Operation* Bakuli in Bakuli. Surja Sahu arranged with Biddibabu to dig two tubewells and three wells within the compound of his two houses. No water anywhere, draught in Birbhum. Unlimited water at Surja Sahu's house, as clear as a crow's eye.
>
> Get your water with a canal tax, everything is burning…
>
> Get out of here. I don't accept your Panchayat nonsense. Increase cultivation with water. You want half the paddy for sharecropping. Everyone is happy with free paddy. Then give me paddy at home, give me money. I've learned my lesson trying to do you good.
>
> What good did you do?
>
> Have I not given water to the village?
>
> You've given it to your kin Bhagunal.
>
> Don't you get water?
>
> No. The untouchables don't get water.
>
> The quarrel began there. In the drought human patience catches easily… . Surja Sahu's house was surrounded at night. Surja Sahu had brought out his gun… . Dulna had said, I'll have the first blow, brothers. My great grand father took a bit of paddy from him, and still gives him free labor to repay that debt. (142)

Dulna and Dopdi escaped the firing and fled whereas many others died. They continued to flee in exile from village to village, forest to forest—half-fed, unfed and sleepless. Yet they did not surrender. Their hearts broke to see Bakuli burning; men, women and children put to merciless death in the name of law and order and their resolution strengthened. So the army officer is at his wit's end to decode what the dying Dulna meant by his last shout of "Ma-ho" or in what language did Dopdi sing her song of jubilation. In the presentation of the two army officers, too, the author uses irony. Captain Arjan Singh, the "architect" of Bakuli, develops a mortal fear of dark-skinned people and turns an inveterate drunkard. Senanayak, in charge of *Operation Forest* Jharkhani, is a more cautious and careful man who maintains a typical elitist position regarding his "theory" of the peasant revolt. He keeps his theory separate from his practice and dreams of writing a bestseller in future in which "he will demolish the gentlemen and *highlight* the message of the harvest workers." Though today he is engaged in killing the young by *apprehension and elimination*, nevertheless, theoretically he believes that the world changes by degrees and its legacy is in the hands of the youth. He proposes, "In order to destroy the enemy, become one." But underneath such pseudo-philosophical realizations there runs the basic instinctive urge for self-preservation. And Senanayak wants to keep himself ready to shift allegiance to the other side, just on the scent of a change.

So the question of understanding does not arise. If Arjan Singh is a pronounced coward, making a fool of himself by public display of his fear, Senanayak is no braveheart either. He is a hypocrite posing as a great leader and tough soldier whose guise fails him when confronted by the naked Dopdi, the illiterate peasant, the defiant rebel, the defiled woman. He has no answer to her challenge. The uselessness of his fake theory of warfare and even worse practice becomes apparent as he cringes in dread in front of Draupadi, the enemy he wanted to subdue, "for the first time Senanayak is afraid to stand before an unarmed target, terribly afraid."

Draupadi, in *The Mahabharata* had five husbands who failed to protect her. The dalit Draupadi of Mahasweta Devi's story had her husband killed and the protectors of the law of the country violating her body repeatedly: "Shaming her a tear trickles out of the corner of her eye. In the muddy moonlight she lowers her lightless eye, sees her breast, and understands that, indeed, she's been made up right. Her breasts are bitten raw, the nipples torn. How many? Four-five-six-seven—then Draupadi has passed out."

Both the Draupadis have realized the male claim for protecting them to be mere eyewash. And so, they reject it. *The Vastraharan* or the stripping (be it at the metaphorical level or the actual), therefore, frees these women from the burden of family legacy, shame and honour. These patriarchal constructs that had restrained the physical, psychological and emotional growth of women within the barriers of the family, have lost their significance to these two women. The epic Draupadi comes back to the fold of family life enriched by her experience of exile but the other Draupadi has no place to go back to, even if she survives the torture; her husband and kin dead in police firing, her comrades taking shelter at some remote corner of the state.

Both of them, however, have seen through the sham of the social hierarchy and thus, are in no need for any further pretension. They can call a spade a spade, can ask questions and laugh unashamedly. They both are dalit outcasts, one because of her social position, the other because she has rejected the society that has wronged her. And literature invests them with courage and a voice to speak. Thus the prolonged parallelism between the epic heroine and the common labourer from the paddy field leads to a revealing realization regarding dalit identity and the nature of their protest. The resistance of a people fighting for their self-respect and their right to live an honourable life takes the form of Dopdi and Dulna and hundreds of people killed at Bakuli, Bankrajarh, Jharkhani and a thousand other unknown places. To do good to them or support them in their struggle may appear to be a self-congratulating pastime to the cultured *bhadralok* of elite Bengal. But in all such insincere attempt there is the possibility of exposing oneself even farther. As Tagore said a long time back, in his essay on public good:

> We cannot do good to others at will. We need to have the right to do good to them. The mighty can harm the weak very easily but in order to do good to the weak and the lowly, it is not enough to be merely mighty, one has to be weak and lowly oneself, an equal. Man will never accept actual good as alms or even as

> borrowing but may receive that only as his rightful claim...The common people of the country today, have to depend on the kindness of the landowners, moneylenders, aristocrats, in a word the genteel society and in doing so, they have lowered the position of the gentility. We can easily beat the servant, plague the tenant, cheat the poor illiterate; to behave justly to the lower order or to be polite to the non-respected multitudes depends solely on our sweet will and not on the strength of the other side, in order to save ourselves from this precarious crisis do we need to strengthen the lower classes of the society. (*translation mine*) (548-553).

Works Cited

Butalia, Urvashi. *The Other Side of Silence: Voices from the Partition of India.* New Delhi: Penguin, 1998.

Davis, Charles. T. *Black is the Color of the Cosmos: Essays on Afro-American Literature and Culture* 1942-1981. Ed. Henry Louis Gates, Jr. Washington, D.C.: Howard University Press, 1989.

Eliott, Carolyn M. "Introduction," *A Space of Her Own: Personal Narratives of Twelve Women.* Eds. Leela Gulati and Jasodhara Bagchi. New Delhi: Sage Publications, 2005.

Mahasweta, Devi "Draupadi." trans. Gayatri Chakravorty Spivak. Cooke, Miriam and Roshni Rustomji-Kerns. Eds. *Blood into Ink: South Asian and Middle Eastern Women Write War.* Oxford: Westview Press. 1994: 135-146. All textual references to the story are from this edition.

Menon, Ritu and Kamla Bhasin. *Borders and Boundaries : Women in India's Partition.* New Delhi: Kali for Women, 1998.

Spivak, Gayatri Chakravorty. "Draupadi by Mahasveta Devi" *Critical Enquiry*: University of Chicago Press. vol. 8 no. 2, Winter 1981.

Tagore, Rabindranath. "Lokahita"(Public Good). *Rabindra Rachanabali* (Collected Works of Tagore). Kolkata: Visva-Bharati Publication Section. 1910. vol. 12: 548-553.

9

Mahasweta Devi's Pterodactyl, Puran Sahay and Pirtha: A Reading in Dalit Resistance to 'Development'

Joyjit Ghosh

In *Towards an Aesthetic of Dalit Literature* Sharan Kumar Limbale writes, "By Dalit literature, I mean writing about Dalits by Dalit writers with a Dalit consciousness" (Limbale 19). According to Limbale, a dalit writer is bound to be an activist for dalit literature is action. In his words:

> When we expel the activist from the writer, he is no longer a Dalit writer. A Dalit writer must posses a particular consciousness. Yes, he must have commitment. When we remove consciousness and commitment, he will no longer be a Dalit writer. Therefore, the primary requirement for Dalit writers is that they must be committed to their society and they must have Dalit consciousness in their hearts and minds.
>
> (Limbale 158)

Mahasweta Devi though of upper caste origins is a dalit writer in her own right. Can any reader of Mahasweta's writing about the tribals be indifferent to the author's 'Dalit consciousness'? A celebrated writer, journalist and tireless activist Mahasweta Devi believes that "a creative writer should have a social conscience"[1] and her conscience is troubled whenever she sees the tribals all over India in crisis and agony.

Mahasweta's involvement in the tribal movement started in 1965 when she first went to Palamu, one of the poorest districts in India, where the bonded labour system still survived. In her own words, "Palamu is a mirror of tribal India." She organized the bonded labourers and in 1979 the Govt. of India liberated a handful of bonded labourers in Seora village.[2] She, however, did not stop her battle. For the last two decades she has fought on behalf of the denotified tribes of India whom the British colonial state branded as 'natural criminals' because they lived in the forest and did not take to cultivation. At present, she is in her late eighties and Mahasweta still fights for the rights of the aboriginal peoples of India.

Resistance is a central theme in the stories of Maheswata Devi. And the theme of resistance addresses the fundamental issues like feudal oppression, female subjugation, Hinduism as Brahman exploitation as revealed in the stories like "The Hunt", "Douloti the Bountiful", "Breast Giver" etc. "Pterodactyl", "Puran Sahay", and Pirtha, our present concern, is a story where resistance is designed as an act to rid a people of its oppressors / exploiters, and it so thoroughly pervades the experience of living under exploitation, subjugation and oppression that it becomes an almost autonomous aesthetic principle.[3]

The title of the story is longish and a bit unusual. Three proper nouns come in a single bracket: Pterodactyl is a prehistoric animal, Pirtha is an obscure block in Madhya Pradesh and Puran Sahay is a journalist (an alter-ego of the author), who visits Pirtha as he is asked by his old friend Harisharan, now the Block Development Officer. In the opening pages of the text the reader is given an idea of the map of the block:

> The survey map of Pirtha *Block* is like some extinct animal of Gondowanaland. The beast has fallen on its face. The new era in the history of the world began when, at the end of the Mesozic era, India broke off from the main mass of Gondowanaland. It is as if some pre-historic creature had fallen on its face then. Such are the survey lines of Pirtha *Block*. (*IM* 98)

The language of the passage quoted above is starkly unsentimental and it has a rocky bareness. Mahasweta once wrote, "Language is a weapon, it's not for shaving your armpits."[4] This is exactly where the writing of Mahasweta emerges as literature of action—action against the callousness, corruption as well as heartlessness of the government officers, businessmen, contractors, MLAs in charge of tribal welfare — all of those who cheat the aboriginals of Pirtha, eat the money that is their rightful claim, and leave them hungry, naked and poor. The government does not even know that there are human beings in Pirtha. And the state government is cautious about declaring famine even if people die. Puran is therefore asked by the S.D.O. not to make a noise in the newspapers : "if you say anything ... more journalists will come. There will be a furore" (*IM* 98).

Pirtha is an obscure tribal village in Madhya Pradesh like Madhola, Derha or Dholki where people die of starvation and malnutrition every year, where the tribals sell their infants and girl children to touts, where education is as much an impossibility as cultivation. The land given to the tribals is barren. And the neighbouring fertile land has been distributed in the name of fake tribals. There is neither school nor hospital, neither irrigation nor industry. The people of Pirtha live as if in an exile.

At this point we are reminded of another story of Mahasweta Devi — *Kusuma*, included in *Bachai Galpa by Mahasweta Devi*, edited by Soma Mukhopadhyay. It is the name of a village which once had the forest of kusum trees. Now it is an arid desert. The village does not figure in the map of West Bengal nor in that of Jharkhand. On the lips of the tribal people of Kusuma, the author puts the inevitable question: "Kusuma is not in Manbajar, Manbajar is not in Purulia, Purulia is not in the state. Are we then no-humans?" (translation mine). These tribal people are thus always socio-politically excluded. The Government of West Bengal does not own them as the rightful people. They do no have access to the district headquarters for any kind of help or support. The place they belong to is as if outside the borders of geography for there is neither road nor health center, neither market nor police station. They remain in dark middle ages.

So is true of the condition of the tribals belonging to Pirtha. They do not receive anything from modern India. And they are:

> nowhere implicated in Indian education, development, science, industry, agriculture, technology. They remain spectators. India marches towards the twenty-first century. (*IM* 178)

The author in the novella thus draws our attention to a nation which is, to quote the words of Homi K. Bhabha, "split within itself."[5] G.N. Devy is absolutely right when he comments:

> The history of tribals during the last sixty years is filled with stories of forced displacement, land alienation, increasing marginalization, the eruption of violence and counter-violence by the state. Going by any parameters of development, the tribals always figure at the tail end. (Devy XV)

This is too true. The nationalist discourse not only ignores the representation by the tribal communities, it in a way contributes to the organized oppression and exploitation of them. Throughout the story it is evident that the main culprit is the fundamental failure or ruthless unconcern of the tribal welfare department from state to district to sub-division. The people of Pirtha thus suffer the man-made poverty and famine. They are even forced to 'ration' their drinking water when both nature and the man-made administration turn against them. At this juncture a few lines from L.S. Rokade's *To be or not to be Born* may come to one's mind :

> Mother, this is your land
> flowing with water.
> Rivers break their banks,
> Lakes brim over,

> And you, one of the human race
> Must shed blood
> struggle and strike
> for a palmful of water.
> I spit on this great civilization
>
> (Dangle *Poisnoed Bread* 4)

This is the angry voice of protest protest against the innumberable ways of exploitation and oppression to which the dalits are subjected all over India.

The aborigines of Pirtha, however, do not protest in the same way. They wait in suffering. They are patient like nature even whey they receive no help and support from the government only what they resist is 'development' which is synomymous with displacement and disaster to them. The women fight against population control. And the men staunchly resist dispossession of land. Thus when the government along with the contractors, businessmen and moneylanders make a diabolical nexus and plan to move the tribals to the plains where there are many supports for survival they starkly refuse :

> ... we will not leave Pirtha ... why should we leave? Isn't this our place? Now no tribal will leave ... if they want to give us aid, let them give it to us here ... if not let them forget, let them forget us. At most we'll die, nothing worse can happen. (*IM* 195–96)

A superficial reading of the passage quoted above may suggest that the tribals are rigid and irrational particularly when they refuse to go for the development meant for them. But any sensitive reader can understand that the word 'development' is pregnant with a 'hermeneutics of suspicion.'[5] In fact, the subtextual meaning of the word under concern lurks in the idea of Kausalji, a corrupt contractor: "If you can move them, and plant some more trees, this spot with the river, the hills, and the trees will make an excellent *picnic* area" (*IM* 151). Kausalji is confident because his relative is the Managing Director of State Tourism. Thus the nexus between the vested interests of people in both private and public enterprises is brought home to the readers. To echo the words of Gayatri Chakraborty Spivak, Kausalji is "the worst product of postcoloniality, the Indian who uses the alibis of Development to exploit the tribals and detroy their life-system."[7] The message of Mahasweta Devi is perfectly clear and unambivalent: the people of all sectors of a state use the aborigines as appearatuses for their own profit. Thus when the Govt. builds metallic roads for them, the road becomes a metaphor of invasion: "Oh, we climb hills and build homes, the road comes chasing us" (*IM* 119). So the tribals are tortured and harassed by the men in power and administration in numerous ways.

But perhaps the worst happening to the tribals is that they are threatened with extinction. "To survive they must mingle in the mainstream" (*IM* 181). This is what the dwellers of Pirtha stoutly resist. They desperately cling to their sense of ethenic being. And this sense of ethnicity is embodied in their myth.[8] The Pterodactyl is not romanticized by the author. She only depicts with loving despair how the creature is represented as the soul of ancestors in the tribal imagination. Among the aborigins, however, only Bikhia has an access to the mystery of the Pterodactyl but he cannot communicate it to others. And it goes beyond the "wisdom, reason and feelings" (*IM* 157) of Puran, the 'outsider'.

But what dawns upon Puran (when he has a vision of the Pterodactyl) is no less signficant. He realizes that Bikhia is a 'tribial', an 'aboriginal' but the Pterodactyl is "much more ancient, more originary than his experience." Puran is enlightened as he discovers a 'contact' between Bikhia and the pre-historic creature: "both your existences are greatly endangered" (*IM* 156). The Pterodactyl dies and with its death, as Ashley Philip succinctly says, "the myth assumes a sense of urgency and is driven to connect with general history. In short, it passes into ideology" (Philip 124). This passage from myth to history to ideology is infinitely interesting. In the oral tradition of the tribals, a myth/ mythical story passes from voice to voice; it becomes a song; and the song enters history; and in the last analysis their history constitutes ideology—that is, the beliefs, values, and ways of thinking and feeling through which the tribals perceive, and by recourse to which they explain, what they take to be reality. The Pterodactyl might be "an empirical impossibility" for the modern educated Indian but for the modern tribal Indian it is a reality.[9] It represents the restless soul of their ancestors—restless because the barbaric civilization "descecrates the ancient peoples' burial-grounds by building roads and bridges, cutting down forests" (*IM* 156).

The tribal resistance to the aggressive advance of 'civilization' thus has strong ecological implications. The tribals will fight for the forest, they will fight for the land. And they will not move an inch from Pirtha because Pirtha is their 'last shelter' and their 'domain' (*IM* 179). They will die yet they will not leave the hills, caves, and river. For Mahasweta Devi, the tribal is not embedded in nature. Nature is part of his / her self.[10]

But the last word which completes the message of the story is love:

> Only love, a tremendous, excruciating, explosive love can still dedicate us to this work when the century's sun is in the Western sky, otherwise this aggressive civilization will have to pay a terrible price, look at history, the aggressive civilization has destroyed itself in the name of progress, each time. (*IM* 197)

The tribals all over India expect love, fellow-feeling and a human recognition from those who belong to the mainstream. They deserve honour as well for their civilization is ancient and the foundation of the civilization of India.

Pterodactyl, Puran Sahay, and Pirtha fits well in the description of the aesthetics of dalit literature. The story is born of the author's own experience of Indian tribal society. But the author's experience has the strength to cross provincial boundaries of Pirtha, and it ultimately embraces the agonies and expectations of all the indigenous peoples of the world.

Notes and References

1. For this idea I am indebted to Stephen Slemon's 'Unsettling the Empire: Resistance Theory for the Second World' in *The Post-colonial Studies Reader*, ed. Bill Ashcroft, Gareth Griffith and Helen Tiffin, London & New York : Routledge, 1995, p.107.
2. This statement is from 'The Author in conversation' in *Imaginary Maps*, p.ix.
3. These autobiographical details have been borrowed from 'The Author in conversation' in *Imaginary Maps*, pp. iv-v.
4. This statement is taken from A study guide for the film: "Mahasweta Devi : Witness, Advocate, Writer" by Shaswati Talukdar, color, 27 min, 2001. Please see *http://www.der.org/films/mahasweta-devi.html*
5. Homi K. Bhabha in *The Location of Culture*, London : Routledge, 1994, discourses on "the nation split within itself, articulating the heterogeneity of its population." (p.148)
6. The phrase is borrowed from the French Philosopher of language Paul Ricoeur. See the entry on 'Poststructuralism' in M.H. Abrams, *A Glossary of Literary Terms*, eighth edition, with contributions by Geoffrey Galt Harpham, 2005 Thomson Wadsworth; first Indian reprint 2007.
7. These words are borrowed from Gayatri Chakraborty Spivak's 'Appendix' to *Imaginary Maps*, p. 208.
8. One may at this point be reminded of Mahasweta Devi's *Reservation* ('Sonrokshon'), a story where Sepai, a 'lodha' (one of the tribal communities), wants to go back to the myth of 'Kalketu' and 'Fullora' and thereby bringing back the past glory to their culture.
9. For this insight I am indebted to the 'Appendix', p. 209.
10. The idea is taken from 'Listening to the Pterodactyl', an essay by Shiv Visvanathan, in *Indigeneity: Culture and Representation*, ed. G.N. Devy, Geoffrey V. Davis and K.K. Chakravarty. Hyderabad: Orient BlackSwan, 2009.

Works Cited

Dangle, Arjun. Ed. *Poisoned Bread : translations from Modern Marathi Dalit Literature.* Hyderabad : Orient BlackSwan (New Edition), 2009.

Devy, G.N. 'Introduction'. *Indigeneity : Culture and Representation*, ed. G.N. Devy, Geoffrey V. Davis and K.K. Chakravarty. Hyderabad : Orient BlackSwan, 2009.

Limbale, Sharankumar. *Towards an Aesthetic of Dalit Literature : History, Controversies and Considerations*. Translated and edited with a commentary by Alok Mukherjee. Hyderabad: Orient Longman, 2004.

Philip, Ashley. 'Aesthetics of Incommunicability: A Study of Mahasweta Devi's *Pterodactyl, Puran Sahay, and Pirtha*'. In *Litcrit: An Indian Response to Literature*. Ed. P.P. Ajaya Kumar. Volume 34, No. 2, Issue 66, December 2008).

10

Of Maternal Inheritance: Dalit/Coloured Women and Strategies of Rewriting Cultural Identity-scapes

Sarottama Majumdar

The cusp at which the varied, multilayered discourses of black American, dalit and postcolonial feminism seem to interject, though spasmodically, is in identifying and unraveling strategies of exclusion. In this paper I shall try to set a course by which exclusion as means of establishing reverse identity may be studied both in the context of Homi Bhabha's definition of 'hybridity', it's development into 'hybridisation', and Gayatri Spivak's insistence on heterogeneity within feminist dialectic. Bhabha is interested primarily in identifying collateral movement between differently empowered p1eople; though in the cited instance the reference is to the colonizer and the colonized in strict 'canonical' terms and movement is seen to be two dimentional. This in turn signals a productive dialogue because it both confirms and shakes "calm assumptions of continuance of authority".

The dimension of culture, gender and class specificity to the aforementioned dialogue is Spivak's construct from which I shall of course draw also. The heavily nuanced dialectics between the center and the margins is again a trope which undercuts essentialist certainties about the identities of the oppressor and the oppressed and this is one debate which the literature dealing exclusively with the subaltern feminine, concerns itself with.

Finally, I shall attempt to work into the scope of this matrix, the idea of de-cerebralization; Fanon's powerful construct, signifying an enforced attempt to make the recipient see herself as the 'other' alienated from her own culture, language and land a state from which violence is the only form of self translation; the subjectivisation of the erstwhile object.

An increasing number of cultural historians and postcolonial theorists now contend that there is a gradual but discernable global shift in cultural, social, political and intellectual perspective: white Protestant America is being hispanized. Hispanic and black America have become the dynamic motors of a good deal of live western culture that operate beyond the shifting confines of white heritage industry, across Europe; north African and west Asian influence has leavened, in places beyond recognition, dominant classical Caucasian civilizational assumptions, while in India politically and in the broad societal spectrum, the historically dispossessed and the oppressed are beginning to consolidate their own distinct cultural space. Gramsci's prophetic dictum to histiographers that "Every trace of independent initiative on the part of subaltern groups should therefore be of incalculable value for the integral historian"(Gramsci 55) seems therefore to be framing a new narrative of hybrid interrelations.

Alice Walker's short story *Everyday Use* and Mahasweta Devi's *Saajh Sokaler Maa* belong to that sub genre, whose membership is growing, of "post colonial woman writers cognizant of the aporias or ethico-historical dilemmas in woman's de-colonialization" (Spivak xxiii). Both Dee, the coloured financially underpriviledged woman, desperate to be recognized as mainstream cultural icon; and her mother, the narrator, who ironically is (though unconscious of the fact) what her daughter aspires to be, of *Everyday Use* is narrativised within the context of the black woman her daughter aspires to be) crisis at the moment of identity formation. The formidable and understated pragmatism of the narrator/narrative deliberately piles images juxtaposing violence with endurance, deliberate emotional repression with sudden visceral triumph and invests the absences with poignance that is bereft of sentiment. Comparisons with Celie(protagonist of Walker's novel *The Colour Purple*) and Draupadi (Mahasweta Devi's eponymous protagonist) are of course immediate and obvious. The quiet confidence of the matriarch narrator is a function of the rhetoric rather than a conscious attempt at imposing authority within the narrative but that is precisely what it achieves. What she reveals unassumingly about her lack of feminine graces, her bitter struggle to raise and educate her daughters are transformed in the unadorned dignity of the narrative, and become anecdotes about resilience, courage and honour.

The cadences and tone of narrative as voice in *Saajh Sokaler Maa* are more plangent, more obviously elegiac. The structural complexity of this short story, with overlays of myth making at many, often elusive levels, are less accessible to cultural translation. Without trying to essentialise the text however, it is possible to detect in the text, tropes that suggest manners in which 'maternal vulnerability' act in both cases as catalysts for strategizing empowerment. Mahasweta Devi has expressed, in the introduction to her anthology, her regret that this story, set within folk traditions, history, oral tales, old stories, myths and canonical narratives of the past, has been much neglected with a few notable exceptions like the critic Arunkumar Mukhopadhayay who had selected this texts from among other more politically charged ones for critiquing. Joti, the protagonist's identity as a marginal woman is important, inspite and because of her peculiar social standing within the oppressed, exploited, economically vulnerable stratum that constitutes most of tribal India. She is a 'kowamara', a 'pakhmara' (literally killers or catchers of crows/birds) a tribe which traces it's origin to Jara the hunter assassin of Krishna; deified hero of Hindu mythology. The racial purity and ancient lineage of the Kowamaras whose strongest taboos are related to mating outside the tribe, coupled with the stigma of their shared past create a boundary around them which is partly deliberately nurtured. The tribe *embodies* taboo within the marginalized society as a means for survival. Joti rebels against it by breaking into the largest substratum of the marginal through her marriage outside and above(in the caste hierarchy of tribal society) the clan which amounts to an act of emancipatory self-exile. The author adds a revealing rider: caste elevation is equated with class change. Celebrating the possibility of parenthood Joti and Utsab (her husband) think about further elevation on the caste ladder by a process of metropolitan assimilation that is an important strategy of social appropriation: he proposes that they move to the big city and legally alter·their surname to one without casteist handles. Utsab's death and further tribulations (which Joti suffers due to her gender, not social position) later Joti takes the decision that completes and seals her transformation. She transforms/disguises/subsumes/sacrifices her identity/es as a woman, a mother and a human being; for talismanic signifiers from the hegemonic upper caste Hindu holy woman a source: the trident and red robes of *athakurun*. Joti's apotheosis must be understood in the context of her vulnerability in the maternal role; she could not save her child from starvation if she continued in her role as a human mother. In an ironic subversion whose polyphonic propensities are immense, Joti denies her biological motherhood through and because of her appropriation of the hegemonic privileges that come with the assumptions of godhood. The discussion may also be taken further and the irony multiplied in Joti's tale: in order to sustain the fiction of her forged identity as a divine being and feed her not-to-be acknowledged son; she reverts to the traditional medical knowledge and skills of her birth clan.

This disavowal/appropriation trope is played out also in the 'deep southern black inheritance' metaphors of *Everyday Use* in an entirely different way. Dee, the 'new' black woman straining at the bounded existence imposed on her by colour, race and poverty is observed with irony and dispassion by the mother who sees her as an armed rebel, her weapons being education and through it adaptation of hegemonic mores. Walker is scathing and wry by turns as she rhetorically fixes the implications of such an education to an illiterate hardworking churchgoing middle-aged southern woman: "She used to read to us without pity, forcing words, lies, other folk's habits, whole lives upon us ... . She washed us in a river of make believe, burned us with a lot of knowledge we didn't necessarily need to know". But finally it is Dee's self-transformation which is interesting. Firstly, like Joti, she recreates herself around a socially acceptable idea of the "exotic other": the historically aware African-American, consciously paying homage to her cultural roots in far off Africa—however half-baked her notion of those roots are. Seminally, however, in order to do so, she fetishises reductively an authentic part of an ethnic American tradition to which she can rightfully claim inheritance, but which she despises as not exotic enough. Dee's desire for a quilt in her family's possession (created for everyday use, not decoration) to decorate a wall in her town house, is a final act of disavowal and hence betrayal. The matriarchal narrator's decision in refusing to hand over the article to her eldest born is in effect, an act of ritual disinheritance of Dee, in favour of the other daughter, the shy and retiring Maggie who is however a part of the authentic, living tradition of African-American life as an organic entity. The acknowledgement of this act as significant, is seminal to our comprehension of the dominant concerns in the discourse of subversive appropriation.

The conclusion one reaches, opens the discussion into the postcolonial arena among other appropriation discouses posing the following conondrum: if in colonialism "the transformation of an indigenous culture into the subordinated culture of a colonial regime, or the superimposition of the colonial apparatus into which all aspects of the original culture have to be reconstructed, operate as processes of translational dematerialization", then is it possible also to posit or accommodate the possibility of agency by colonised subjects in the reconstructive process which undercut the hegemonic discourse and colonial ambition in unexpected ways?

Works Cited

Bhabha, Homi. *The Location of Culture.* London: Routledge, 1994.

Mahasweta, Devi. *Saajh Sokaler Maa* (Ponchshti Golpo), Ed. Mahasweta Devi et al. Kolkata: Pratikkhan Publication, 2001. 91-110.

Fanon, Franz. *The Wretched of the Earth,* tr Constance Farrington. London: Macgibbon & Kee, 1965.

Gramsci, Antonio. *Notes on Italian History: Prison Notebooks.* New York: International Publishers, 1971.

Haug, Frigga. *Beyond Female Machochism: Memory, Work and Politics,* tr Rodney Livingstone. London: Verso, 1992.

Spivak, Gayatri Chakravorty. Translator's Preface, *Imaginary Maps.* By Mahasweta Devi. Calcutta: Thema, 2001.

Walker Alice. "Everyday Use", *The Secret Self: Short Stories by Women*, Ed: Hermione Lee. London; Everyman's Library, 1991. 244-252.

Young, Robert J.C. *Postcolonialism: A Very Short Introduction.* Ind Ed. Oxford: OUP, 2006.

11

Representation of the Dalits and Other Marginal Classes in the Plays of Girish Karnad: A Study

Abhinandan Malas

Girish Karnad has established himself as a literary stalwart who, through his plays, has explored several aspects of modern Indian society which he has presented as his dramatic themes sometimes through history and sometimes with other thematic motifs and patterns that relate to the modern social tradition and also to the psychology of the characters presented in his plays. The presence of the dalits or the marginalized classes of society is prominent in these plays. Through them Karnad discusses several other issues like politics, family relationships, morality, religion and the desire of the unconscious.

The marginalized classes represent a level in society with which the mainstream society fails to interact. Through his plays Karnad prepares a ground where a space is created for the interaction between the main stream and the marginalized sections of society. Karnad provides the suppressed voices of the marginalized classes with expressions through which new things are revealed and myth and history are reinterpreted anew.

Girish Karnad, one of the major post-independence Indian English dramatists, has used the Indian history, myth and the postcolonial society in his plays to bring out the various aspects of human existence, social interactions, class discriminations and their conflicts, and violence. He provides a voice to the marginalized sections. In my paper I intend to study and analyze the presentation of the Dalits and other marginalized classes in the plays of Girish Karnad. I also explore the issues dealt by Karnad while exploring the Dalits and 'other' sections of Indian society. My paper also focuses on how Karnad succeeds in making the Dalits and other subalterns move from the margin to the centre.

The word 'Dalit' is very significant regarding the presentation of the marginalized classes in Indian society. The term 'Dalit' is a Hindi and Marathi translation of 'depressed classes', a term used by the Britishers (during the colonial period) to refer the marginalized classes who are now specifically known as the scheduled castes in the modern India. Later in 1970s the 'Dalit Panthers' revived the term and included scheduled tribes, poor people, women and all those who are being exploited socially, politically, economically and in the name of religion. So the word 'Dalit' does not refer to any particular caste or community but to those people who become the victims of oppressions in society through different social agencies and institutions.

The primary motive of the 'Dalit' writing is the liberation of the marginalized classes from all kinds of oppressions and discriminations and to create awareness among the people in society regarding such vices. Girish Karnad himself does not belong to the Dalit sections. But he is one of those writers who have contributed a lot in the development of the Dalit discourse which now reveals itself as a text that runs parallel to the mainstream writing. The presentation of the several marginal sections and people become a major component of Karnad's thematic motifs. Plays like *Tughlaq*, *Hayavadana*, *The Fire and the Rain*, *Tale-Danda*, *Naga-Mandala* and others present a picture of the marginalized classes and the individuals and focus on their struggle, their sufferings and other complexities that arise due to the conflict between mainstream society and the oppressed classes. These problems may arise in family relations, marriage, government, society and other institutions which can threaten the individual's existence as a whole.

In *Tughlaq* we see that the dalits or the marginalized classes generally include the common people who present their opinion about Muhammad Tughlaq and his rule. It is important to note that the play *Tughlaq* deals with the conflict between the outer and the inner selves of Tughlaq. The inner self of Tughlaq is made up of his desires and dreams to become an ideal ruler and to create a utopian nation. The outer self on the other hand is basically the image formed in the mind of the people about Tughlaq through his actions and rule. The fact is that there lies a huge difference between the Tughlaq as an idealist (the inner self) and Tughlaq as a ruler (his outer self as presented before his subjects). The common people fail to understand Tughlaq's inner self and the latter has to remain in conflict with the image formed by the people regarding him as a tyrannical ruler. This difference and conflict lead Tughlaq to total disillusionment, failure and the ultimate downfall. The play *Tughlaq* deals with the theme of search for identity, alienation and loneliness. Tughlaq, an idealist, shrewd politician, impartial ruler, practical in understanding the situation, and modern in attitude towards life, fails to establish his identity as any one of these and turns out to be 'Mad Tughlaq'. This difference between his idealist self and his real self is drawn through the opinions of the masses who reflect the character of Tughlaq and influence his psychological development as well that leads him to his utter disillusionment and downfall. Thus, the marginalized class plays an important role in building the character of Tughlaq. The discussion between the Old Man and the Young Man at the very beginning of the play points out the doubts that is there in the heart of the common people about the Sultan,

> OLD MAN: God, what's this country coming to!
>
> YOUNG MAN: What are you worried about, grandfather? The country's in perfectly safe hands—safer than any you've seen before.
>
> OLD MAN: I don't know. I've been alive a long time, seen many Sultans, but never thought I would live to see a thing like this.
>
> (Karnad *Collected Plays* vol. I, 5)

This conversation refers to the steps taken by Tughlaq to establish a utopia through his impartial rule that includes his equal attitude to the people of every community. The irony is that the people (the marginalized lower classes), for whom Tughlaq tries to bring so many reforms in the state by keeping his kingship at stake, fail to understand his good intentions. This occurs due to the lack of communication between him and the common masses. The common people take him as an imperial oppressor. Tughlaq always remains in indirect conflict with his subjects on the psychological level. This gives rise to the eternal discourse of the conflict between an oppressor and the oppressed. Here the dalit discourse comes into play since any oppressed individual can be termed as a dalit. His decision to shift his capital from Delhi to Daulatabad and his measures to reform the economy by introducing copper coins equal in value to silver dinars turn out to be his greatest blunders that make the people suffer tremendously and that clear his way towards destruction. The enormous sufferings of the common people, while shifting from Delhi to Daulatabad, as depicted in the play, describe the picture of death, decay, corruption, hunger and all sorts of devaluations.

The economic reformations also give rise to severe corruptions that affect the life of the common people who suffer as a consequence. The common people become marginalized, oppressed and discriminated which Tughlaq fails to understand. The difference between the royal class of Tughlaq and the lower class of these oppressed common people stops Tughlaq from realizing the actual situation and reality. He dreams about bringing a revolution in society and government, but fails to realize the importance of the marginalized classes who form a majority of his subjects and they include both the Hindus and the Muslims. The class difference is prominent over here. The Sultan, who belongs to the most privileged class of society, fails to get associated with his subjects who include the marginalized and the dalits. As a result of that the people become suspicious about his real intentions. Even his positive steps also seem to be marked with dark designs to the people of the opposite community. It becomes prominent from the words of the Hindu who speaks doubtfully about Tughlaq thus, expressing his worries about the whole situation. It shows that Tughlaq fails to convince the Muslims, the community to which he belongs, and also the Hindus, the community which he favours to establish himself as an impartial ruler at the cost of the wrath of his own community. The Hindu says,

> HINDU: ...when the Sultan kicks me in the teeth and says, 'Pay up, you Hindu dog', I'm happy. I know I'm safe. But the moment a man comes along and says, 'I know you are a Hindu, but you are also a human being'—well, that makes me nervous.
>
> (Karnad *Collected Plays* vol. I, 6)

The situation is ironic in the sense that it depicts the strange predicament of the Sultan when he fails to prove the authenticity of his intentions to the people. The privileged suffers among the marginalized. But, the seriousness of the situation lies in the fact that it depicts the failure of a wise ruler to establish a society free from class and communal discriminations. Karnad, through his play *Tughlaq* brings out the present situation of the postcolonial Indian society. He basically focuses on the Nehruvian era which brought chaos and confusion among the people of India of every class regarding the Indian politics and government in the post independence era. While talking about his autobiographical motif in the play Karnad says:

> In a sense the play reflected the slow disillusionment my generation felt with the new politics on independent India: the gradual erosion

> of ethical norms that had guided the movement for independence, and the coming to terms with cynicism and realpolitik.
>
> (Karnad 'In Search of a New Theatre' 98)

The voices of the marginalized others play important role in carving the character of the protagonist and also the course of the play. Thus, in this play the voices of the marginalized section are heard with effects.

In case of the play *The Fire and the Rain* the situation is little different. In this play we do not find any major conflict between classes as we see in *Tale-Danda* or *Yajati*. In this play the marginalized class or the Dalits are represented by Nittilai, a low caste girl, who form a ground where these classes can interact with each other to discuss their various problems and issues and can come to some solution. Nittilai act as a listener and also become a symbol of sacrifice, morality and nonviolence which is lacking in the people of both the classes. Upper class people like Raibhya, Paravasu, Vishakha and Yavakri indulge in violence and immoral activities. The people of Nittilai's class also exercise their power to discard the domination of the privileged classes and remain in conflict with the latter. Arvasu, belonging to the upper class, ultimately incorporates within himself all the virtues of Nittilai irrespective of her low class, and becomes one like her.

In *The Fire and the Rain* Nittilai, a Dalit, becomes a source of acceptance, forgiveness, wisdom and sacrifice. With the death of Nittilai (a lower caste girl) her lover Arvasu (a Brahmin) becomes wiser and sacrifices everything for the humanity. Nittilai is Karnad's 'new woman'. The character of Nittilai is a creation of Karnad and it does not exist in the "Vanaparva" of *Mahabharata*. Through her Karnad creates a space for dalits to interact with the mainstream society. In *The Fire and the Rain* Karnad puts forth the important issue of the class differences. The conflict between the upper caste Brahmins and the lower Dalits is prominent but not violent. Arvasu and Nittilai transcend the barrier of this eternal conflict. Through them Karnad creates the domain where these conflicts dissolve. On finding that Vishaka (Paravasu's wife) and Yavarki (Paravasu's cousin) having illegal relationship, an engraged Raibhya (Paravasu and Arvasu's father) summons a Brahma Rakshas, a demon to kill Yavarki. The demon does so, and Arvasu has to cremate him; this delays his appointment with Nittilai's father and her village elders, and as a result she is married to someone else. After this we see the theme of sacrifice. Nittilai leaves her family, her community and remains with Arvasu though not as his wife but as his sister. She cannot defy her lawful husband. But she cannot accept the oppressions of society either. That is why she comes to Arvasu's rescue when the latter is attacked by the mob which was infuriated against Arvasu by Paravasu. Paravasu killed his father Raibhya and put the blame on his brother Arvasu. Arvasu is attacked by the people of his own caste. Nittilai acts as a link between Arvasu and the low class people. She acts as a listener. While being found with Arvasu by her husband she is killed. She sacrifices herself for the sake of her love for Arvasu.

The character of Nittilai is a part of Karnad's theatrical innovations. Through Nittilai Karnad brings forth the issue of tolerance, love and sacrifice. Society must listen to the problems of all the communities. It is Nittilai who shows Arvasu the way to sacrifice. Ultimately when Lord Indra appears and blesses Aravasu and asks him to ask for any boon Aravasu does not ask for the lives of his family members and Nittilai. He asks for the release of the Brahma Rakshasa. The rain suddenly comes. The land is relieved of the draught for which the Yajna was being performed by Paravasu and other Brahmins. Arvasu has become wiser. He has transcended the boundaries of social differences. He has united himself with Nittilai spiritually through sacrifice. He now becomes one of the dalits. He becomes a bridge between the two communities. The knowledge which he could not gather from his community ultimately achieves them after achieving the love of Nittilai, a dalit, and losing her physically for ever.

By the end of the play Arvasu stands as an enlightened man who is enriched with the knowledge of humanity and universal brotherhood. It is a fact that Karnad has always placed his themes in the context of the modern Indian scenario.

In *Tughlaq* we have seen the subjects of Tughlaq expressing their skepticism for the Sultan's rule. That refers to the post independence situation of modern India where people expressed their doubts regarding the rule of Jawaharlal Nehru.

In *The Fire and the Rain* Karnad brings out the relevance of the theme of the demolition of class differences and acceptance of humanity which is very relevant in the postcolonial Indian society which is marked by such discriminations and riots. Arvasu and Nittilai become the casteless beings. They do not meet physically but their love attains spiritual fulfillment. This is required for the regeneration of the whole society. That is indicated by the rain which comes at the end of the play. The joy of regeneration, freedom and fulfillment is expressed through the crowd and also by Arvasu who calls Nittilai to share this moment of freedom from all kinds of barriers and discrimination,

> CROWDS: What's that?—You smell that?—Yes. Yes. The smell of wet earth.
>
> Of fresh rains. It's raining. Somewhere. Nearby. The air is blossoming with the fragrance of earth. It's raining—it's blossoming with the fragrance of earth. It's raining—it's raining—Rain! The rain! (Wind blows....It pours. People dance with joy. They roll in the mud. Arvasu sits clutching Nittilai's body.)
>
> Arvasu: It's raining, Nittilai! It's raining!
>
> (Karnad *The Fire and the Rain* 62)

This shows the dissolution of the differences between the communities and the creation of a utopia. Arvasu and Nittilai become the harbingers of that classless society. The rain comes as a purifying element that demolishes the barriers of class differences and purifies the whole society.

In the other three plays *Hayavadana, Yayati*, and *Bali: The Sacrifice* the conflict of classes is shown through extramarital affairs, adultery and illegal relationships that bring other several issues like, nonviolence, incompleteness, and racism. *Hayavadana* deals with a triangular love relationship between Devadatta (the upper-caste brahmin), Padmini (Devadatta's wife) and Kapila (the lower-caste dalit). Padmini's love for both these men indicates the prevailing incompleteness in society. The play *Hayavadana* becomes an important ground where the issue of the conflict between different classes becomes prominent.

The action of the play begins in the city of Dharmapura where we see Devadatta and Kapila are two close friends living in this city. Devadatta is the son of a wise Brahmin Vidyasagar. He is wise intelligent, educated, fair and handsome but lacks muscular body, physical beauty and the attractive features of his friend Kapila. Kapila is the only son of an ironsmith named Lohita. He is dark and plain to look at but is unmatched in physical strength and skills. He is a Dalit.

Through the conflict between the two friends Karnad brings out the issues of class conflict, identity crisis, female desire and adultery. Devadatta falls in love with Padmini and marries her. The conflict arises when Padmini, unable to suppress her female desires gets attracted towards Kapila. Meanwhile Padmini becomes pregnant and the three of them decide to go on a short visit to Ujjain. Padmini gets greatly impressed by Kapila's physical charm, strength and skills during the journey. Devadatta becomes aware of Padmini's intense longing for Kapila. Devadatta cannot withstand his wife's love for another man, nor can he say anything to his dearest friend Kapila. Kapila and Padmini decide to go to the Temple of Lord Rudra. After they are gone, Devadatta goes to the Temple of Goddess Kali, asks for forgiveness and beheads himself. Apparently it seems that the problem is adultery which is true to some extent. It becomes impossible for a husband to tolerate his wife's love for another man. He cannot say anything to his friend Kapila. But unknowingly the issue of class difference comes into play. Kapila is a dalit. His culture is different. His ways of life are different. He is hardworking and close to life and nature.

Padmini finds more adventure, more libidinal force and more security in Kapila than her husband Devadatta who is a sophisticated person far away from the earth. This creates a difference in the attitude of Padmini for both the men. Unknowingly Padmini gets attracted towards Kapila due to his physique and character for which his class is responsible. This becomes clearer after the heads are exchanged between Devadatta and Kapila. After becoming alive Kapila with Devadatta's body claims Padmini because he thinks body is superior to head and head contains the actual identity of the individual. While Devadatta with Kapila's body claims Padmini considering head to be more important than body. A sage tells them that the head is superior to body. Padimini and Devadatta are overjoyed while all is lost for Kapila. Kapila goes away into the forest. Gradually Devadatta, having Kapila's body, loses his muscular physique due to his reading and writing while Kapila, with Devadatta's body, becomes strong and muscular with labour and hard work. So the head governs the body and the head is governed by the culture and tradition that are related to the respective classes. Devadatta with Kapila's body loses his muscular physical beauty due to his way of living which is according to his high class.

On the other hand Kapila with Devadatta's body (which is weak and unattractive) grows his body into a muscular one with his way of living as a dalit. Earlier Padmini could not marry Kapila because of the class difference. But now she cannot ignore Kapila anymore. She again feels the attraction for Kapila and finally goes to him. At that moment Devadatta also appears and both declare their love for Padmini. They fight with each other and die. Padmini hands over her son to Bhagavata and performs Sati. The core of the problem lies in the difference that lies between

Devadatta and Kapila. Even the head also cannot control the menace of this discrimination. The head is finally governed by the class. That is why even after the exchange of the heads the problem of imperfection returns. Wh[illegible] this matter in the 'Introduction' to *Collected Plays,* Volume Two Aparna Bhargava Dharwadker writes:

> In the human world of Devadatta and Kapila, transposition offers a symbolic but temporary resolution to the problem of mind/body dualism: for a brief period of time, Devadatta-Kapila possesses the ideal mind as well as the ideal body, while the other hybrid being, Kapila-Devadatta, is deficient in both respects. But when each man's body reverts to its original qualities, the problem of dualism returns, and the human condition appears as essentially one of disunity and imperfection culminating in death. Karnad diffuses this human 'tragedy' by placing it alongside two other realms of experience—the divine and the animal.
>
> (Karnad, *Collected Plays* vol. I, xxvi-xxvii)

The 'dualism returns' because the influence of the class is there which governs the psychology of the individual. That is why when the heads are exchanged the bodies also change according to the classes to which the heads belong. But, through the presentation of these three characters Karnad tries to emphasize on the fact that all individuals, irrespective of their class and caste, are equal. It is society which is responsible for such discriminations and acts as an external power to impose its ideological constructs on the individuals. That is why the problem remains the same even after the exchange of the heads. Karnad dissolves the concept of class differences by mixing up the heads and the bodies thus discarding the constructs of the Hindu society. While talking on this matter J.S. Rohan Savarimuttu writes:

> It is to be noted that Karnad uses the caste name to denote the class of Devadatta but gives room for the audience to work on the caste of the other two characters by suggesting it through their class names. Thus it is brought forth in this play that all the three actors in the participatory interactive process are of equal status neither

> high nor low reinforcing the theme that all creatures are of equal value and beauty even though the conventional caste system in the recent days pretends to be vertical. Karnad also breaks this vertical relationship by the marriage between a Brahmin and a non-Brahmin.
>
> (Savarimuttu 42-43)

In *Tale-Danda* the class struggle becomes prominent and severe. The play is based on the history of the revolution against the caste, religious and other social discriminations that took place in the twelfth century ancient India. The play draws a parallel between the present postcolonial situation in India's socio-religious, political and economic scenario (the issue of mandir-mandal conflict) and the struggle against class differences and discriminations that took place in Southern India in 12th century A.D. The story is set eight hundred years ago in the city of Kalyan when Basavanna, an influential Brahmin, assembled a group of poets, mystics, social revolutionaries and philosophers, with distinguished skills and abilities in their respective fields. They opposed idolatry, rejected temple worship, upheld equality of sexes, and condemned the caste system. They started a movement against the class discriminations. But the movement took a violent turn when a Brahmin girl married a 'low caste' boy. The movement ended in bloodshed.

Tale-Danda (*Rakt Kalyan*) deals with those days during which the Indian society plunged into anarchy and terror that evolved due to the oppressions inflicted upon the dalits by the ruling class and the resulting rebellion against such discriminations that came as a form of protest. The tragedy lies in the fact that the subaltern voice is suppressed while society remains silent. The fact is that the oppressive instruments of society act without the consent of society and the masses suffer. The movement started by Basavanna for a casteless society ends into failure and bloodshed. The voice of the subaltern is oppressed with an iron hand.

As we have seen in his other plays here also Karnad relates his theme to the postcolonial Indian scenario. Class conflict and the oppression of the marginalized and the dalits have always been an important issue in the Indian context. Karnad has presented the negative side of this conflict and the pessimistic view of Karnad pervades through the play. But, on the other hand Karnad has shown that the emancipation of the oppressed classes and the demolition of the class barriers will become easier only when the privileged class gets ready to listen to their problems and take initiative for the enhancement these marginalized classes. In this play Basavanna plays the role of a listener to the suppressed voices of these marginalized classes. He is a brahmin and belongs to the privileged class of society. He prepares a ground for the development of the dalits discourse. That ground needs to be recognized by society.

It is interesting to see that while in *The Fire and the Rain* Karnad presents a dalit woman Nittilai as a listener who tries to become a bridge between her own Dalit community and the community of her brahmin lover, in *Tale-Danda* Karnad presents a Brahmin, Basavanna, with the same role that of a listener. What Karnad tries to focus over here is that the responsibility to consider the problems and to devise a solution to the evil of class discriminations lies on both the sides which are in conflict.

While in *Tale-Danda* the struggle ends in utter disillusionment and bloodshed, in case of *The Fire and the Rain* dissolution of these differences through spiritual regeneration and reunion is presented. This ground for reunion of the quarreling communities is never achieved in *Tughlaq*. The continuation of the difference between Tughlaq and the common masses ultimately leads him towards his disillusionment and frustrations. In *Tale-Danda* King Bijjala is an important character through which Karnad demolishes the concept that the superiority of a person is related to caste or heredity and shows that personal ability is responsible for the superiority of an individual. While discussing this Lakhwinder Singh Gill observes:

> Bijjala is also instrumental in striking at the very base of caste system i.e. the men from the higher-castes have born superiority over those of the lower-castes. And the men from the lower-castes lack the ability to rule. Bijjala, the king, is not from any higher caste. He is a barber and still he is full of kingly insight. He is of the view that for kingship heredity is no qualification. He rejects Sovideva as his descendant on the ground that he does not have the qualities of a ruler.
>
> (Gill 95)

In his another important play *Bali: The Sacrifice* Karnad presents the ideological conflict between the Hinduism and Jainism. Blood sacrifice (bali) in Hinduism is challenged by the Queen who is a Jain and a follower of nonviolence. On the other hand the Queen Mother is a devotee of Hinduism and a supporter of 'bali' (blood sacrifice). The King converts himself into Jainism after his marriage to the Queen but is unable to come to terms with the new faith. The Queen is always in psychological conflict with the Queen Mother on the question of bali (the blood sacrifice). One night the Queen, enchanted by the voice of a low caste ugly Mahout (the Elephant-Keeper), visits him and indulges in physical relationship with him. When found the Queen Mother considers it as a heinous crime and decides to perform 'bali' to appease God. The Queen refuses to support that. The King opts for a mock sacrifice of the dough cock. The sacrifice of the dough cock turns into the sacrifice of the Queen herself and she dies. The act of adultery made by the Queen indicates the climax of the conflict between her and the Queen Mother. The act of adultery committed by the Queen is an act of aggression or revenge on the ideologies of violence in 'bali' or the blood sacrifice. It is not that the Queen is not satisfied with the King or she is adulterous.

The indulgence in extramarital affair is a protest against violence, and in this case the Mahout, a dalit, plays an important role as a medium for the expression of that protest. This act of the Queen points out her desire to break away from the shackles of the religious morality practiced by the Queen Mother and followed by the King. The class difference between the King and the Mahout points out the fact that the question of the affectation of morality and the practice of violence through bali varies from class to class. The Mahout belongs to a lower class and is not obsessed with the question of physical morality and the purification rituals like sacrifice.

The Queen finds a relief from the shackles of violence that is performed in the name of bali or the blood sacrifice among the people of the aristocratic class to which the King belongs. Her physical relationship with the lower class Mahout does not affect her spiritual purity and challenges the ritual of bali in Hinduism which is an act of violence according to Jainism. The self-sacrifice of the Queen by the end of the play indicates the point of climax of the conflict between the ideologies of violence and non-violence. But, this also emphasizes on the fact that the conflict of ideologies vary from class to class.

The ideological tussle is intense among the upper class aristocratic people than the low caste dalits. The meeting of the Queen with the dalit Mahout also points out an interaction between the two classes and also the union of the two classes (on the question of nonviolence) thus, discarding all differences. While talking about the King and the Mahout and drawing a parallel with Devadatta and Kapila in *Hayavadana* in the 'Introduction' to *Collected Plays* Volume One Aparna Bhargava Dharwadker writes,

> The two male characters in the play, in contrast, are arranged in relations of perfect antithesis and hierarchical reversal: the cultivated, sensitive, and valiant but impotent king versus the crude, amoral, and cowardly but potent mahout with his irresistible song. The dualisms of mind and body, culture and nature that Karnad had addressed in *Hayavadana* reappear in this play, but as unavoidably separate qualities that cannot be brought together. Furthermore, the radical disparities between the mahout and the royal couple underscore not an egalitarian message about the union of a queen and her servant, but the eventual irrelevance of that act to the long term disequilibrium of the royal marriage.
>
> (Karnad, *Collected Plays* vol. I, xxxiv-xxxv)

Thus, the difference between the two classes (the royal and the dalit) and the difference of the two individuals, the King and the Mahout, become prominent issues in this play.

The master-slave relation and the consequent conflict that lead to several questions regarding the class divisions of a Hindu society is presented through a *Mahabhharata* myth in Karnad's play *Yayati*. In *Yayati* the class conflict becomes a serious issue which is related to the other problems like male desire, adultery, extramarital affair, responsibilities and sacrifice. Like *Bali: The Sacrifice* once again Karnad brings the question of class differences on the family level. King Yayati marries Devayani, a Brahmin and the daughter of Shukracharya the Guru of the demons. Sharmishtha, the princess of the Rakshasas, is a friend of Devayani. Sarmishtha comes to the palace with Devayani as the latter's maid (slave). Jealousy intoxicates Sharmishtha's mind and she seduces King Yayati to indulge in physical relationship with her. The physical relationship of Yayati with an attendant girl infuriates Devayani and she leaves the palace and goes to her father Shukracharya. Shukracharya curses Yayati with old age. Yayati becomes old. He suffers. Shukracharya says that he can get back his youth if some one is ready to exchange his youth with Yayati's old age. Meanwhile, Yayati's son Pooru has arrived in the palace along with his newly married wife Chitralekha. Pooru agrees to exchange his youth with his father's old age. Yayati gets back his youth and Pooru becomes old.

The conflict between Devayani (a Brahmin) and Sharmishtha (a low caste Rakshasa princess) becomes the central motif of the play on which the other issues are based. The conflict between the two women lies rooted in the class difference between the two. Sharmishtha is aware of her low class. But she is also a princess of her Rakshasa clan. She cannot tolerate the contempt that Devayani has for her in spite of being a friend. Once, before marriage Devayani pointed out the class difference with contempt when the dresses of the two ladies were exchanged. Sharmishtha attacked Devayani and the latter fell into the well. But Devayani was rescued by Yayati who married her. Thus, Sharmishtha became an instrument for Devayani's good fortune which the former cannot tolerate. In spite of being a slave to Devayani Sharmishtha seduces King Yayati to indulge in physical relationship with her. Thus she replaces Devayani and challenges the superiority of Devayani's class. Devayani is infuriated and from here starts the conflict of the play. Here Karnad presents a balanced picture of an individual's social right, irrespective of the class, which, if not granted normally, must be achieved through tricks. From that point of view it is obvious Yayati has not committed anything wrong. While talking about the issue Dr. Falguni P. Desai observes,

> Devyani thought Yayati had violated his Dharma, when he married Sharmishtha. She was right in her own way. But if a man is bogged by a woman for Dharma's sake to pour in the seed he must do so, as a king & a Kshatriya Yayati followed his Dharma in doing so.…Sharmishtha asks from Yayati her ritu right, ritu embrace, so that her ritu may not be in vain and in such circumstances Yayati rightly follows his dharma and grants her an offspring by practicing world's highest holy law of their union.
>
> (Desai 51-52)

Thus, while Devayani can achieve her right to become the queen through dharma, Sharmishtha can also claim her right in the same way though belonging to the lower class. The play *Yayati* becomes a dalit text that also redefines the feminine discourse as well. In the play we see how the conflict develops between two ladies due to the class difference. King Yayati's sexual relationship with Sharmishtha is a crime against his wife Queen Devayani. She carves out an oppressed figure of herself. But if we consider the feminine discourse then we see that the paradigms of class differences also occur among the women as well. So, oppressions are occurring at different levels. While Sharmishtha is a dalit by her class Devayani becomes an oppressed individual in her own aristocratic class. Thus, the dalit text intersects the feminine text.

In the play *Naga-Mandala* the feminine discourse proliferates largely where we see the emancipation of a woman from the torturous oppressions of the patriarchal society. Her journey from the darkness of exploitations to the light of freedom makes her an embodiment of women empowerment and enlightenment. Here class does not become the centre of conflict. The eternal issue of the exploitation of women in the hands of patriarchy appears to be the central motif of the play where the woman becomes a dalit not by her caste but by her sufferings, humiliations and exploitations in the male dominated society. Rani is that female character who becomes the oppressed dalit and also the symbol of emancipation. Like Nittilai and Padmini Rani also appears as Karnad's 'new woman'. Rani suffers like Nittilai and boldly expresses her inner desires like Padmini and Vishakha (*The Fire and the Rain*). She also becomes a symbol of other suffering classes and Dalits. In the beginning of the play we see that Rani is tortured by her cruel husband Appanna. Rani transgresses the norms of patriarchy. The concepts of chastity, virginity, marital status and adultery are social constructs which Salvoj Zizek terms as the 'ideological fantasy'. Rani breaks away all these ideologies and social constructs by indulging in sexual relationship with Naga, a Cobra that comes to Rani in the disguise of her husband Appanna every night, who makes love with her in the absence of her husband. Though it apparently seems that Rani is unaware of the Naga's real identity, it is almost impossible to accept that Rani cannot identify the difference between the cruel husband in Appanna and the caring lover in the Naga.

Rani's indulgence in extramarital affair seems to be an aggression against the patriarchal ideologies and a protest against the oppressions of her husband that brings out the unfulfilled sexual desires of her unconscious. Through Rani Karnad presents an oppressed self which is equated with a dalit. In the play a role reversal takes place where we see poetic justice happens where, by the end of the play, Rani becomes the dominant figure and her cruel husband Appanna becomes her obedient slave.

Through Rani Karnad reverses the oppressive system of patriarchy where the oppressed or the dalit, in that sense, becomes the superior one while privileged one, here the male figure, now takes the subject position of the oppressed which the latter deserves. Karnad even goes to the extent of justifying Rani's act of adultery and keeping two husbands Appanna and Naga, according to the second ending, which is a sure violation of the establishments of Hindu patriarchal society. Rani emerges as a 'new woman' and her empowerment and the consequent subversion of the patriarchal discourse symbolically indicate the emancipation of a dalit from the oppressions of the privileged class and also the subversion of the latter. Rani's attainment of sexual and social superiority is reflected through the words of Fatima Sugarwala:

> At the end Appanna worships his wife and accepts the child. Now he is at peace, he has resolved his differences, but faces the dichotomy of her real and ideal self. She pats her hair, and tells Naga, "This hair is the symbol of my wedded bliss, live happily for ever." She wants the love and the status of her wedded husband and she also yearns for the warm sensuous love of the Naga.
>
> (Sugarwala 22)

Thus, Rani converts the male into a slave, which we see in case of her husband Appanna, and also into a sex object which we see in case of the Naga. The oppressed thus, takes control of the oppressor. The dalit discourse subverts the mainstream discourse and takes control of the latter.

Apart from these there are other minor dalit characters in these plays who perform minor but dramatically significant roles. In *Yayati* Swarnalata, the slave, acts as an informer in this play. Though her role is small but still she participates in the discussions among the other characters and also acts as a listener to these problems. In *Naga-Mandala* Kurudavva, the old blind woman, becomes the rescuer for Rani from the oppression of patriarchy. She is a common low class lady but with experience and wisdom of life. She gave the root of the love potion to Rani which was given to the cobra by Rani by mistake. After eating the potion the cobra (the Naga in the form of Appanna) starts visiting Rani every night in the absence of her husband Appanna thus leading to her emancipation and also making her pregnant. In *The Dreams of Tipu Sultan* the common people plays the role of chorus from whom we get information about Tipu Sultan.

Thus, the dalit discourse and the representation of the dalits and other marginalized classes by Girish Karnad remain among the major thematic aspects and motifs of Karnad's plays. The dalits gradually acquire a central position thus, making the 'other' discourse a part of the mainstream society. Different conflicts presented in these plays show the development of the discourse that includes and brings into consideration the voice of the 'other' which is generally suppressed by the mainstream society. Karnad puts them simultaneously and brings forth the importance of recognizing the marginalized and the dalits for the progress of society itself.

Works Cited

Desai, Falguni P.. "Girish Karnad's Yayati." *Contemporary Vibes* 4.16 (Jul-Oct 2009): 50-53. Print.

Gill, Lakhwinder Singh. "Portrayal of Indian Polity in Girish Karnad's Plays: A Comparative Study of Tughlaq and Tale-Danda." *The Commonwealth Review* 15.1 (2004): 87-97. Print.

Karnad, Girish. *Collected Plays*. vol I. New Delhi: O.U.P., 2010. Print.

_______. 'In Search of a New Theatre.' In *Contemporary India: Essays on the Use of Tradition*. Ed. Carla Borden. Delhi: O.U.P, 1989. Print.

_______. *The Fire and the Rain*. New Delhi: O.U.P., 2009. Print.

Savarimuttu, J. S., "The Liminar in Girish Karnad's Hayavadana." *The Atlantic Literary Review Quarterly* 10.2 (Apr-Jun 2009): 38-45. Print.

Sugarwala, Fatima. "The Real and Ideal in Karnad's Plays." *The Quest* 12.1 (June 1998): 19-25. Print.

12

The Expendable Dalit in Hindu-Muslim Riots: A Critical Reading of Nabendu Ghosh's Partition Story "The Saviour"

Debasri Basu

This paper seeks to explore the position of the depressed castes or dalits during the 1947 Partition of India with special reference to Nabendu Ghosh's short story "The Saviour". Faced with the looming prospect of attack from Muslim quarters during the Partition riots, caste Hindus of a Calcutta neighbourhood approach the leader of a local untouchables community with an eye to enlist active cooperation. They stress on unity as the need of the hour and call upon him to marshal his men in the event of any violence. This is shrewdly accomplished through harping on their common religious affiliation, and also an explicit offer of money as inducement. During the subsequent clashes these dalits act as the proverbial shield and save members of the gentility who are escorted to safer havens under military protection.

Ghosh here exposes the high-politics at play during those turbulent days when caste-differences, strictly enforced at other times, were conveniently put aside in a bid to shore up adequate numbers by certain sections of the Hindu *bhadralok* community. Taking recourse to both Machiavellian glib talk and bribery, they mobilized members of the depressed castes in a show of strength with the ulterior motive of turning these hapless foot-soldiers into cannon-fodder in the likelihood of direct confrontation. In course of this reading, the paper highlights the problematics of exploitive inter-caste relations which have sadly come to characterize Indian society.

The Partition of British India in 1947 to create the new states of India and Pakistan, though a political process, gave way to massive societal upheaval involving displacement of millions of people and accompanied by heinous acts of violence. This paper seeks to explore the position of the depressed castes or Dalits during the Partition riots with special reference to Nabendu Ghosh's short story "The Saviour" ("Traankarta" in the original Bengali). In course of this, it engages with critical responses to understanding the attendant violence and its inherent politics that have, more often than not, been subsumed in the larger picture.

Set in a Hindu Bengali *Bhadralok*[1] locale that lay in close proximity to a Muslim area in Calcutta,[2] Ghosh's story begins at a point of crisis when the latter community has suffered an initial setback in the ongoing riots: "The other neighbourhood was up in flames–severed heads soaked in blood landed here and there, breasts of 16-year old virgins had been cut off, angelic infants were bashed against the hard concrete, in pitch-dark hell the devil was being ceremonially installed tonight over there" (131). Retaliation was more or less inevitable; in fact "news had reached this locality" that "tonight those others from that neighbourhood would attack these people here" (131). There was a palpable unease in the air as battle-lines between the two warring parties were being drawn: "Shivers ran down their spines when they heard this–what could they do? How could they save themselves?"(131).

In the story, this atmosphere of foreboding is crystallized in the characters of the barrister Mr. Bose and his family-members who seem to be greatly apprehensive about the impending assault and live in a state of fearful trepidation. An emergency meeting of the local Defence Committee, of which Mr. Bose is the president, is convened at his house, duly attended by all the "heavyweights" (135) of the area. They deliberate on the "course of action" (136) to be taken, and chalk out plans to divide the neighbourhood into four patrol units, each to be guarded by a group of young men from the locality. But when one of them proposes that "a group of people always has to be on guard on the street ready to fight, should the enemy attack...they have to be prepared to lay down their lives all the time" (137) and asks whether all able-bodied men were willing to do that, it causes a veritable "explosion" (137), with none of them forthcoming to sacrifice their lives. Providing a way out of this seemingly insurmountable problem, one of the young men assembled there, Jatin, suggests recruiting the "doms" who lived "in between this respectable, aristocrat enclave and that other neighbourhood" (133).

The *doms* are traditionally scavengers and funerary specialists, and hence consideredunclean or polluting by upper-castes. They are also known for their physical strength, though often condemned as criminals. In Ghosh's story, it is specifically mentioned that these people "swept and sprayed water on the streets, cleaned the drains and the sewage lines, cleared the clogged manholes, collected garbage riding on municipal trucks" (133). The renowned sociologist G.S. Ghurye in his book *Caste and race in India* had categorically stated that "no Hindu of decent caste would touch a ...Dom" (8). However, stricken with panic in view of the impending confrontation and acutely aware of their own lack of resistance, the caste-Hindus are left with little option but to seek the assistance of these supposed low-castes. In accordance with Jatin's strategy, the leader of the *doms*–Jhogru Sardar–is personally invited by three of the Committee members and escorted to the meeting where Mr. Bose delicately broaches the topic of the coming danger: "You know there have been riots, don't you?...They may attack us tonight" (140). Being a barrister from England, he employs his lawyerly wiles in the subtlest manner to harp on their common religious affiliation: "We are Hindus, both you and us...If Hindus don't help each other, who will?...If they come will you put up a fight? We...are going to join in too and fight united" (140). Aware of their proclivity towards liqueur, he also assures them of a drinking binge as a form of advance remuneration: "Listen Jhogru, we'll give you and your people lots of cash for buying booze–as much as you want. We'll give you money not only for booze but for a feast as well" (140). To further bolster his cause, Mr. Bose even gets up from his seat and holds Jhogru's hand to make him sit down along with the other caste-Hindus, speaking in a voice choked with emotion: "What if you are a dom? You are a human being just like us and a Hindu–sit down my brother" (140).

Not surprisingly, his histrionics have the desired effect on Jhogru who till then, on account of his supposed lower caste and menial profession, had been used to sheer indifference if not actual contempt from those like Mr. Bose. He is easily led to believe that the upper-castes, whom he reverentially regarded as *hujoor*,[3] have finally embraced men like him as one of their own: "Jhogru tried to speak, but couldn't utter a single word. He was used to speaking non-stop even while he was dead-drunk. But today he was bereft of words in amazement, gratitude and a kind of happiness he had tasted for the first time" (141). He feels overwhelmed at this prospect of inter-caste solidarity and stops by the temple to express his gratefulness: 'While returning home he stopped short in front of the Shiva temple near their slum and went nearer. He caressed the damp walls of the temple and smiled. Mumbling he said, 'Shivji, you are great, truly great' " (141).

Interestingly, it is the same Shiva temple which forbade the entry of lower castes like him. It is obvious that Jatin had intended to exploit their yearning for recognition and assimilation into the caste-Hindu fold when he shrewdly suggests turning them into pawns at the hands of the Defence Committee. His strategy is clearly laid out in these words: "In fact, they consider themselves belonging to our area and though they are denied entry into the Shiva temple at the entrance of our lane, they offer prayers to the idol. In other words they are Hindus" (137). Badri Narayan in his book *Fascinating Hindutva: Saffron Politics and Dalit Mobilisation* cites one of the principal reasons for the success of people like Jatin in mobilising dalits by pointing out the strong urge of the Dalits themselves to seek acceptance from the upper-caste Hindus who had always culturally and socially marginalised them, by linking themselves with their temples, rituals, gods and goddesses and also by replicating many of them. This appropriation of the cultural resources of the very people who oppress them and from whom they want liberation might be a means to elevate themselves in their eyes and thereby gain acceptance in their exalted circle (Narayan 23).[4]

The long-anticipated attack from the Muslims comes around one in the night. Slogans of "Allah-ho-Akbar" and "Long Live Pakistan" (141) rend the night sky as they slowly approached to this neighbourhood: "They were holding up blazing torches… . They first advanced towards the Shiva temple with the intention of destroying the temple before wiping out the locality" (141). Jhogru, who had been waiting with his men in silence, now marshals them into the fray as the two groups clash in the middle of the night: "Come on brothers, let's clear the garbage" (142), perhaps in a grim allusion to their daily job of waste removal which assumes a greater import now that they have also been delegated the task of disposing off the "rivals" (141) by their caste-superiors. His battle-cry of "Har Har Mahadeo" (142) implying "Glory to our Lord Shiva" underscores the inherent irony of the situation, which Ghosh is quick to point out in the preceding lines: "The Shiva temple which they had never been allowed to enter, the damp walls of which they were only too happy to caress and seek blessings of the mute stone idol who had never protested against the blatant discrimination they face–Jhogru raised his slogan to hail that God" (142). Incidentally, legend has it that once Lord Shiva asked one of the sons of Kalu Rai, regarded as the forefather of the *dom* caste to bring water from the Ganges. When he arrived at the river bank, he found some people preparing to cremate a corpse. He helped them prepare the funeral pyre using bamboo sticks in lieu of money. On his return Lord Shiva cursed him that he and his descendants would earn a living only by cremating dead bodies.[5] Viewed in the light of this, the simple-minded devotion of Jhogru and his ilk to Shiva and other gods of the Hindu pantheon acquire a tragic dimension, more so when one juxtaposes it with the guile of the upper-castes who take advantage of such naivety to further their own cause.

The ensuing riot is a bloody one: "There were rivers of blood. Limbs and head flew here and there. Grey matter oozed out of crushed skull; sharp knives kissed the soft tissues of the heart and came out victorious…corpses lay strewn on the battlefield. The air was heavy with the stench of fresh blood" (141), though eventually the attackers are forced to retreat as "Jhogru's men had managed to teach them a lesson. The Shiva temple was untouched" (142). The death toll in both the camps is rather high; however, "those who died on this side were the doms" (142), including their leader Jhogru. Their tenements fill with lamentation for the dead, for "many a woman had lost her father, brother, husband and son" (143). This is in stark contrast to the genteel sections of the neighbourhood which show no sign of ravage on account of the riot. One cannot miss the note of mordant irony when Ghosh discloses that "the respectable babus were holding fort behind the frontline–the fight didn't reach that far. If it had, they would surely have fought they said, laid down their lives" (142).

Mr. Bose and his family members slip away in their motorcar to Bhabanipur, a predominantly Hindu locality, accompanied by a military truck with four soldiers to ensure a safe passage. En route, it is only his son Arun who gratefully acknowledges the role of the doms when he says "Jhogru saved us Baba–oh, how he fought!" to which Mr. Bose nonchalantly replies that "we gave him good money. *He was well-paid*" (143, emphasis in original). His daughter Ruby is equally apathetic to Jhogru's fate; instead of feeling any tinge of sadness for those who laid down their lives for the sake of the gentility, she is merely relieved that the riot did not mark "an end to picnic and movies in her life. The social butterfly hadn't died an untimely death" (143). She appears to be the least bothered about the gravity of the situation, and her superficial view of life can further be judged when we remember her initial response after catching a glimpse of Jhogru at the meeting of the Defence Committee: "She screwed up her nose and mumbled, 'How ugly and dirty' " (140). It is the shrewd manipulation of religious sentiment and subsequent gross indifference towards the sacrifice of Jhogru and his men which arouses the righteous indignation of the author and reader alike. Ghosh highlights this gross exploitation when he declares that "Jhogru was dead because people like Jhogru were always born to save the likes of Mr. Bose', in a sardonic reference to Mr. Bose's earlier remark that '...it was their job after all..." (143). In perhaps the most telling comment in the concluding lines of his story, he declares that "the Pandavas would never have lived if the five Nishads had not died in their place" (143), alluding to a similar episode in the mythical Indian epic of *Mahabharata* where five men of a hunting tribe–the Nishads–and their mother are deliberately allowed into the lacquer house and let to die in a fire, to establish the deaths of the Pandavas in the eyes of their rivals, the Kauravas. The above analogy reinforces the appalling tradition of exploitation on the basis of social hierarchy that has been continuing since ages.

Social history, and more particularly, the history of the Partition bears testimony to the fact that in times of conflicts it is the lower section of society that has to bear the greatest brunt, and this is particularly true of the riots in Bengal. This is evident from documentary proofs too; Major L.A. Livermore of the Eastern Command who notes in his diary that while Calcutta during the August 1946 riots was the battlefield between mob rule versus civilization and decency, "the casualties of that stricken field were for the most part the poor, the low-caste illiterates and those too weak to defend their property from the looter, the vulture of the mob" (qtd. in Tucker 597). The subaltern sections took the beating either owing to their unprivileged position in society, primarily owing to the nature of their livelihood which compelled them to come out in the streets even during times of communal conflagration, or else fell naïve victims to the machinations of the upper castes and classes at in Ghosh's story.

At this juncture, a pan-India survey of the position of the depressed castes amidst the raging communal turmoil brings to the fore certain revelations of a paradoxical nature. The received wisdom on violence and on traumatic events is that they are great equalizers. Violence, it is assumed, does not recognize caste and class differences when it is on such a large scale as the Partition riots of 1947. None the less, in some respects, this is not the wholly correct. During these horrendous riots, dalits were rarely attacked by Muslims in northern India as they were not considered an integral part of the Hindu mainstream. In her book *The Other Side of Silence: Voice from the Partition of India*, Urvashi Butalia narrates the case of Maya Rani, a dalit young girl, who testifies to the fact that dalits of her village in Punjab, including her own family of sweepers, were not affected by the ongoing Hindu-Muslim riots. Butalia adds that this was perhaps the outcome of the social invisibility that was characteristic of stable times and which, fortunately for these people, continued even in those days of tumult (Butalia 223-258, *passim*). Sind in West Pakistan too exhibited a similar leniency toward these castes; in fact, the administration in its capital city of Karachi actively discouraged the exodus of members from these castes to India in a bid to retain their traditional menial services, and thereby ensure a class of subservient workers.

However, the situation in Bengal was markedly different from the rest of India, with the lower castes being equally vulnerable to Muslim attack as caste-Hindus, especially in the minority areas of eastern Bengal/East Pakistan–a startling fact that has led historian Sekhar Bandyopadhyay to investigate this incongruity in greater detail. In his essay "Partition and the

Ruptures in Dalit Identity Politics in Bengal", he expounds that while untouchability as a social phenomenon was a rampant throughout Bengal despite its apparent progressive aura,[6] the unique conditions prevalent in this region at the time of the Partition brought about a forced homogenisation of intra-communal social identities. Barring a few leaders like Anukul Chandra Naskar in southern Bengal and Jogendra Nath Mandal in eastern Bengal who opposed the Partition Plan, most of the other scheduled caste members of the Bengal legislative assembly viewed with apprehension the rising tempo of anti-Hindu sentiments amongst Muslims ever since the Dhaka riot of 1941, which eventually reached its culmination with the call to Direct Action given by Mohammad Ali Jinnah in Calcutta on 16th August 1946 to press for the demand of Pakistan. Bandyopadhyay maintains that under those circumstances, Partition and the creation of a Hindu majority province in West Bengal were seen as the only viable option for economic and political survival by them. The fact that twenty-five of the thirty scheduled caste members voted for the Congress-Hindu Mahasabha sponsored Partition resolution in the Bengal legislative assembly on 20 June 1947 reinforces this view (Bandyopadhyay 459). Inevitably, this resulted in the loss of neutral-status and attendant immunity during riots for the Bengali dalits which had been extended to their counterparts in other parts of the country.

The overtly Hindu political groups were equally eager to appropriate these people into their fold to bolster their claims in the nationalist discourse. The eminent social historian Ashis Nandy has not only explored the nexus between the middle class and the slum, but offered the startling insight that the middle class itself constitutes the most intractable slum of Indian political life. In his essay "The Death of an Empire", Nandy contends that the slums are the natural bastions of people, as a result of which the middle classes expected the slum dwellers who had acquired new loyalties amidst their dislocation to die, if necessary, in the common cause of the defence of the nation and the faith; but they were themselves not prepared to offer any such sacrifices. He further reminds that the masculinist, middle-class and majoritarian enterprise of Hindu nationalism was riddled by other anomalies. The British had declared the Bengalis to be an effeminate people; thus according to Nandy, in the evolving social milieu "the lower caste musclemen and the criminal elements previously considered social outcasts or outsiders, apart from the castes with low-status vocations–butchers, blacksmiths and fishermen–and even up-country Hindus, Sikhs and Nepali Gurkhas now became the heroic protectors of middle-class, sedentary, upper-caste Bengali Hindus" (7).

Along with Ghosh, the famous litterateur Munshi Premchand had also raised this issue in his very first Hindi novel *Sevasadan* which exposes the Hindu politics of befriending the *doms* who are otherwise treated worse than animals to counter Muslim votes on account of political expediency. What is perhaps even more regrettable is the fact that such manoeuvring of religious sentiments has remained a prominent feature of not just the Partition riots but also subsequent communal conflagrations in post-Independence India. R.D. Sonkar, a dalit intellectual and retired IAS officer, who had served as the advisor of the governor of Uttar Pradesh, explains that the underlying motive for promoting wrestling and appeasing the wrestlers living in the *akharas* is that at the time of communal riots these forces come forward to defend the Hindus (Narayan 67). Similarly, Asghar Ali Engineer in his essay "Communal Fire Engulfs Ahmedabad Once Again" makes a mention of many Dalit leaders who had admitted to their being willing instruments at the hands of caste Hindus during the Ahmedabad riots of 1969 (1117).

During the post-Godhra riots of 2002 in Gujarat, there were charges from certain sections that dalits and tribals had been recruited in the fight against Muslims under the garb of religious fraternity. The recurrence of such a phenomenon has led Badri Narayan to highlight the various tactics resorted to by the political parties in an express attempt to unify the dalits "under the broader

Hindu identity and communalise them by separating them from the Muslims, who they portray as foreign invaders who polluted the pure Hindu culture coming down from the Vedic period" (13). Such an appeal to the common Other has borne palpable dividends in the decades past[7] and is bound to perpetuate in an environment of spiralling mutual suspicion and hatred, unless one is astute enough to deconstruct the overwhelmingly monologic voice of fundamentalism which treats these depressed sections like Jhogru and his men in Ghosh's story as disposable chaff in the grind of inter-communal hostilities.

Notes and References

1. *Bhadralok*, literally meaning civilized person in Bengali, denotes the exclusively upper-caste and predominantly upper- and middle-class of the Bengali Hindu populace which constitute its gentility.
2. Modern-day Kolkata was earlier known as Calcutta. The name of West Bengal's capital city was officially changed in the year 2000.
3. *Hujoor* means master in Hindustani, an amalgamation of Hindi and Urdu.
4. Narayan refers to G. K. Karanth's essay 'Replication or Dissent? Culture and Institutions among "Untouchable" Scheduled Castes in Karnataka' to propose that saffronisation of Dalits is often mutually complemented by the desire of the lower castes for upward social mobility (24).
5. As recorded in Ganesh Gupta's *Padabi Abhidhan* [*Dictionary of Family Names*, in Bengali]. Kolkata: Annapurna Prakashan, n.d. 52.
6. When M. C. Rajah moved the Untouchability Abolition Bill in the Central Assembly in 1933, every Hindu member from Bengal reacted violently against it. Pandit Satyendranath Sen took the view that "...these untouchables owe their origin to serious violations to the marital laws...[and] by their avocation, by their habits and their culture they can never come up to the standard of caste Hindus..." and B. P. Singh Roy denounced the Bill as "a direct encroachment on the religious rights of the Hindus and an attempt to undermine the foundations of Hindu society." This reaction lead M. C. Rajah ironically to observe, "It is surprising...that the bulk of the opposition comes from a province, Bengal, where they say there is no untouchability" (qtd. in Chatterji, 40).
7. Badri Narayan refers to the fact that of all the people who have fought and died for the Hindus in the communal riots that have taken place

> in since Independence, the maximum have been the Dalits and Backward Castes. Their houses were burnt down the most, implying that they were the ones who stood their ground or were manipulated to fight against the Muslims (31).

Works Cited

Bandyopadhyay, Sekhar. "Partition and the Ruptures in Dalit Identity Politics in Bengal." *Asian Studies Review* 33.4 (2009): 455-67.

Butaia, Urvashi. *The Other Side of Silence: Voice from the Partition of India.* New Delhi, Viking, 1998.

Chatterji, Joya. *Bengal Divided: Hindu Communalism and partition, 1932-47.* Delhi: Cambridge UP, 1995.

Engineer, Asghar Ali. "Communal Fire Engulfs Ahmedabad Once Again." *Economic and Political Weekly.* 20. 27 (1985) : 1116-1120.

Fraser, Bashabi, ed. *Bengal Partition Stories: An Unfinished Chapter.* London: AnthemPress, 2008. 131-43.

Ghosh, Nabendu. "Saviour." *Bengal Partition Stories: An Unfinished Chapter.* Fraser 131-43.

Ghurye, G. S. *Caste and race in India.* Mumbai: Popular Prakashan, 2008.

Gupta, Ganesh. *Padabi Abhidhan* [*Dictionary of Family Names,* Bengali]. Kolkata: Annapurna Prakashan, n.d. 52.

Karanth, G. K. 'Replication or Dissent? Culture and Institutions among "Untouchable" Scheduled Castes in Karnataka.' in D. Gupta, *Caste in Question: Identity or Hierarchy, Contributions to Indian Sociology Occasional Studies 12.* New Delhi: Sage, 2004.

Nandy, Ashis. "The Death of an Empire." Saint, *Bruised Memories* 5-13.

Narayan, Badri. *Fascinating Hindutva: Saffron Politics and Dalit Mobilisation.* New Delhi: Sage, 2009.

Premchand, Munshi. *Sevasadan.* [Hindi]. 1919. Allahabad: Hans Prakashan, 2003.

Saint, Tarun K, ed. *Bruised Memories: Communal Violence and the Writer.* Calcutta: Seagull, 2002.

Tucker, Sir Francis. *India's Partition and Human Debasement.* Delhi: Anmol

13

Saga of the Downtrodden (Dalit): Protest against Exploitation in Mulk Raj Anand

Oindrila Ghosh

> . . . the Indian nation is on the course for a civil war, a civil war that has been simmering as an undercurrent of the caste-based cultural system that Hinduism has constructed and nurtured for centuries.
>
> (Ilaiha: Blurb)

This simmering undercurrent born of centuries of oppression and deprivation gave birth to a literature, dalit Literature, of protest, shame, anger, sorrow and indomitable hope for the upheaval of a social order based on human exploitation. Its attempt was and is to pose a treat to brahminic hegemony in literature and aesthetics. Besides the four main castes, there is a fifth group in India – the dalits – treated as the untouchables in society. Oppressed, downtrodden and exploited, the dalits were hardly considered to be part of the Indian society even some time back.

Although the Constitution of India grants and assures every individual equal rights and opportunities, many among the dalit community are yet to take for granted, receive and exercise such natural rights (Chakraborty 2). The dalits have always seen as polluting society and were generally segregated and ostracized physically from participating in Hindu social life. While some change has taken place, the lot of the majority of this section of

Indian society continues to be woeful, to say the least. Against these atrocities the dalits have initiated several movements in the course of Indian history. All these movements aimed at the liberation of dalits from the shackles of inhuman exploitation, rejection of the sub-human status imposed on them by the Hindu social order and securing dignity due to them as human beings. The subject of dalit writings – novels, prose and poetry – be it in Marathi, Kannada or Bengali has chiefly been focused on the depiction of the plight of the dalits and stressing on the need for human dignity.

However, even before the flourishing of a literature of their own, the plight of the dalit, the untouchables, the downtrodden of India found its voice in the writings of Munshi Premchand and Mulk Raj Anand. Though when they were writing about the have nots of society there was no specific bracket of Dalit thought in literature. A pioneer among the upper-caste Hindu writers is Munshi Premchandwho identified untouchability as one of the worst evils of the existing Indian society dominated by the Hindus. In his short stories and novels, *Godaan*, *Thakur ka Kuan*, *Sadgati*, he expresses his strong condemnation against the insensitivity and heartlessness of the upper caste educated people against the dalits. Premchand and Anand were in fact instrumental in forming the base of dalit literature, in the sense that they wrote about the plight of the mindless cruelty and oppression meted out to the so-called outcastes.

Speaking about the real test of the novelist Mulk Raj Anand contemplates that a writer should be the fiery voice of the people, and be able to give a new vision of life realizing the pains, frustrations and aspirations of others, and by cultivating his incipient powers of expression, transmutes in art all feelings, thoughts and experiences. Anand's poignant involvement in the miseries of these subaltern subjects in pre-independent India is evident through his characters Munoo (*Coolie*) and Bakha (*Untouchable*) whose sagas of injustice and exploitation sought to shake out the white sahib as well as the Indian upper caste. He was in fact instrumental in ushering the first wave of dalit literature emulated by regional dalit writers in the years to come. In Anand the subaltern remains voiceless and he, an upper caste Hindu, enlightened by the liberal philosophical thoughts of the West, takes it upon himself to convey the former's emotional, physical and social trauma. However, what makes him a pioneer is the near-empathy achieved by him while retaining objectivity. In fact E.M. Forster wrote, in the Preface, about *Untouchable*: "*Untouchable* could only have been written by an Indian who observed from the outside . . . And no Untouchable could have written the book, because he would have been involved in indignation and self-pity Mr. Anand stands in the ideal position. By caste he is a Kshatriya, and he might have been expected to inherit the pollution-complex. But as a child he played with the children of the sweepers attached to an Indian regiment, he grew fond of them, and to understand a tragedy he did not share." (*Untouchable* vii).

As early as in 1788, Edmund Burke had commented about India and its caste system: "In that country the law of religion, the laws of the land, and the laws of honour, are all united and consolidated in one, and bind a man eternally to the rules of what is called his caste",[2] revealing thereby the all-pervasive sway of the caste-system over Indian lives and minds. In the Indian social structure, caste system has always played a prime force in the determination of the role which individuals are required to perform. The status of an individual on social, cultural and political levels is assessed on the basis of his birth in a particular caste, rather than on the basis of his human worth or potential. What follows naturally from this is social injustice and oppression based not on individual merit or demerit but social determinism. The suffering of the untouchables is unspeakable as they are segregated and discriminated against on the basis of birth, the menial work they do and are made to undergo physical and mental tortures. Bakha right from the start of the novel is shown as a dutiful, alert and diligent, doing his work with dedication and unlike his father he never concocts fibs or excuse to stay away from work. For all these Bakha is not appreciated but rather showered with abuses and treated as vermin. Dr. Farhana Khan comments: "Anand's desire to see these people are given an equal status in the society impells him into the messianic role of championing their cause" (Khan 59). Having seen these downtrodden people from close quarters, since many of them were his childhood companions, he had knowledge of and cause for vehemently attacking the evils of a society which generated and perpetrated such inhuman exploitation. Anand attempts to encompass the saga of the miseries of the downtrodden from his first novel *Untouchable* to *Coolie* and then with an eruptive forcefulness in *Two Leaves and a Bud*. His diehard socialism often leads him to use his fictional art as a vehicle of propaganda to arouse the latent humanism in his readers and "to improve the conditions of the people, to uplift India's dispossessed to social dignity" (Khan 59).

In his novels Anand, like Dickens, attempts to project social reality, often resorting to melodrama to highlight the inhumanness, and ultimately seeking to do away with social inequalities inherent in the caste-system which perpetrates such cruelties. Anand as a writer belongs to the tradition of the Indian Renaissance (Rajan14), belonging to the long train of such writers as Tagore, Iqbal, Bankim Chandra, Sarat Chandra and as already mentioned, Premchand, and inheriting and embodying the ambivalence that was born out of the East-West encounter.

Untouchable is a fictional representation of the real tragedy faced by the untouchables in India of the 1920s and 1930s, through the story of a day in the life of Bakha a sweeper boy. Bakha, the untouchable, has to rebel against the social prejudice and the ossified Hindu caste-system which has marginalized him and Anand makes him wage a crusade against caste in order to attain a selfhood based on his intrinsic worth and merit. It has been suggested that "[i]n Untouchable the intended meaning seems to be a rejection of the Hindu Society, with its age-old lies and brutal discrimination against millions of untouchables. This rejection is to be accompanied by an acceptance of the modernist values of the western world. Right from the beginning of the narrative till the end, Bakha's dream is to be like the sahibs; the world of the Tommies is his ideal world" (Rajan 38) and his struggle is a crusade for attaining selfhood by rebelling against the social prejudices which have marginalized him and led to his persecution and humiliation. Anand had read about and carried numerous memories from his childhood days of the untold suffering of the untouchables and he tried to put them all in his novels making them such violent critiques of casteism and a bitter exposure of inhuman treatment meted out to the so called 'lower castes' or shudras. Rama Jha observes:

> *Untouchable* is Anand's first novel in which he is concerned with the evil of untouchability in Hindu society. Anand is the first Indian novelist to have depicted in the novel form, the stigma of this evil which isolates man from his own society creating an archetypal image of the untouchable. . . . the novel's emphasis on an individual's attempt to emancipate himself from the age old evil of untouchability . . . . Anand projects his theme through characterization.
>
> (Jha 59)

Anand's purpose is to bring out empathy in his readers through the poignant descriptions of the unrelented suffering and hardships of his protagonist Bakha. The author's humanistic outlook and sincere efforts to end ostracism in the name of something created by man to subdue other men is evident from his depiction of his lowly characters in heroic light as they traverse through their oppressive lives with heroic perseverance. Bakha finds no source of inspiration or respite from the caste-dominated society, he rebels against it but with the innate sense of futility accompanying it. Thus, for him the only road to emancipation appears to be the emulation of the British, who with their superior lifestyle and democratic and caste-less society naturally lures the oppressed and tortured Bakha. Kancha Ilaiha has said something in this regard and in the same strain. He says:

> The Hindu thinkers never realized that in the course of human history, Hinduism would die much before the other religions exhaust their potential to influence the human masses. . . . The Hindu scholars never realized that the Indian Dalit-Bahujan masses, who constitute a great majority of the national population, are slowly but surely moving away from Hindu spiritual fascism. . . . The Shudras who fall 'below' these[upper] castes in the social hierarchy, have an ambiguous relationship with Hinduism, and . . . once they realize that the religion is dying, they will abandon it as one abandons a sinking ship.
>
> (Ilaiha xii)

Though written about the caste system and its impact on Indian lives in the early decades of the twenty-first century, these lines seem to be a theoretical expression of what Anand the intuitive artist had sought to posit through his fictional art. Bakha's efforts to rebel against the rigid caste-structure and the appeal of the lifestyle of the sahibs already seem to foreground the lack of faith of the downtrodden castes in the Hindu spiritual system. The '*Varna*dharmic' system built into it by brahminic hegemony lent to it an anti-egalitarian and anti-scientific character which Hinduism till date has been unable to transform and update,[3] leading to the exclusion, exploitation and marginalization of the Bakhas.

The appeal of Christianity in Bakha's mind is momentary, vague, mixed with the sense of awe for the British sahibs who follow it and based on his half-formed opinion that "yesuh messih (Jesus) must be a good man . . . if he regards a Brahmin and a Bhangi the same" This feeling is soon undercut by the missionary's wife voicing not the liberal egalitarian sentiments of Christianity but refers to Bakha as "dirty Bhangi . . ." revealing the fact that the onus of generating a sense of equality and fraternity rest not on institutionalized religion but on the followers of religions. But for Anand literature is but an extension and expression of society and the questions raised by him in his fiction are social questions.

Untouchable broke the tradition of the earlier Indo-Anglian novel which was mainly based on romance or history and meant for light reading. Anand wrote with the zeal of a social reformer, who did not believe in 'art for art sake' but chose to wield his pen in order to arouse the reader's sympathy for the suffering, misery and oppression of the underdogs of society exploited by the caste system or the capitalist forces.

Around the 1930s when the freedom movement was gaining momentum under Gandhi's leadership, the famous fast undertaken by him as a mark of protest against the introduction of separate electorates for the untouchables was perhaps the climax of protest against caste system in India. This was an impetus for Anand, who was seething with righteous anger against this age old evil system, to write a novel of protest. But, the climactic slapping scene in the novel shows how the rebellion of Bakha ultimately fails as he submits to the ruling caste ideology. "His first impulse was to run, just to shoot across the throng . . .but then he realized that he was surrounded by a barrier, not a physical barrier, because one push from his hefty shoulders would have been enough to unbalance the skeleton-like onlookers, but a moral one. He knew that the contact with him . . . would defile a great many more of these men" (*Untouchable* 20). Anand presents the conflict in Bakha's mind between revolution and submission to timeless moral codes, however oppressive. The solution offered at the end of the novel is also viable and realistic, the introduction of the flush system, water-closets and main-drainage, simple-sounding mechanical solutions to remove the stigma or cause of branding a class of people as untouchables for the menial work they do. K.D. Verma comments:

> While the only way to understand the value of Bakha's work, if there is any significance at all, is to see Bakha' destiny in the context

> of the theories of casteism and karma, there is no possible plan for Bakha's liberation, unless of course, he, after Rousseau's ideal plan, I placed outside the social order. But despite the best possible expositions of the philosophy of karma one would find it rationally indefensible to believe that Bakha's ignominious existence and hi pain and suffering should be the result of ignobleness of his caste, the dalit, the Harijan, into which Bakha is born. Significantly, Anand has tried to show that none of the Western theoretical models, including the Hegelian and Marxian models, is appropriate to theorizing the tragedy of Bakha's deterministic existence and the stubborn order that is responsible for the creation of the Bakhas of society.
>
> (Verma 93)

Anand's fight was against all forces of oppression and deprivation, be it the caste hierarchy or the forces of Capitalism and Imperialism. His opposition to the later force becomes evident from his 1935 novel, *Coolie.* Farhana Khan comments 'in the past few centuries the emergence of rigid class system based on money power, beside the age-old caste system, proved to be more decisive in India, which in turn led to the permanent cleavage between the haves and have nots. It pervaded to all aspects of social life . . .' (Khan 76). It is the larger social reality, of class struggle in India, which becomes the subject of *Coolie*, which seeks to project this macrocosm of Indian social life through the struggles of a single boy – Munoo – to attain self-esteem and self-identity.

Anand chooses Munoo, a young impressionable and sensitive boy, as his central character. The young boy comes from a village, brought up by his insensitive uncle and aunt. He is full of the usual innocence and restlessness of a child. He is hounded out of the village by the pressure to earn a livelihood, which initially turns him into a domestic servant, then indentured labourer, a worker in the cotton mills of Bombay, a rickshaw puller and finally as page to an Anglo-Indian woman in Simla, where he meets an untimely death at the age of fifteen through consumption. A gruesome tale of unmitigated suffering and the heartlessness of society which destroys the potential of a young boy and nips his growth at the bud, it has been said that in *Coolie*, "the purpose of the novelist is not to present a gloomy picture of life. On the contrary, he wishes to arouse the conscience of humanity against the ruthless exploitation of the weak." (Sinha, 33).

Both Munoo and Bakha, especially Munoo, remain passive characters, with things happening to them and even in their opposition to society they remain passive while society remains active. This sense of passivity of the protagonists in Anand's novels emerges from the purpose of the novelist to graph out the process of their incessant exploitation[4] rather than recording their growth through experiences and encounters, as in a bildungsroman. His protagonists become the mouthpiece for his social critiques as Anand mercilessly exposes the evil and putrefied customs of society. "Anand's condemnation of untouchability derives its strength from his passionate involvement in, and identifications with, the problem of the socially-boycotted individuals. He shows the utter futility of attaching a tag . . ." (Khan 71).

Anand was a humanist from the bottom of his heart and was often so moved by the suffering of the downtrodden victims of caste or class prejudices, to sacrifice artistic refinement and quality to social criticism. K.R. Rao comments:

> Anand is irresistibly drawn by the social motives, and his attitude to life is so particularly dominated by socialistic theory that it is difficult to bypass or isolate his commitment . . . so strong is his sense of commitment to this creed, that he is not ashamed to admit that he is 'using literature as a means rather than an end in itself.'
>
> (Rao 134-135)

Thus, long before the emergence in India of a dalit literature, he was writing almost with the realism and reformative zeal of Dickens about the plight of the downtrodden, the causes of their bitterness borne out of centuries of oppression and deprivation, with near-empathy. There is the absence of any attitude of patronizing or pity in Anand towards the downtrodden because his childhood had been spent in close camaraderie of the untouchables, who were his friends. Mulk Raj Anand's childhood friends were mainly children from the cantonment area. They included a dhobi boy Ramcharan, a Muslim child called Ali, a Cobbler's son Chota, and a sweeper boy Bakha.

Works Cited

Chakraborty, Prashanta.'Dalits and Indian Literature'. *Language in India*. Volume 11:4 April 2011. www.Languageinindia.com. Web. 5th November, 2011.

Das, Sanjukta. 'Mulk Raj Anand: Coolie' in *Derozio to Dattani: Essays in Criticism*. Sanjukta Das. Delhi: Worldview, 2009. Print.

Dirks, Nicholas B. *Castes of Mind: Colonialism and the Making of Modern India*. Delhi: Permanent Black, 2002. Print.

George, C. J. Mulk Raj Anand: *His Art and Concerns*. New Delhi: Atlantic Publishers and Distributors, 1994. Print.

Ilaiah. Kancha. *Post-Hindu India: A Discourse on Dalit-Bahujan Socio-Spiritual And Scientific Revolution*. New Delhi: Sage, 2009. Print.

Jha, Rama. *Gandhian Thought and Indo-Anglian Novelists*. Delhi: Chanakya Publication, 1983. Print.

14

Kanyadaan: Daring beyond Politics of Casteism?

Srideep Mukherjee

My presentation here is more the outcome of an urge to share certain disturbing areas of thought on the dalit question with an informed audience/reader community, rather than it being in the nature of a research paper per se.

I was drawn by a report on *Mail Today* on 10th October 2011 of a wealthy dalit family in Uttar Pradesh having Ram Pyari, a less affluent dalit woman, paraded naked in Chandwapur village of Lakhimpur Kheri district. Apparently, her bane was that they believed Ram Pyari's husband had helped a daughter of their family, who was a divorcee, to elope with a local youth. The natural justice of 'innocent until proven guilty' did not obviously apply to her case and political bigwigs were quick to comment – "The victim is a poor Dalit woman while the accused are wealthy Dalits with political links..." It was also rued that such an incident could happen in a state where the Chief Minister herself was a Dalit woman.

Almost around the same time, I was at a staging of Vijay Tendulkar's *Kanyadaan* in Bangla translation, with the lead role being enacted by the noted thespian Bratya Basu. I was told he had stopped staging the play for quite some time before the elections, the apparent reason being that the role of Arun Athavale which he enacted was a negative shade of character. I find certain striking similarities between these two episodes, though a time gap of nearly three decades separates Tendulkar's writing of the play and the news report I have just referred to.

Kanyadaan is primarily the story of Arun Athavale, who hails from a family of Johaars and says that generation after generation; his family has been fed on stale stinking bread got from begging while their tongues have relished the flesh of dead animals. He has been more comfortable being huddled up with a large family in an eight feet by ten feet room, clotheless, foodless; being warmed in winter only by the heat of their bodies. So the damn houses of the city people seem to him like the bellies of sharks and crocodiles with each one alone in them. There can be no debating that Gandhi's term 'harijan' is indeed too soft and cosmetic to describe the plight of Arun and his likes, however much young politicians of shinning India might ceremoniously break bread at the homes of such fellow countrymen! It is also true that theoretically at least, Ambedkar's demand for the abolition of *Varnas*hram structure from the Hindu social order could have brought a semblance of dignity for the depressed classes. But in the more immediate context of the play, Arun's past is all brought out by his 'telling' of it, while his present comes along through the method of 'showing'. He is doing his B.A in Pune and works part time for Sramik Samachar; he is also a frequenter at the Socialists' Study Group where he has met Jyoti Devlalikar, the daughter of Nath a socialist ideologue and Seva who is an activist for the womens' cause and a pragmatic individual at that.

Arun and Jyoti are not very sure if they share the love of being a cosy twosome but they have decided to get married. As the play unfolds, it becomes clear that Jyoti, who has been brought up on her father's doctrines of socialism, looks upon this marriage as her means of contributing to social equality by declassing herself; while Arun looks upon marriage as conquest. He says in a merry rhyme:

> Hasli re hasli, ek bamaneen fasli! It's a jolly game, Caught a Brahmin dame.

Marriage is surely no bear-squirrel game, nor should it be a space for class warfare and so there is no real logic behind this coupling. But we must also remember that even though Jyoti likes Arun's dabbling in poetry, she has no illusions about his being an intelligent boy. Nor does she lay any claims to knowing much about Arun the man; in fact her discovery of the individual is almost concomitant to our understanding of him. The problem on our part however arises with the question of where to place Arun Athavale who stands at the interstices of his past and present. One understands that for all his education, his deliberations on dialectical materialism or his flirtations with socialist ideology, it is not easy for Arun to put behind the ignominy of his past with a virtual sweep of the hand.

At the macro level the dalit movement has never been a natural ally to the Communist movement in the Indian context for the simple reason that the latter has always rested on dictums like class struggle, dictatorship over the proletariat and notions of base-superstructure without getting into the underlying complex inequalities in a manner that subaltern studies have. As such the emergence of an autonomous dalit movement never found favour with the Communists for it was interpreted as dividing workers and diffusing the focus of the anti-imperialist struggle.

At the micro level therefore, if the focus of Tendulkar's play be taken as dialectic on class relations, then emancipation from it is only a societal pose that the protagonist strikes. As an individual however, he draws his real sustenance (even justification in the larger context of the play) from being enshrined as the oppressed; or even as one of the oppressed who has acquired a 'voice'. It is therefore clear that both parties to the marriage stand on fault lines and in such a situation the outcome makes for interesting study.

Whatever be her motivations behind the marriage, Jyoti is self motivated in her resolve, she is no Madhavi or Draupadi, both women who have had to passively accept the commodification of their female bodies to uphold the much vaunted reputations of their respective patriarchal lords. So Jyoti's function is much more than just bodily, even though Arun does use her, both mind and body, to parade that he can be a dangerous mix of (projected) caste violence and subversive patriarchy. He may be giving her a very realistic picture of how different life in a dalit household can be from the secure confines of her world – eating stinking bread and spoilt dal without vomiting, begging from door to door for grass for the buffaloes or even shitting in the village toilet. By such parameters, Jyoti truly inhabits an 'unwrinkled Tinopal world' and any kind of 'give and take' is difficult between Arun's ways and her 'fragrant, ghee spread, wheat bread culture'! But as one who has stepped out of his community and knows the differences between the two 'nations', Arun is surely an informed person. Having seen through her progressive socialist mindset and armed with the knowledge that Jyoti regards this marriage as something beyond the conventional act; Arun virtually throws the gauntlet at her with his romanticised self-degradation and difference. I am compelled to call it romanticised because Tendulkar's strong 'showing' brings out only a "Brahmin among Dalits" in the emergent figure of his protagonist, but I will come to that at greater length.

Arun's elation at having caught a brahmin dame in itself means nothing unless he can use it to show his otherness through the relatively soft option of marriage. Jyoti becomes to him an easy target through whom he can fulfil his vaunted desire of revenge:

> I want to set fire to the whole world, strangle throats, rape and kill. Drink up the blood of the beasts, your high class society.

There are signs of violence of myriad kinds even before the marriage and Jyoti understands it is quite a journey she must undertake to become the wife of a man who sees her as brahmin femininity that must be subdued to his dalit masculinity. With seva, he loses his calm for she tries to strip him of his caste-class identity and sees him as an educated young man who is expected to fend for the family. His mocking retort of brewing illicit liquor for a living if need be, might point to a pre-capitalist mode of family based production where any surplus is subsumed within the family; but it definitely posits him as what Kancha Ilaiah calls panii paata leenoodu (a person without work or song). Ilaiah categorically asserts that in the dalit bahujan culture, song is an integral part of labour and therefore all activity is a pleasurable community affair. In threatening to sponge upon the fruits of his wife's degraded labour, Arun thus goes against that very grain of his dalit origins that he seems to hold so dear. Seeking small victories in shallow achievements like the subversive use of discourse, he singles himself out as a sinister individual much more than a member of the repressed class.

If resistance brings out animosity and acceptance unleashes violence, then yielding to Arun prompts him to adopt arm twisting techniques and Nath learns this the hard way. More a doctrinaire than an individual, Nath embodies the deep rooted malaise of all mainstream movements as he appropriates the voice of the marginal and inadvertently becomes self-declared agency for emancipation. This cannot however justify the progressive degeneration of Arun from a wife beater to a sinister peddler of emotions who touts himself as the mouthpiece for the dalit community. Sharankumar Limbale, one of Maharashtra's pre-eminent dalit writer activists, characterises dalit literature as 'purposive' in the sense that it is a literature of commitment. He describes its purpose variously as 'revolutionary', 'transformational' and 'liberatory'. In Limbale's view, dalit literature serves its radical function through an authentic representation of dalit reality; a representation that empowers the untouchable Other with a voice to speak across the caste line and thus destroys the vaunted purity of the sa*Varna* space. Such a deconstructive enterprise is expected to give visibility to the dalit and enable him to bare the processes of history and society that have been used through centuries to legitimise. the caste system. Like Negritude, dalit movement too is supposed to be a complete revolution; in fact Bahurao Bagul looks upon the term as synonymous with 'revolution incarnate'.

Cut back to Kanyadaan and we find Arun Athavale, the rising star of the community is now a famed writer with a ravely reviewed autobiographical novel under his belt. As literature per se, it seems authentically dalit – precise, unsentimental, full of the true living language and 'belongs one hundred percent to our own soil' as Nath exclaims. But authentic dalit literature is necessarily the outcome of felt experiences and there is no space either for the trappings of bourgeois literary theories of depersonalisation or any kind of posers! So, almost immediately when Seva returns home after having had Jyoti hospitalised for she has been kicked by Arun in the sixth month of her pregnancy, Nath is perplexed just as we are:

> Such heinous behaviour by one who wrote this beautiful autobiography? How can he? Here in these pages he describes the humiliations he has undergone with extraordinary sensitivity...and the same man kicks his pregnant wife on her belly? How...?

In a virtual incantatory tone, Arun's earlier words recur in our minds – that marriage to Jyoti is a conquest of sorts and it gives him an opportunity to unleash his bestial instincts of strangling, raping and killing. At once the term 'Dalit' transcends the limits of a creed and becomes a paradigm where caste is not the only identifier; class and gender become equally important. The oppression of dalit women in particular might have specificity about it, as Padma Velaskar points, but broadly speaking, every woman at the intersections of caste, class and patriarchy is always at the receiving end of power relations in the politico-economic, social and cultural domains. Tendulkar thus makes the dalit identity a metaphor, the full implications of which are realised at the end of the play when Jyoti proclaims:

> I am not Jyoti Yadunath Devlalikar now, I am Jyoti Arun Athavale, a scavenger. I don't say harijan. I despise the term. I am an untouchable, a scavenger. I am one of them. Don't touch me.

We must realize that this identity is not one that comes just vis-s-vis her husband; it is a paradigmatic expression of her state in life, so she virtually re-defines the contours of dalit entity by taking upon herself the onus of reversing the Brahminical custom of kanyadaan. Nothing can be simpler than these words which contain the basic understanding that it is neither possible to improve people, nor to change society. Understandably, responses to *Kanyadaan* have been extremely diverse – it earned the playwright both the Saraswati Samman and a pair of slippers! At the Saraswati Samman acceptance speech, Tendulkar said of the play that

> it (was) the admission of defeat and intellectual confusion. It (gave) expression to a deep-rooted malaise and its pains.

It is evidences of this 'deep-rooted malaise' which haunt me as a conundrum that I have tried to raise in my reading of two texts—the barely two month old report at the outset and Vijay Tendulkar's *Kanyadaan* written in 1983. The title of my paper is not in the form of a statement; it is an interrogation. If dalit literature is all about a journey 'From Erasure to Assertion' as Alok Mukherjee says in reading Limbale's *Towards an Aesthetic of Dalit Literature*, and if such 'representationality' can truly make for figurative denominations beyond the mimetic, then where do these two texts lead us? How do we wish away the words of R. Upadhyay at the South Asia Analysis Group meet in 2001:

> Instead of looking on the growing consciousness among the educated caste Hindus against the social evil of caste discrimination against Dalits and appreciating this positive change, the Dalit activists ignore and understate the development. Their sole aim is now pointed towards personal ambitions at the cost of their community. This has created a new class of Brahmins among the

> Dalits, who are now exploiting the actual Dalits by grabbing the benefits meant for the latter. This may look like a paradox, but it is the hard reality.

That brings us back to the eternal debate of caste or class as the real index of progress or retarding of communities and individuals. To that I would definitely add the third category of gender which is sociologically determined for all classes; its representation in societal terms includes not just the material but also several non-material indexes of life. Are we headed towards the necessity of sub subaltern studies in the days to come?

15

From Maid to Literary Star: A Dalit Woman Writes Back

Sravasti Guha Thakurta

The dalit community has been at the receiving end of abuse and maltreatment from society from time immemorial. However, a fact which eludes our notice most of the time is that there exists another category of "dalits" amongst dalits. This category comprises of the women of the dalit class, those who suffer discrimination and cruelty at the hands of the males of the community. Very few amongst these women are educated enough or aware enough to give a voice to their sufferings and bring those before the notice of the world. Baby Halder is one such rare exception. Through her autobiography, *A Life Less Ordinary*, she lays bare before the eyes of the world the life of the average dalit woman—the poverty, discrimination and violence which are necessarily a part of their lives.

Simone de Beauvoir's observations on women's subjugation to men, their existence as "inessential [beings] which never becomes the essential"[1] appear in this context to be surprisingly relevant even to the contemporary egalitarian society. The feminist thinker and writer, Christine Delphy's observation that just as the lower classes are oppressed by the upper classes in society as a whole, so also women suffer oppression within their own families, where they are treated merely as subordinates, seem surprisingly apt in this context. Married women, especially, according to

Delphy, are made to act as unpaid domestic labour, and their hard lifelong labour is looked down upon and trivialised, and not considered important enough to be a topic of any serious discussion, or debate in its own right. Delphy points out that:

> societies [all over the world] depend on the unpaid labour of women for domestic services and child-rearing. These services are furnished within the framework of a particular relationship to an individual [the husband]. They are excluded from the realm of exchange [i.e. these services are not treated like the jobs people do for money outside their own home] and consequently have no value. They are unpaid. Whatever women receive in return is independent of the work they perform, because it is not handed out in exchange for that work [i.e. as wages to which their work entitles them], but rather as a gift. The husband's only obligation, which is obviously in his own interest, is to provide for the wife's basic needs, in other words he maintains her labour power.[2]

An acquaintance with Baby Halder's writing forces one to recognise the undeniable truth in the theses of de Beauvoir and Delphy. And a unique position is accorded to Halder's case by virtue of the fact that she is a woman, and also a "dalit". Dalits as a class have suffered for centuries at the hands of the "superior" classes; and yet among the dalit class, the women are subjected to an extra degree of subjugation, of repression. It is as if women form a separate, more inferior class- who somehow deserve that extra bit of repression. Baby Halder's autobiography therefore becomes an unique and important document which showcases the sufferings of the most repressed and subjugated homo sapiens- the dalit woman.

Baby Halder's autobiography, *A Life Less Ordinary*, originally published in Hindi as *Aalo Aandhari* and later translated into English by Urvashi Butalia, talks of the tyranny, abuse and repression she was subjected to all through her childhood and early adulthood. Halder was born in Murshidabad in West Bengal, to parents struggling with a dysfunctional marriage. Her father, was often absent from home, and even when at home, misbehaved with her mother. Her mother left home when Halder was seven years old. The frightened young child was now left without any comfort or shelter. Poverty and violence were the only two constant factors in her life. Sheela Reddy observes: "It is clear from her random and curiously flat narrative that far from trying to make sense of her senseless childhood, Baby had spent most of her life trying to forget it. The events she recounts so relentlessly are almost horrific in their randomness. Her mother abandons them without an explanation, taking only her youngest child. An older sister is married off just as abruptly. Her father beats her up for confessing that there is nothing to eat at home. ...It is as if, given a pen and paper, and asked to write about her life, Baby is assiduously extracting, with a surgeon's precision, and professional lack of sentiment, all the hurts and traumas that made up her childhood."[3] Beaten up by her father, and then beaten up by her husband, to whom she was married when she was "twelve years and eleven months old"[4] she knew nothing abuse, pain and fear all her life. An interesting thing to observe is the fact that although Halder writes about her own experiences, she often lapses into the third person. Perhaps that is the only way in which she can bear to graphically evoke once again, the searing, suppressed memories of her painful life.

About her marriage, an institution glorified across all classes and castes of society, Halder has this to say: "Now when she thinks back, Baby wonders how she spent that day [of her wedding] of sorrow in such merriment. Little did Baby know that this was the beginning of her days of grief and pain."[5] The "marriage" with an under-teen does not deter the much older Shankar from claiming what he obviously deems as his marital rights. Halder is forced to endure what can only be termed as a form of sexual slavery. Three children are born in quick succession to the underage bride while bouts of violence continue to recur. Baby's account of her marital life reads like continuous reruns of episodes like the following one: "He [her husband] didn't say a word when he saw me, but roughly caught me by my hair and started kicking and beating me…People walking past on the road could see what was happening but no one stopped him. In fact, some of them even seemed to be enjoying the spectacle. I lay on the ground, quietly, while my child wept with fear."[6] Another episode of horrific violence is narrated in the same apparently unemotional voice: "Silently, he picked up a stone from the ground and hit me on the head with it. My forehead split apart, and blood gushed out….All I asked my husband was what I had done to be beaten like this. The words were barely out of my mouth when he picked up a sturdy piece of wood and began hitting me on my back. A short while later, I felt a piercing pain in my stomach. By the evening, it was unbearable and I lay whimpering and crying for my father and mother. The pain was so severe, that I could not sit or stand or do anything. I howled in agony all through the night while my husband slept on without a care in the world. Either he did not hear my cries or couldn't be bothered to do anything about them. I was now shouting saying I was going to die, but he was utterly indifferent. I begged him to call someone. I told him I had not felt like this even when I gave birth to my child, but he just said, 'Who can I call at this time of night?' turned over and went back to sleep.[7] Halder's quiet, impassive voice hides a minefield of turbulent emotions within.

In this context one may recall the theses of Colette Guillaumin, the French feminist author. Guillaumin observes that the primary form of women's oppression which also reveals their function as property is appropriation. She observes that it is not merely the case that women are exploited in the labour market, (where as everyone knows, they are paid less than men for the same work) and in the home, where their daily labour goes unpaid, but they are also oppressed by what she calls "direct physical appropriation". By this phrase she refers to the "reduction of women to the state of material objects".[8] This she compares to slavery and serfdom. In reference to the case of women, Guillaumin terms this appropriation "sexage". According to her sexage occurs in four main forms: (a) the appropriation of women's time, (b) the appropriation of the products of women's bodies' (c) women's sexual obligation, (d) women's obligation to care for whichever member of the family cannot care for themselves as well as for the healthy male family members. Guillaumin further observes that the marriage contract places no limit on the time women will have to work. No holidays are specified on which they will not have to work. In fact all other women living in a family, such as daughters, aunts, grandmothers have to adhere to the same rules. By and large, the number of children that a couple will have is decided by the husband; also the children from a marriage are also the legal property of the husband. Guillaumin observes that women's sexual obligation to men occur both in marriage and in prostitution. However, she points out that in the case of prostitutes, there is a limitation placed on the time for which for which the prostitute's body may be used, and also, the prostitute must be paid for her services. Wives emerge as losers on both counts. Also, she points out, it is women who look after babies, children, the elderly, and the sick. The overall effect of all four areas of appropriation is to deprive women of their sense of individuality as well as of their independence and autonomy. Baby Halder is a case in point. It is as if women form a "class", or a "caste" by themselves—the most oppressed and repressed of all classes.

It is only after several more painful years of intolerable suffering, in the course of which her elder sister is beaten and finally murdered by her husband, and she herself is often subjected to brutal beatings—in the course of one such beating her head is split open on being struck by a rock – that Halder finally decides to leave her husband's house. Taking her children with her she flees to Delhi. She worked as a maid to earn her living, and many unsympathetic employers later found employment in the household of Professor Prabodh Kumar, the grandson of Prem Chand. Professor Kumar realised her inherent literary potential and encouraged her to write her life story. The rest, to use a much abused cliché, is history. However, not many victims of social repression are able to articulate their repression in the manner of Halder. Most, as we are all well aware, are forced to suffer and endure in silence. Society does not care for the sufferings of the weak and the underprivileged—and both dalits and women fall into this category. And for those unfortunate enough to be dalits and women, the repression and the suffering is without limit.

References

1. Oliver, Kelly. Ed. *French Feminism Reader*. New York: Rowman and Littlefield, 2000, p.10.
2. Delphy, Christine and Diana Leonard. *Close to Home: A Materialist Analysis of Women's Oppression*. Amherst: University of Massachusetts Press.1984, p.60.
3. Halder, Baby. *A Lifeless Ordinary*. India: Penguin Books,2006,p. Ix.
4. Ibid., p.33.
5. Ibid., p.34.
6. Ibid., p.80.
7. Ibid., p.84.
8. Guillamin, Collette. 'The Practice of Power and belief in Nature'. *Sex in Question: French Materialist Feminism*. Ed. Diane Leonard and Lisa Adkins. London: Taylor and Francis,1996, pp.72-108.

16

Is the Subaltern Heard? Interrogating Spivak's Translation of Mahasweta Devi's *Draupadi*

—Anirban Guha Thakurta

In conversation with her interviewer Pankaj Singh, Mahasweta Devi mentions:

> I was attached to the so-called criminal tribes, but when I wrote 'Aranyer Adhikar' I got real acceptance among them as they felt that what I wrote was their voice....
>
> In India's history it was the first time that the tribals began to get recognition. They drummed up support for me in every village and began to visit me. It was in 1979. Since then I had an easy access to tribal society. When 'Shri Shri Ganesh Mahima' and other books of mine were translated into the Telugu language and my sympathy for the Naxalite movement became known I got wider recognition. I also had contact with those tribals who were active Naxalites.
>
> In this process gradually I understood those whom they call 'criminal tribes'.... I have great affection for them. They are wonderful people... really wonderful!
>
> Tribal life is my last destination. The more I moved towards it, the more I got disenchanted with the middle class. My inner self cried out - 'No, I don't want these things, no... no... no...!' Now I do not want anything from there....[1]

Mahasweta Devi's aesthetics cannot be understood as mere literary outputs that have raised aesthetic debates; they are to be stated as extensions of her political workshop, as products of a mind that does not oscillate between oppositional loyalties towards the state and the tribes which cannot find themselves accommodated within that idea of a state run by law and disciplines. Her fictional world is a world of disturbing realism, a world that problematises the very conception of the independent Nation, that we had been nurturing and nourishing since 15 August, 1947. She has been interpreted severally as a sympathizer of the so-called militant tribes that have put internal security of India under grave doubts, and have caused shivers within the conception of parliamentary democracy by violent acts of rebellion. Rightly or wrongly, her literature is that of a propagandist who does not advocate in favour of the discourse of healthy democracy in a politically free nation like India, since she puts the very idea of freedom under question. Her act of writing is not merely a medium of voicing her own concerns, but a way of giving voice to a community of people never heard of in the contemporary India and never heard of in history.

A term like 'Dalit' should not be viewed as having originated from discourses in sociology. It is a term that has immense possibilities. It is not a qualification, but a status. It is political, since the group it tries to refer to is born out of a political negation, a negation that marginalizes and often obliterates the presence of a group of people by way of various strategic strangulations. In a dictionary sense, dalit would necessarily refer to a lower caste of people, a caste which is not integrated into the mainstream of culture. However, the term must be viewed in economic and political senses as well. Firstly, the group that remains unrecognized by the dominant mainstream, is economically suffering from malnutrition; secondly, such a group is given access to no mainstream medium of self-articulation in political fronts. They remain passively an object, devoid of any essential humanity, and when they choose to be directed by their spontaneous desire to voice themselves in spontaneous terms, their spontaneity becomes a violent self-assertion, which goes against the 'civilized' paradigms of the state. This violent process is for them a way of self-discovery, and since their practice remains detrimental towards the conception of a developing nation, it is bound to be branded as 'unparliamentarily' manufactured to bring in the downfall of the nation. Now, in any way, their voice is never heard in spite of their violent act of rebellion against the state.

Mahasweta Devi widens the scope of the term 'dalit', if we only choose to reconsider the term and her attitude towards the tribes that she works with. If we are to find her as a dalit writer, then primarily we have to reconsider conceptions of a dalit subjectivity. She is not born as a dalit, and neither is she a woman without a voice. The conception of a Dalit subjectivity is not to be internalized by the mere accident of birth, it must be bounded in by experiences of repression. Then, is she 'repressed'? Probably not, but in spite of being part of the civil middle class of Bengal and a studier of the English literature (details which would normally fix her to be an elite), she seems a person, dissatisfied by the political independence of the nation that she inhabits and her main concern therefore is to give voice to the tribes who are often viewed as 'criminals' according to the laws of the land. Her subjectivity is therefore extended to the so-called 'criminal' tribes of the Austro-Asiatic Munda origin who remain voiceless, repressed, marginalized and merely interpreted by the mainstream rather than given the opportunity to raise their own voice and interpret themselves alongside the mainstream. In this sense, her writing is about the voiceless, and if we liberate ourselves from viewing the term 'Dalit' to be referring to a condition and status in the world of castes to widen its scope by accommodating more politically and economically controversial issues regarding the repressed, she would appear to be a dalit writer.

Mahasweta Devi's short story *Draupadi* is a political assessment of the condition of the tribes in India, especially in Bengal. The story, written in Bengali, bearing a linguistic realism that is often a challenge to speakers of the mainstream Bengali language, is of immense complexity, since it probably refuses to see the tribal subject as a mere monolithic and linear substance ruled by laws of singularity. Devi problematises conceptions regarding the position of the tribal subject, bringing in issues of gender, a post-modern device of subverting the grand and epical narratives, and a new-historicist perspective on the histories of the tribe under the scanner. She does not decide to write in English, probably because of the impossibility of impregnating and defamiliarising the language to such an extent that would suit her activism and express her conceptions regarding the tribal experience. Rather, in *Draupadi*, she could create in the regular Bengali, a zone of excessive irregularity that would undeniably voice the experience that she wants to voice. The linguistic structure of the urban middle class Bengalis is so well defamiliarised in the story that her enunciation and interpretation appear largely authentic. However, Gayatri Chakravorty Spivak chose to translate the story alongside others under the title 'Breast Stories', into English. It is of immense interest if we try to investigate what probably had motivated her translation, and how well did her translations champion the cause of the tribal female subject in *Draupadi*. Did she find enough literary material in Devi to propound her own case and idea regarding the subaltern? Did she globalize Devi's rather localized assertion? Is her English an obstacle to her goal? Does English choke rather than evoking the tribal sensation? All this would welcome a parallel study of the versions of Devi and Spivak, and problematise and reconsider ideas regarding authenticity, originality, virtuality and representation.

The three contentions that began the discussion on *Draupadi* by Devi, must be re-registered now in order to be relocated and reconsidered in order to investigate what pushed Spivak to translate the same in English. As stated earlier, Devi problematises the repressed uniformity of the tribal subject by bringing in the idea of gender. While discussing the Spivak's concept of the subaltern Gina Wisker mentions:

> 'The subaltern' is a term used by Antonio Gramsci to indicate groups in society subject to the control of ruling classes. While subaltern classes traditionally include peasants, workers and others denied access to controlling power, Gramsci, interested in politics and the state, focused on their historiography. Spivak specifically linked the notion of the subaltern to that of eastern women, silenced, marginalized and disenfranchised economically and socially.
>
> 'The subaltern' would involve some indication and acceptance of individual subjectivity, while also refusing the notion of the subject itself, since we are all constructs and results of time, place and influences rather than bourgeois subjects. These tensions make her work difficult to read but also dialogic and inspirational. [2]

Spivak's subaltern accommodates within its scope the ideas related to gender, and Devi's protagonist is not merely a tribal, but also a woman. Spivak probably sees it as a potent literary evidence to propound her own theoretical position. She uses three of Devi's tales and keeps them bracketed within the title "Breast Stories". She declares:

> The breast is what the stories have in common. What they don't share is shown by staging of the names of the three protagonists: Dopdi, Jashoda, Gangor; in 'Draupadi', 'Breast Giver', 'Behind the Bodice.'[3]

There is always the idea of a double-marginalization and this makes the tribal subjectivity more dialogic than merely uniformed. The dialogism is extended even further if we try to see it from the perspective of Devi's subversion of the *Mahabharata*. This would bring under consideration our second contention. She utilizes the heroine of the Aryan epic, Draupadi, whose dishonor caused the great war of Kurukshetra, and addresses the protagonist of his story as Dopdi. This acts as a potent reminder of the epical scale and cult of female subjugation and its aftermath. This is a method that is not merely dialogic but also potentially that of the pastiche since Devi reinterprets the epic and its celebrated heroine through an act of literary subversion. This again pluralizes the subjectivity of the tribal woman, and the very insistence on the subversion of the epical or the grand narrative of the Aryan kind as a method of giving voice to the tribal non-Aryan woman, is very much a part of Devi's project of rehistoricising the tribal position.

If we come to our third contention, then it will not be inappropriate to announce what Devi herself considered to be her position. In an interview she is asked by Archana Masih:

> How did you get involved with working with the tribals, how did it begin? Was it difficult to gain acceptance from them in the beginning?[4]

and she declared:

> It happened very naturally. My book *Jungle ke Davedar — Aranyer Adhikaar,* written with Birsa Munda's rebellion as the background, won the Sahitya Akademi Award. Then the tribals, specially in West Bengal, and other states when it was translated to other languages, felt that for the first time...
>
> You see tribal rebellions are never mentioned in the history of the freedom struggle. This was the first time that the mainstream came to know about the tribal heroes, their rebellions. This gave them a sense of joy. Sense of pride in themselves.
>
> After that it became easy. They were coming to me, I was going to them.[5]

Devi's activism and the desire of telling their unheard story were enough inspirations for Spivak who saw in her *Draupadi* the potential of her own theory. Devi's protagonist neither bears a singular position of the female, nor is she a mere tribal woman. She is a woman as much a part of the contemporary, as she is of the past. Her pastness is subverted through the mythical method that Devi uses, while the same device makes her present identity equally unstable. And since Devi's method of historiography brings in issues of the 'dialogic' in the consideration of the subjectivity, Spivak's subaltern can be best voiced even if the same is not given a voice of her own.

However, the use of English in voicing the subaltern or giving voice to the same brings in problems of its own and those resulting out of the application of an alien linguistic apparatus to the aboriginal. Though in theory we can never say that language can voice subjectivity, though we profess that language imposes a certain structure of its own rather than expressing the self, and though in theory language never describes but represents the condition of the subject, we can dare to argue that Devi did not have to invent a new structure of the Bengali language in order to represent Dopdi and the tribe. She did not have to aboriginize the Bengali language, as within its very structure she could find the aboriginal dialect suitable enough for her narrative. She uses various linguistic sub-structures existing within Bengali. She uses the dialect of the tribe, which is often incomprehensible for the mainstream Bengali reader; she uses the officious English as the voice of the army, carnivalises the same by having officials who trivialize their English by way of a mimicry; she uses a song by Dopdi, which remains un-deciphered throughout the text.

In Devi's story, there is a language for the narrator, a different one for the officials, one for the Senanayak, another for Dopdi, a rhetorical one for the song, and various others for the entire work. All these structures of the Bengali language are used and continually metamorphosed according to the epical sub-text and Devi's proclaimed activism in favour of an aboriginal historiography. And all these are further re-examined in the final message (if any) of the story, and the spectacle of the repressed and ravaged tribal heroine, rising naked. The language in Devi's tale is problematically multidimensional, since it is given even a biological extension at the end of a story which already has heterogeneous entities of the linguistic within it.

For Spivak, this problematised heterogeneity in language appears to be of immense challenge, in spite of the fact that it is the same heterogeneity in Devi's text that probably had attracted her critically aesthetic attention. To exemplify, we can compare the very beginnings of the two versions. The story begins with a description of Dopdi, given by the higher authorities to the officials. After the short description, ending in an equally political ellipsis, the man in the uniform in Devi's version, ejaculates:

> *snaotalir naam Dopdi, kyan?*[6]

an interrogation (or exclamation, amounting to a sense of surprise), which is translated by Spivak as:

> What's this, a tribal called Dopdi? The list of names I brought has nothing like it! How can anyone have an unlisted name?[7]

Firstly, even though in Devi's original has the second statement made by the man in uniform as an interrogation (with the sentence ending in an interrogation mark), Spivak takes the translator's liberty to replace the same by an exclamation. However, what appears to be of even greater complication occurs in the very structure of the entire argument. In Devi, the interrogation is more of an exclamation which does not occur out of the presence of the name 'Dopdi' as an entity outside the list given to them. The wonder expressed in the exclamation is extended as a commentary that is part of the epical sub-text in the consideration of the subject. The wonder is aroused by the fact of a tribal woman is being branded as the controversial Draupadi.

Devi begins by way of pluralizing the subjectivity of the protagonist. Moreover, this brings in the comparison between the marginalized and the disreputable Aboriginal female protagonist whose dishonor is not avoided by any divine intervention, and the Draupadi of the *Mahabharata*, whose dishonor caused the rise of patriarchal fratricide where glorious maleness is put into practice as part of male exhibitionism of boldness. As the story leads itself and gets unfolded, this branding and the sense of wonder announced at the beginning by the man in uniform would prove the presence of the un-uniformity prevalent in it. Devi must have intended the same. Spivak's translation does bring in the issue, but beside such an idea, there is in the same translated statement, a presence of wonder at the presence of an unlisted name, rather than purely being a representation of the ethnic issue involved in it. The wonder in Devi is aroused by the possibility of accommodating the Aboriginal into the Aryan scheme of things by the signifier 'Dopdi'. In Spivak, this sense does not appear to have been brought in clear terms. The problem of the translator does not merely resolve here in the mere branding of the non-Aryan in Aryan terms as the same is extended later as well.

Devi's story stages few gaps and they are hardly revealed and defined. Such words like 'Maho' appear in the texture of the story and since strategically enough, Devi herself does not herself reveal its meaning, and neither gets them deciphered by the officials, they remain unrecognized. This is a method for Devi, who perhaps understands that all that the civil society and the state can do is only to launch an attempt to investigate and interpret. They cannot decipher the heart and the mind of the tribal. Spivak too intends to keep such statements undeciphered. Thus even though the Senanayak announces that he has almost deciphered Dopdi's song even though he could never have done so, Spivak does not translate the song and keeps it as Devi left it.

Samaray hijulenako mar goekope

and,

Hendre rambra keche keche
Pundi rambra keche keche[8]

Devi's linguistic structures in the text are part of the flexibility of the dialects available in Bengali itself. I don't want to mean that English is always an urban language, and there are no dialects as sub-structures within the normative design of the language. We cannot say that English cannot be used to translate the story because it still bears the colonizer's imperial status, and operates as a medium of cultural control. Rather, in this text, the problem of the English language occurs due to the absence of linguistic sub-structures that would suit this translation. The presence of the linguistic sub-structures inside the Bengali language as dialects helps and empowers Devi, while Spivak can only translate the sense of the story, since she cannot use the various English dialects for this purpose. Her translation is an attempt at globalizing the local, and she does the same only in spreading the sense of Devi's story, and remains unable to have the linguistic fluidity that Devi enjoys. This is part of a larger problem of any translation and even a theoretician like Spivak is not immune from it.

However, it is going to be improper to state that Spivak's attempt is a failure. Spivak's idea of the subaltern is part of her post-structuralist contention regarding subjectivity. The sheer unstable nature of the subjectivity, as previously mentioned, attracts her, and the positive that lies in the translation is partly due to the final episode in the story. The episode does not merely project Devi to be of great caliber in housing inside the text the idea of the subaltern, that of gender, and the subversion of the epical grand narrative, but unites the same heterogeneous structures with Spivak's theoretical concerns.

In spite of the Aryan branding, the non-Aryan Dopdi is apprehended, her honour is not merely tainted but murdered as she is gang-raped by the officials. The lust of the Nation, personalized by the uniformed, is mercilessly portrayed. Both the original in Devi and the translation in Spivak detail the visual *opsis*, and this probably acts as Devi's mode of unmasking the predatory masculinity of the state. All these acts probably occur as ways of not mere subjugation, but as methods of silencing. The Aboriginal woman is severally marginalized, and in Spivak, she can never 'Speak'. Such should have been Dopdi's finality. In *Mahabharata*, Draupadi's dishonor is not manufactured merely by the Kauravas. She is given a 'swayambar sabha' where she can only decide according to the rules set by the males. This is a limited liberty. To be more specific, it is only an illusion of liberty. When she is 'won' by Arjuna, she is divided between the Pandavas. She is dishonoured by her husbands when she is thrown as a prize in the game of dice. These are all indignities, and only her visual dishonoring in the hands of Kauravas is avoided by Krishna. In Mahabharata, Draupadi is the spectacle of dishonor, even when her 'dishonour' is avoided. She is dominated according to the whims of the patriarchy and gets toyed, and remains utterly marginalized and rooted in the identity of the subaltern. Such should have been the plight of the 'criminal' apprehended Aboriginal Dopdi, if she had resembled her Aryan counterpart. Draupadi in *Mahabharata* is a metonymic representation of Spivak's subaltern, since she is marginalized by the outside as well as by her in-laws. Dopdi, the tribal woman, in regular sense should have been exactly the same. She should have been ruled by the state and the Aryan worldview from the outside, and should have been toyed by patriarchal land lords within her tribes. However, she contests such discourses, as Devi absolutely subverts her expected position.

Discussing gender and the armed conflicts, Anuradha M. Chenoy and Kamal A Mitra Chenoy, writes:

> The commonest image of women in all conflict zones is as victims. Sexual violence occurs even though it is recognized as a crime. Tribals complained of rape by Salwa Judum activists and paramilitary against alleged Maoist women.[9]

and

> Men are taught to display strength and assertiveness to control the public and private spheres. Femininity is meant to complement, support and supplement this version of masculinity, to safeguard and give public face to it, even though they may be victims of violence and oppression. These roles are accentuated during times of armed conflict.[10]

When we come to Devi's story, the practical and ideological space that contains the events is the same. In reality, the Aboriginal woman is silenced, and her silence is a product of institutional control that advocates in favour of a patriarchal conception of the world. The phallocentric doctrines of the epic and the reality are contested by this 'Dalit' female. She refuses to be silenced by subjugation. She is raped, humiliated, and pushed into the tent of the Senanayak. Did she find voice? Has the subaltern spoken? Devi's text finds its best translation into English in the final descriptions by Spivak. With her un-deciphered song, Dopdi would have till now appeared to be uncanny to the civilized Senanayak. Now, she is an enigma.

Draupadi of the *Mahabharata* wanted clothing, and the apparently marginalized Dopdi refuses to clothe her nakedness. She contests the male gaze, subverts the theory that registers the woman as a passive receptacle. Her activism transcends voice in the linguistic sense of the term. Devi provides her with a voice, more biological and visual, than merely linguistic. She refuses to acknowledge the masculinity of the official who raped her. 'There isn't a man here', she has an 'indomitable laughter' and the 'Senanayak simply cannot understand'.[11] She has spoken, not in a language really used by men, but her body, its nakedness and the inscriptions of perceived masculinity have spoken such a language that has been heard and not understood by the Senanayak. Yet it has made him afraid. Probably, it is this unheard and uncomprehended language that becomes her voice. Probably, Devi did not intend the ending to be tragic.

Spivak's subaltern probably finds a voice, and since it is not understood, or does not fall under the categories of speech, it will remain unheard. However, the finality is not a tragedy that raises pity and fear at the sight of this violent site of the woman's dishonor. Devi's heroine has found the most effective self-assertion that contests the Aryan epic, patriarchy and the state. Probably, here lies justification of Spivak's translation of Devi's story, since the globalizing (even though there are limitations in the English translation) of the very possibility of a replacement of a linguistic self-assertion by a more politically revolutionized conception of the female body has made an 'unarmed *target*' a potential threat to all superstructures.

Notes and References

1. "Mahasweta Devi: An Intimate Interview." September 1999 <http://www.revolutionarydemocracy.org/rdv5n2/devi.htm>, 2nd September, 2011.
2. See Gina Wisker, *Key Concepts in Postcolonial Literature*. New York: Palgrave Macmillan, 2007 p.206.
3. Gayatri Chakravorty Spivak, Introduction. *Breast Stories*, Calcutta: Seagull, 1997, viii.
4. *The Rediff Interview*/Mahasweta Devi, "Independence has failed", December 24, 1997 <http://www.rediff.com/news/dec/24devi.htm>, 2nd September, 2011.
5. Ibid.
6. Mahasweta Devi, Draupadi(1976), *Mahasweta Debir Chhotogolpo Shankalan*(1993), New Delhi: National Book Trust, India, 2002, p. 29.
7. Gayatri Chakravorty Spivak, *Breast Stories*, Calcutta: Seagull, 1997, p. 19.
8. Ibid.
9. Anuradha M. Chenoy and Kamal A. Mitra Chenoy, 'Gender and Armed Conflicts', *Maoist and Other Armed Conflicts*, New Delhi : Penguin Books India, 2010, p. 193.
10. Ibid., p.181.
11. Gayatri Chakravorty Spivak, *Breast Stories*, Calcutta: Seagull, 1997,p 36.

Works Cited

Chakraborty, Prashanta.'Dalits and Indian Literature'. *Language in India*. Volume 11: 4 April 2011. www.Languageinindia.com. Web. 5 November, 2011.

Das, Sanjukta. 'Mulk Raj Anand: *Coolie*' in *Derozio to Dattani: Essays in Criticism* . Sanjukta Das. Delhi: Worldview, 2009. Print.

Dirks, Nicholas B. *Castes of Mind: Colonialism and the Making of Modern India*. Delhi: Permanent Black, 2002. Print.

George, C. J. *Mulk Raj Anand: His Art and Concerns.* New Delhi: Atlantic Publishers and Distributors, 1994. Print.

Ilaiah. Kancha. *Post-Hindu India: A Discourse on Dalit-Bahujan Socio-Spiritual And Scientific Revolution.* New Delhi: Sage, 2009. Print.

Jha, Rama. *Gandhian Thought and Indo-Anglian Novelists.* Delhi: Chanakya Publication, 1983. Print.

Khan, Farhana. *Mulk Raj Anand: A Critical Spectrum.* Jaipur: Shree Niwas publications, 2005. Print.

Rajan, P. K. *Mulk Raj Anand: A Revaluation.* New Delhi: Arnold Associates, 1994. Print. Print.

Rao, K. R. *The Fiction of Raja Rao.* Aurangabad: Perimal Prakashan, 1980. Print.

Verma, K. D. T*he Indian Imagination: Critical Essays on Indian Writing in English.* London: Macmillan, 2000. Print.

17

Unarmed Mutiny through Literary Writings: The Role of Dalit Literature in Promoting the Dalits' Struggle for Dignity, Justice and Equality

Soumitra Chakraborty and Gouri Das

In the traditional Hindu society which is categorized into four main hierarchical caste groups: Brahmins, kshatriyas, vaishyas and shudras, the dalits or 'ati shudras' are forced to occupy the lowest position beyond the periphery of this fourfold caste hierarchy. Dalits are treated as 'untouchables' as per this abhorrent social order and behaved like animals by the people of the upper classes.

Although the Constitution of India outlawed caste system in 1950, still the dalits are subjected to extreme social and economic exploitation in the country; physical and mental torture.

So the dalits raise their voice against this casteist tradition and demand the equal right with those of the people of upper classes. In fact, the dalit movement is an anti-caste movement fighting for building a modern secular and democratic Indian identity.The literature, which supports the dalits' legitimate demand and promotes their traditional struggle for dignity, justice, equality etc., criticising this shameful social-segregation is known as the 'Dalit Literature'. It was born from the womb of caste-system, the primary motive of which is the liberation of the dalits. Chokhamela, Mahatma Phule, Prof. S. M. Mate, Dr. B.R. Ambedkar etc. were deeply concerned with the plight of the untouchables and fought against all unjust divisions in the society through their writings. However, in this paper our avowed aim is to analyse the role of dalit literature in combating social discrimination and harsh humiliation done to the oppressed dalits and promoting the dalits' traditional struggle for dignity, justice and equality in the society, with exclusive reference to the significant literary creations of some of the important dalit writers.

The word, 'Dalit', meaning 'oppressed' or 'broken', had firstly been derived in 1930 by the British to indicate the 'depressed classes'. But the term is now revived and not used to indicate a particular class, rather the scheduled castes, tribes, poor peasants, women and all those who are being exploited socially, economically, politically and in the name of religion. The dalits, who constitute more than 16 per cent (i.e. around 160 million) of Indian population, belong to poor communities and are used to be known as untouchables to the elite feudal brahaminic society under the Indian caste system, the history of which has been spreaded over 3000 years.

Historically, the caste-system is the socio-cultural menace of Hinduism. The traditional Hindu society is categorized into four main hierarchical caste groups: brahmins, kshatriyas, vaishyas and shudras. Beyond the periphery of this fourfold caste hierarchy, there is a category of ati-shudras or dalits, which is forced to occupy the lowest position in this abhorrent social order. Although the Constitution of India outlawed caste system in 1950, still the dalits are subjected to extreme social and economic exploitation in the country; physical and mental torture.

In his article, *Dalit Literature: The Voiceof the Downtrodden*, Mr. Razi Abedi has portrayed the position of the dalits in Indian society. According to him, "The Dalits are treated worse than animals. Their presence is usually banned from upper-class localities. Even then they are bound to hang clay pots from their necks so that they may not pollute the streets of the privileged by their spittle. They carry brooms tied to their bodies so that while passing through such 'upper lanes' they can wipe away their footprints". Their attempts of exercising their constitutional rights are often obstructed by the people of the upper classes. Resistance is often resulted in inhuman torture, rapes, massacres and other atrocities. The official statistics are enough to assess the plight of the dalits in India. One million dalits are manual scavengers who clean public latrines, roads, drains and dispose dead animals, 80 per cent of dalits live in rural areas and 86 per cent of dalits are completely landless. Whereas 60 per cent of dalits are dependent on casual labour, only 37 per cent of dalits are literate. Three dalit women are raped every day. At least one crime is committed against a dalit every day. Poems, short stories, novels and autobiographies written by dalit writers provide useful insights on the question of dalit identity.

The dalits raise their voice against this casteist tradition and demand the equal right with those of the people of upper class. In fact, the dalit movement is an anti-caste movement fighting for building a modern secular and democratic Indian identity.It is a movement of demanding equal right with the people of the upper class and fighting for building a modern and secular Indian identity. A movement of that nature was the 'Dalit Panther Movement', the motto of whichwas to protect dalit people in all over India. This movement gave a revolutionary colour to prevent discrimination against dalits still exists in our society. This movement borrowed its moral support from the writings of Dr. B.R. Ambedkar who accentuated that "the root cause of untouchability lies in a pronounced cultural or racial difference of contempt and hatred coupled with a close dependence of the inferior society on the superior one".

The literature, which supports the dalits' legitimate demand and promotes their traditional struggle for dignity, justice, equality etc. criticising this shameful social-segregation is known as the 'Dalit Literature'. It was born from the womb of caste-system, the primary motive of which is the liberation of the dalits. It focuses on two main functions: 'demolition' and 'reconstruction'. dalit literature is deeply concerned with the plight of the untouchables and fight against all unjust divisions in the society through writings. Infact, it is a crusade to combat against cruelties, humiliation, and discrimination done to the dalits. The dalit literature questions the mainstream literary theories and upper caste ideologies and explores the neglected aspects of life. Depicting the plight ofthe dalits in the caste-based Hindu societyand their struggles for dignity, justice and equality, this literature is by nature oppositional. Although the dalit Literature achieved a firm foundation in the mid-twentieth century, but its framework was established in the early nineteenth century.This literatureof the oppressed class forms an important and distinct part of Indian literatureand gradually comes as a powerful literary genre in the Indian literary scene.

Though dalit narratives have been a part of the Indian social narratives since eleventh century onwards, dalit literature gained prominence and importance as a collective voice after 1960, starting with Marathi, and soon appeared in Hindi, Kannada, Telugu and Tamil languages, through self-narratives, like poems, short stories and most importantly autobiographies known for their realism, and for its contribution to dalit politics. In its depiction of issues of racial segregationand injustice,as seen in Slave narratives, Dalit literatureis often compared with the Afro-American literature.

Poems, short stories, novels and autobiographies written by Dalit writers provide useful insights on the question of dalit identity. The writers of dalit literature denounced the 'conviction', popularized by the non-falit writers, regarding caste hierarchy and depicted the whole dalit issues like the social reality of appalling poverty and oppression of the caste Hindus. Uttam Bhoite and Anuradha Bhoite have described the dalit literature as aplatform to organize a protest movement against the traditional Hindu social theories of life and liberation. A sense of collective identity and solidarity are seminal for a protest movement. Dalit literature was evolving in a dialogic structure towards this direction as a communication system for various segments of the movement, the dalit writers and dalit intellectuals. Dalit writings addressthe oppressed, the untouchables, the victims, and the oppressors. It is notonly our intention that what we write should beread only by the untouchables, but our writers aspirethat it should be read by the touchable, too. (Raosaheb Kasbe in his essay, *Some Issues on Dalit Literature*).

Chokhamela, Mahatma Phule, Prof. S.M. Mate; Dr. B.R. Ambedkar etc. were deeply concerned with the plight of the untouchables and fought against all unjust divisions in the society through their writings. The great Renaissance leader, the architect of the Constitution of India and an ardent critic of the Indian caste-system, Dr. B.R. Ambedkar demolished the myth of divine origin of caste hierarchy and advocated for the total emancipation of the dalits. He inspired and initiated the creative minds of India to enforce the socio-cultural upsurge for the total emancipation of the dalits from the bondage of slavery and oppression. Not only Dr. Ambedkar, the other dalit writers too, have protested against this inhuman convention, expressing sorrow, anger and shame in sharpe language through their writings and pleaded for the abolition of this age-old oppression.

The dalit literary movement has been given shape by the dalit feminist writers along with other elite writers. Dalit literature shows us triple exploitation of dalit women based on caste, class and gender in our society. This paper attempts to unfold the issue of dalit women'sconsciousness by amplifying the way of literature provided by dalit women and men writers. Dalit autobiographical writings structure the subjectivity of dalit women who have over the decades evolved their own understanding and their situation is constitute as a part of dalit studies. These writings show the feministic argument about masculine influence and the egalitarian principle and many of the expressions of marginalization of the dalits are displayed through women. These autobiographies are consideredas dynamic expressions of the social worlds of dalits and their co-relation with the dominant class in the society. The main focus is on writings of women and men dalit writers to see the patriarchal hegemony in the context of autobiographical writings because it gives us life stories of dalit women.

Daya Pawar's *Baluta*, published in 1978, has generated ripples in the literature circles and has earned many awards at all levels. *Baluta* is a story by Dagdu Pawar as narrated to the literate Daya Pawar, both are personas of the author. The novel recounts the experiences of an untouchable struggling for a peaceful existence, mentally tormented but incapable of retaliation in word and deed. It also reveals the sexually exploitation of dalit and non-dalit women in urban and rural life. In this story we see, his father, Dada, an alcoholic, does not come home for around 15 to 20 days after getting his salary from his brahmin landlord. So his mother has to go out to collect waste paper for the survival of their family. Dada, here, sexually exploited women as they came to him for their scythe which was hiding by Dada. Simultaneously, we observe that there also low caste young people like 'Mahars' were sexually utilized by rich and generous Maratha women only to satisfy their erotic lust. Whereas that very 'Mahars' people were treated as untouchables to those women when it came to provide them food and water. The same logic was applied for the dalit women by the Hindu male.

Here, we have also seen Daya Pawar's traditional patriarchal character – how he left his first wife, Sai at her village because he had a wrong feeling that his wife had a relationship with a Muslim boy. After over the period Sai got remarried with an elderly person and continued to work as a labourer throughout her whole life. On the other hand, in a prostitutes' area, Daya was introduced with his 'Maushi'(mother's sister), Jamuna who was stunningly good looking and it was the only reason that she was used to be beaten up, ill-treated and finally sold to that area by her husband who was highly suspicious by nature. These two incidents indicate how dalit women are controlled and suppressed by dalit males. Apart from this, Daya Pawar throws the light on caste discrimination with other marginal communities such as Muslim.

In this way, she conveys and exposes an extremely diverse textualisation of dalit experiences in his novel.

Bama, one of the creators of dalit feminist literature has also become a noteworthy regional voice among the subcontinent women. Bama has personally experienced of two sides – one, she belongs to the marginalized group and two, she is a woman. Her text Sangati, an autobiography of a community, serves as not only a dalit fiction but also a dalit feminist speech that is inclusive of a clarion call for action and transformation. The story deals with multicolored personal experiences of dalit women stringed together and with a community's identity, not about the single self. It has no plot in the normal sense, nor any main characters. Experiences are first counterpointed by the generalizing comments of the grandmother and mother figures, and then by the reflections of the author narrator.

At the very beginning of Sangati, we learn that the oppressed class too has its own gender discrimination where dalit men who are on the margins of the structured society in turn marginalize their women on the basis of fixed gender roles. The text is all about the hardship of women who have worked hard all their lives, from the moment they are able to help with the care of younger siblings, or with responsibilities about the house, or outside. The story shows that how the economic instability of dalit women leads them towards the terrible violence by their fathers and husbands, and sometimes even brothers. Besides these tales of hardship, they do their day to day work together, such as preparing and eating food, celebrating and singing, bathing and swimming. These women including the author Bama regain their marginalized identity and establish their sense of individual self. Bama wants to portray the positive image too by creating certain freedoms enjoyed by dalit women: no dowry is required of them, for example, and widows re-marry as a matter of course. She speaks for women on the whole when she says that women too as individuals have their own desires, and wishes, that if women do not speak for themselves, come forward to change their condition then who else is going to do it for them. Bama focuses the 'difference' of dalit women from privileged upper caste women and also celebrates their 'identity' in their strength, labour and resilience. As a feminist writer Bama protests against all forms of oppression and relying on the strength and resilience of dalit women, makes an appeal for change and self-empowerment through education and collective action.

Mukta Salve, another pioneer of dalit feminist writer of the nineteenth century, who belongs to the Mangcommunity, provides us legitimate evidence in her brief essay, Mang *Maharachya Dukhavisatha* (about the grief of the Mang and Mahar) that explores the plight of dalit women. In this essay she elucidates how dalit women were compelled to give birth their children in the roofless houses and how Brahmans seized the lands of poor 'Mang' and 'Mahar' people who were treated like dogs and cattle, where they built their own houses. The writer lights up the brutality of that society narrating if a 'Mang' or 'Mahar' crossed the 'talimkhana' (gymnasium), his body would be cut into two as a punishment and simultaneously those bodies were used to play. No one had the courage to voice against them and to stop those killings. Brahmins manipulated religion and other caste people to control the knowledge and power in the society.

In Baburao Bagul's *Mother*, we have an experience of fierce battle for life in an urban slum. The story revolves around a young, lower-caste dalit widow and her son Pandu, who face harsh realities of life. Their life was brought in a turmoil because their mutual understanding was breached and also because the upper caste people exploit the innocence of the child by poisoning his mind against his own mother. Their struggle to survive was so intense that there was no time for mutual understanding between the mother and the child. The story shows the pain and loss of the mother. BaburaoBagul portrays the harsh realities of life in a minority's life. He shows the struggle of women in his works. His stories show the external as well as internal conflict faced by the dalit women. He shows the fall as well as the rise of women characters and depicts them in their own self.

Infact, the vision of dalit writers is to develop a community not individuality, revolt not passivity, progress not backwardness, to make dalit masses aware for assertion, protest and mobilization.

Works Cited

Abedi, Razi. *Dalit Literature: The Voice of the Downtrodden.* 12 September 2011 <www.gowanusbooks.com/dalit.htm>

Ahmad, Imtiaz & S.Bhusan Upadhyay, eds. *Dalit Assertion in Society, Literature & History.* New Delhi: Orient Blackswan, 2010.

Aruna, Marie. *Bama's Sangati.* 6 January 2012 <http://www.museindia.com/featurecontent.asp?issid=36&id=2534>.

Chatterjee, Debi. *Dalit Rights/human Rights.* Jaipur: Rawat Publications, 2011.

Dalit – Wikipedia, free encyclopaedia, <http://en.wikipedia.org/wiki/dalit>

Dalit – Wikipedia, free encyclopaedia, <http://en.wikipedia.org/wiki/dalit_literature>

Mishra, Dr. Jugal Kishore. *A Critical study of Dalit Literature in India.* 12 September 2011 <http://www.sasnet.lu.se/EASASpapers/4Jugal Kishore.pdf>

Pawar, Daya. *Balut.* Mumbai: Granthali Prakashan.

Poitevin, Guy. *Dalit Autobiographical Narratives Figures of Subaltern Consciousness, Assertion and Identity.* 11 September 2011 <http://aune.lpl.univaix.fr/~belbernard/misc/ccrss/dalitautobio.htm>

Sankarapillai, K. G. *Voice of the Oppressed- Dalit literature.* 12 September 2011 <http://www.razarumi.com/2008/05/09/voices-of-the-oppressed-dalit-literature>

Sanoop, C.N. A *Dalit Feminist Reading of "Sangâti".* 6 January 2012 <http://www.enmalayalam.com/home/en/topic/academic-papers/2339>

Sargar, S.D. *Dalit Autobiography and Education: An Analytical Study.* 19 October 2011 <http://www.the-criterion.com/V2/n4/Sargar.pdf>

Tharu, Susie & K. Lalita, eds. *Women Writing in India.* Delhi: Oxford University Press, 1995.

Tiwari, Dr. Chetna. *The Portrayal of Dalit Life: A Study of Baburao Bagul's Mother.* 11 September 2011 <http://sites.google.com/site/journalofenglishliterature/archives/vol-1-no-4-april-june-2010/4-the-portrayal-of-dalit-life>

18

Representation and Resistance: A Reading of Omprakash Valmiki's *Joothan*

Bisweswar Chakraborty

Subjugated and segregated for centuries, the dalits in India have occasionally expressed their voice of protest before Independence, and with the inspiration provided by figures like Ambedkar,[1] Jyoti Rao Phule[2] etc. their voice of protest have found an ideological base and political maturity. Accordingly, dalit conscience has developed from this objective reality of a Pan-Indian situation which is deeply rooted in the age-old tyranny of untouchability, inhuman *saVarna* oppression and unabated suffering owing to socio-economic exploitation and deprivation of these people belonging to the 'lesser caste'. In the background of this class-caste division and socioeconomic as well as politico-cultural oppression and exploitation by the privileged sections, dalit consciousness gradually moulded into a shape which has finally given birth to dalit literary endeavour.

Among all the literary genres, it is the autobiography that helps the dalit writers to represent their subjective reality: their experiences of pain and suffering, their history, their struggle and movements etc. Dalit autobiographical writings are primarily narratives of injustice and exploitation, and seek social awakening by incorporating those human values which wage a continuous struggle "born out of anger and rebellion against feudalistic mindsets".[3] Omprakash Valmiki's autobiography *Joothan* showcases how painful his experiences have been throughout his life. In the Preface, he writes:

> Dalit life is excruciatingly painful, charred by experiences. Experiences that did not find room in literary creations. We have grown up in a social order that is extremely cruel and inhuman. And compassionless towards Dalits.

Viewed from this angle a dalit autobiography is a medium of assertion and resistance from a dalit's point of view against an indifferent social order. This paper is a humble attempt to show how Valmiki's *Joothan* is replete with that consciousness of struggle and how does that consciousness resist the hegemony of the upper-caste Hindu people in India today.

Recent critical writings on women and black autobiographies act as a yardstick on the basis of which we could analyze any dalit autobiographical narrative. Unlike the autobiographies of celebrated persons, dalit autobiographies are usually written by anonymous individuals who emphasize the ordinariness and hardships of their lives rather than their uniqueness in order to establish themselves as spokesmen of their community. For dalit autobiography, as for autobiographies of other marginalised communities, the entire life-narrative is based the idea of communal identity. It will be worth-quoting in this respect what Stephen Butterfield writes of African-American autobiographies, "the self belongs to the people, and the people find a voice in the self."[4] He asserts that autobiography is one of the ways through which the black Americans have vindicated their right "to live and grow"[5] and these autobiographies think of the subject as "a member of an oppressed social group, with ties and responsibilities to the other members."[6]

Furthermore, theoretical studies by Barbara Harlow show how narrative and autobiography have been used as a means of political assertion by marginalised groups. Many of their findings reveal important resemblances to the way dalits use their own autobiographies as a political act. They point out how the autobiographical narrative is perceived as the actual site of the power struggle, where the voice of the marginalised individual contests the institutionalized narrative of the dominant sections. Harlow writes:

> If the resistance poetry challenged the dominant and hegemonic discourse of an occupying or colonizing power by attacking the symbolic foundations of that power and erecting symbolic structures of its own—resistance narratives go further still in analyzing the relations of power which sustain the systems of domination and exploitation.[7]

Indeed, the strength of dalit autobiographies has been their act of exposing the continuation of caste-based discrimination and the power structures and belief systems that support this practice of untouchability. For dalit writers, autobiography is a means to sustain their 'history';[8] it constitutes their primary political act of assertion.

In his Preface, Valmiki declares that *Joothan* captures 'those experiences that did not find a place in literary representations.' It is a memoir of his growing up 'untouchable' starting in the 1950s outside a typical village in Uttar Pradesh. Told as a series of vignettes it tells the author's own story bearing real witness to his painful journey that he undertook to get rid of the preordained life of continuous physical and mental persecution and his development towards a faithful chronicler of the exploitation and oppression he endured, not only as a person but also as a member of a stigmatized and oppressed community. He begins his chronicle from his childhood. He was born into the 'Chuhra' caste (aka 'Bhangi'), whose ordained job was to sweep the roads, clean the cattle barns, get shit of the floor, dispose of dead animals, work the fields during harvests and perform other physical labour for upper caste people, including the Tyagi brahmins. The Tyagis did not address them by name, only called out, "Oe Chuhre" or "Abey Chuhre." (2) It was all right to touch cows and stray dogs but if a higher-caste person happened to touch a Chuhra, he/she got instantly "contaminated or polluted." With an unmistakable directness, Valmiki says, "The Chuhras were not seen as human." (2) During his boyhood, his entire family worked hard, yet they found it extremely difficult to manage to put two decent meals a day, not the least because they often did not get paid for their labour and instead got sworn at and abused.

Valmiki narrates one such incident where the Chuhras had refused to work without wages when a high official was visiting the village. The surveyors wanted some people for cleanup work, for which they would not be paid. When they refused this unpaid work, they were forcefully arrested, dragged inhumanly to the panchayet office where they were made to squat in a rooster position and beaten mercilessly. "The women and the children of the basti were standing in the lane and crying loudly.... They could not think of what else they could do but cry" (38). The writer reflects, "Why is it a crime to ask to be paid for one's labour? Those who keep singing the glories of democracy use the government machinery to quell the blood flowing in our veins"(39).

In another similar incident, the boy Valmiki himself was forcibly taken to the field by Fauz Singh Tyagi (aka Fauza) while he was getting prepared to sit for his mathematics examination the following day as if he was a bonded labourer. *Joothan* is filled with such incidents,each one of which left a deep scar in the writer's mind. After witnessing the severe beating of his people in public for refusing unpaid labour, he reflects: "My mind was filled with deep revulsion. I was then an adolescent and a scrach appeared on my mind like a line scratched on glass. It remains there still"(39). And being forced to work by Fauza in the field when he would have liked to study for his examination, he writes: "My mind was set aflame by his swearing. A fire had engulfed my innards that day. The memories of these crimes of the Tyagis continue to smoulder deep inside me, emitting red hot heat"(57).

Probably the most painful aspect of this humiliation is the fact that his teachers were not only a party to it but also aggravated it. These fellows who were sold to the idea of caste hierarchy were blot to the noble profession of teaching. Valmiki was admitted to the school with great difficulty, he was made to sit apart from the Tyagi boys, he was made to squat on the floor while other students sat on the benches, he was not allowed to participate in extracurricular activities, and he was made to sweep and clean the school and adjoining field. During examinations he could not drink water from the glass when he was thirsty. Each day brought new torture and humiliation from his teachers. More than once, he was mercilessly caned. Despite being one of the few good students in the class, he was given such low marks in the chemistry practical test that he failed the Board examination that eventually spelled doom for his promising career. With a pen dipped in acid, Valmiki writes: "It was such ideal teachers that I had to deal with. Moving from childhood to adolescence when my personality was being shaped, I had to live in this terror-filled environment....At times I feel like I grew up in a cruel and barbaric civilization"(48). Education was not for them. Most of Valmiki's family members worked at harvest season. For a hard day's labour, which included harvesting lentils, cutting sheaves of wheat in the mid day sun, and transporting them via bullock carts each person got only two pounds of wheat as wages. For the rest of the work in the cowshed, they got paid in grain and a leftover roti each day (made by mixing flour with the husk rice since it was for the chuhras), and at times scraps of leftovers from their employer's plates, *joothan.*

The Hindi word *joothan* literally refers to the scraps of food left on plates that are usually unfit for any further consumption. Such food would only be characterized joothan, if only, someone else apart from the original eater were to take it. Hence, the term is loaded with implications of ritual purity and pollution as *jootha* means *polluted.* But these were given to the dalits as if they are only takers of such leftover foods in lieu of their toil. Such was the destiny of the Chuhras. In her Introduction to her translation of the original Hindi text Arun Prava Mukherjee writes:

> The title encapsulates the pain, humiliation,and poverty of Valmiki's community, which not only had to rely on joothan but also relished it. Valmiki gives a detailed description of collecting, preserving and eating joothan. His memories of being assigned to guard the drying joothan from crows and chickens, and of his relishing the dried and reprocessed joothan burn him with renewed pain and humiliation in the present.[9]

The word also connotes historical signification. Both Ambedkar and Gandhi appealed to the untouchables not to accept such *joothan*. Ambedkar also points out how the high-caste villagers violently threatened them at their refusal to accept *joothan*. Valmiki has thus restated a common word from the dalit vocabulary to symbolise the demeaning existence imposed on the dalits. He passionately exhorted the dalits against this inhuman custom of the acceptance of *joothan* even at the cost of physical exploitation. The custom thus, simultaneously signifies both oppression against and resistance of the dalits. It is not surprising, therefore, that the incident where the narrator's mother overturn the basketful of *joothan* against the face of Sukhdev Singh Tyagi is the most powerful moment in the text. Her act of defiance inspires Valmiki since his childhood. Dedicating this text to her parents, both portrayed as heroic figures, Valmiki thus gives voice to the indignities suffered by them and other dalits.

The latter part of the book describes Valmiki's experiences as he moved from his native village to Dehra Dun, Roorke, Jabalpur, Bombay and Chandrapur. Caste followed him like an albatross around his neck. He was taken as a decent, educated, and respectable human being as long as people did not know about his caste. The moment they got to know about it they recoiled from him as though he were a lump of shit. The same happened with Savita who fell in love with him but dropped him shamelessly when Valmiki told her about his caste: "Suddenly, the distance between us has increased. The hatred of thousand years had entered our hearts. What a lie culture and civilization are"(98). Being repulsed thus, time and again, he observes: "*Caste* is a very important element of Indian society. As soon as a person is born, *caste* determines his or her destiny"(133). Even the dalits who aspire to be a part of the mainstream society after getting an education are nefariously discriminated. "Doubts are cast on their intelligence, their ability, their performance"(127). Caste cannot be improved by education; "it can only be improved by taking birth at the right caste"(58). In this way, the text, *Joothan* reveals to the reader the rigidity and narrow-mindedness of casteist India, which is as relevant today as it was in the earlier half of the last century.

The author is not evoking compassion towards the oppressed dalits in the mind of the reader, instead, he questions the justification of the existing social order: "why my caste is my only identity?"(134). This one query leads the reader into introspection. In India caste has always defined the socio-political scenario of the country. Whether it is the debate on the reservation policy for government jobs and education to aid the socially and economically backward classes or political gimmickry, everything has an undertone of caste, community, and religion. The sense of caste hierarchy is so ingrained in the Hindu consciousness that it cannot be erased overnight simply by formulating laws of affirmative education, but that a revolutionary change of mind and heart is required. The writer rightly asserts: "Being born is not in the control of a person. If it were in one's control, then why would I have been born in a Bhangi household? Those who call themselves the standard-bearers of this country's great cultural heritage, did they decide which homes they would be born into? Albeit they turn to scriptures to justify their position, the scriptures that establish feudal values instead of promoting equality and freedom" (133-34). Valmiki's struggle described so graphically is symptomatic of the extent challenges involved in the process reclaiming dignity for himself and his community. It goes to his credit that he does not simply give an univocal account of the caste prejudices harboured by members of the upper caste, but also deals with the internal divisions within the depressed classes that point to the fault lines within the movement and draws attention to the ways in which the depressed classes themselves have internalized these prejudices against the castes they consider a notch below themselves. It is also equally undeniable that the rough and raw feelings/experiences narrated in the text with liberal sprinkling of the author's animus against the high caste will raise the hackles of traditional critics who have their eyes glued on the so-called universals, and who, for that reason, will find it sensational and gross, lacking in objectivity.

However, we should take notice of the fact that dalit literature has emerged out of specific historical and social circumstances and that protest and testimony are inseparable elements of it. Valmiki writes:

> Dalit society has been imprisoned for a thousand years in the dark mist of ignorance, deprived of knowledge. Dalit literature is the portrayal of the wishes and aspirations of these oppressed and tormented dalits.[10]

In this sense, it may appear to be propagandist, but there lies its strength. Dalit autobiographical narratives present no constructed 'truth' but factual experiences of terrible grief and oppression: the authentic experience of anguish, pain, deprivation, and exclusion. Autobiography is a privileged site where a dalit writer can represent his/her reality and try to create a true dalit subjectivity besides contesting the caste-discrimination and untouchability. Dalit autobiographies are, no doubt, unstructured and artless outpourings of unmediated experience, but in this way the dalit writers keep their history alive and attempt to resist against this harsh reality in which they are beset. For the dalit community, like other marginalized groups, autobiography is not merely a kind of literary exercise rather a form of assertion and resistance in its own right.

Notes and References

1. Ambedkar, B.R. (1891-1956) fondly known as Babasaheb or father to his followers is considered the greatest leader of the untouchables. He received his PhD from Columbia University in 1917. He became the Minister of Law in independent India in 1948 and prepared the draft of the Costitution of India (1949). He was an indefatigable fighter against the prevailing caste-system wrote many treatises against it. Conflicts with the government made him resign his post in 1951.
2. Jyotirao Phule (1827-1890), a leading social reformer, was born into a 'mali' caste family considered to be inferior by the Marathi brahmins. He founded the Satyashodhak Samaj (1873) to fight for the rights of the lower castes and for women.
3. From Valmiki's *Dalit Sahitya ka Soundryashastra*, where he attempts to justify the role of Dalit autobiography to challenge the caste divisions of Indian society. Translation is taken from the Introduction to *Joothan* by Arun Prabha Mukherjee.
4. From Stephen Butterfield's *Black Autobiography in America* (1974) where he states how autobiography for the black Americans served as a medium to assert their selfhood, history and agency. pp. 2-3.
5. Ibid.
6. Ibid.
7. From Barbara Harlow's *Resistance Literature* (1987) where she attempts to assess the importance of the new 'resistance literature'. By bringing together the poets and writers of the organised national liberation struggle and resistance movements in America, Harlow asserts that literature, no less than armed struggle, is vital to the attempt to wrest back the cultural history expropriated by the forces of colonialism and imperialism. pp. 85.
8. From Valmiki's *Dalit Sahitya ka Soundryashastra*, where he attempts to justify the role of Dalit autobiography to challenge the caste divisions of Indian society. Through autobiographies the dalits can make their history stay alive and portray the agony of their exploitation. Translation is taken from the Introduction to *Joothan* by Arun Prabha Mukherjee.
9. From the fascinating Introduction by Arun Prabha Mukherjee to her English translation of Valmiki's *Joothan*. p. xxxi.
10. From Valmiki's *Dalit Sahitya ka Soundryashastra*, where he attempts to justify the role of Dalit autobiography to challenge the caste divisions of Indian society. Through autobiographies the dalits can make their history stay alive and portray the agony of their exploitation. Translation is taken from the Introduction to *Joothan* by Arun Prabha Mukherjee.

19

Quest for Green Liberation and Enlivening Integral Theology: A Study in Dalit Ecotheology

Sibasis Jana

Dalit theology, the variant form of liberation theology, concentrates mainly on the plight of the 'untouchables' or the 'outcastes' though their lies an ideological clash between the priority of class (as stressed in liberation theology) and 'caste' (as vivid in dalit theology) in the polarization of these two brands of current progressive theologies. Though dalits are marginalized, isolated, estranged, they have greater concept of the rhythm of nature than the elitist and so called post modern intellectuals. They live in harmony with nature and depend on the environment for their basic needs like food, water and shelter. Aristocrats and modernists ravish nature by means of urbanization but Dalit theology stands supreme in protecting and revitalizing the environmental ecology.

Dalit theology, the branch of Christiantheology comes into light among the Dalitcaste in India in the 1980s. It focuses on the liberation theology, which arose two decades earlier, including a self-identity as a people undergoing *Exodus*. Dalit theology finds light of hope in the "Nazareth Manifesto" of *Luke 4*, where Jesus speaks of preaching "good news to the poor ... freedom for the prisoners and recovery of sight for the blind" and of releasing "the oppressed."

Dalit theology was focused by Arvind P. Nirmal (1936–95), a dalit Christian in the church of North India. Nirmal criticised brahminic dominance of Christian theology in India, and believed that the application of liberation theology to India should reflect the struggle of dalits, who make up about 70 per cent of Christians in India. Nirmal also criticised the Marxist element within South American liberation theology. Nirmal drew on the concept of the Suffering Servant in *Isaiah* 53 to identify Jesus himself as a dalit – "a waiter, a dhobi, and bhangi."

Dalit theologians have seen passages in the gospels, such as Jesus's sharing a common drinking vessel with the *Samaritan woman* in John 4, as indicating his embracing of Dalitness. The *parable of the Good Samaritan* is also seen as significant, providing a "life-giving message to the marginalized Dalits and a challenging message to the non-Dalits."

M. E. Prabhakar expanded on the Dalitness of Jesus, stating that "the God of the Dalits ... does not create others to do servile work, but does servile work Himself." He also suggested that Jesus experienced human, and especially Dalit, brokenness in his *crucifixion*. Prabhakar has developed a Dalit *creed*, which reads in part:

> Our cries for liberation from harsh caste-bondage
> Were heard by God, who came to us in Jesus Christ
> To live with us and save all people from their sins.

Vedanayagam Devasahayam (b. 1949) of the *church of South India* followed Nirmal as head of Dalit theology at the *Gurukul Lutheran Theological College*, and further developed Nirmal's ideas, writing a number of books. Devasahayam later became bishop of the church of South India's Madras Diocese. Dalit theology opposes *indigenization* movements within Indian Christian liturgy, since these are seen as reinforcing traditional caste hierarchies. However, the incorporation of some pre-Sanskritic Indian religious traditions is supported.

We, the human beings are endowed with freedom of will, but few of us are ever aware of how to utilize our will force and the power showered through the environment. We are guided by our inherited or acquired tendencies and habits born of environment. If we follow the ecotheological views we can get peace and harmony in this prayer ploughed cosmic world.

Ecotheology, the form of constructive theology focuses on the interrelationships of religion and nature especially in the light of environment studies. It came into light in the late twentieth century in Christian circles with the emergent scientific field of ecology highlighting the whole "household" of God's creation, especially the world of nature, as an interrelated system and it is rooted in early modern theologies of nature conveying the messages –

1. The idea of divine immanence in the whole cosmos;
2. A rational, ecological rather than a hierarchical understanding of God, humans, and the created world;
3. A radically reinterpreted view of human dominion over nature in terms of partnership with nature;
4. A commitment to justice for all creatures, not just humans, highlighting the needs of the impoverished masses and engendered species around the globe.

Christian ecotheology draws on the writings of such authors as Jesuitpriest and Paleontologist Teilhard de Chardin , philosopher Whitehead , and is well-represented in Protestantism by John B. Cobb, Jr. and Jürgen Moltmann and ecofeminist theologians Rosemary Radford Ruether, Catherine Keller and Sallie McFague. Creation theology is another important expression of ecotheology that has been developed and popularized by Matthew Fox, the former Catholic priest. Abraham Joshua Heschel and Martin Buber, both Jewish theologians, have also left their mark on Christian ecotheology, and provide significant inspiration for Jewish ecotheology.

Hindu ecotheology includes writers such as Vandana Shiva. Seyyid Hossein Nasr, a liberal Muslim theologian, was one of the earlier voices calling for a re-evaluation of the Western relationship to nature.

By the year 2002, Christian ecotheology had emerged as a theological movement that had begun to speak with a new and powerful voice on behalf of the whole creation "groaning in travail".

So ecotheology seeks to uncover the theological basis for a fine relationship between God, humanity, and the cosmos. It stresses to uncover our sense of place on the earth, a reminder that the earth is our common home, that the story of the earth and that of humans are one.

Dalit ecotheology shares with liberation theology in its theological explications and biblical interpretations; in that it also adopts a sociological as well as political reading of the scripture, expect that dalit theology does it from a dalit perspective. Dalit theology is based on a faith in a dalit God. God is not the 'wholly other 'or the one who is up there, but is one who is identified with the oppressed, the dalits.

Dalits can also affirm that they are Christian dalits and not just dalits as it it imples that Jesus Christ is a Dalit himself, for the dalits despite his Jewishness. Christ himself preferred the title 'son of man' implying –(1) As an ordinary man, (2) To refer to this immanent suffering and death, (3) And in the eschatological sense of the term.

For dalits, the land is their ecology as they believe that it is God-given. Interestingly the Greek word for "home' (*Oikos*) is the root of ecology.To quotes Nirmal Minz:

> Land here means the land he lives on now, the trees, and plants he relates himself with day and night, and even the whole earth.

Dalits consider the Earth and all its produces as God's gifts, and therefore they can be 'owners 'of the Earth and its gifts.

Dalit theology is expressed in oral tradition, in the form of myths and legends which are rich in ecological insights. It can develop strong ecological network and thus refresh the nature's vital force. Dalits are inseparably coupled with its close proximity to nature, especially to forests and land and with a harmonious relationship between them and their environment. Dalit theology is to reclaim this identity vis-a vis its relationship to a homeland and a friendly and rich environment. According to Sundarlal Bahugana, the father figure of environmental movements in India expressed:

a) Nature is to be worshipped, not exploited.

b) One who takes more from nature and society should receive greater respect than the one who takes less.

c) There is a world inside a person that is richer and more worthy of cultivation than the outside world.

Paulos Mar Gregorios incorporates a modified version. His views are also very much applicable:

a) nature and history are inseparable as the matrix of our origin, growth and fulfillment and so created order is to respected and tended as God's creation. Worship only the creator.

b) Simplicity of life is of high value, but enforced poverty is not.

c) Life is not to be divided into inner life, but to speak of the final fulfillment which is already implied in the present realm beyond our senses, which moves our world as its norm and goal.

Dalit life is based and built upon a vision of human existence in which they are aware that land, forest, and the country they occupy are gifts of God. Dalits festivals like 'mango festivals' or the 'Mocca pindum' (among Moria Gond tribe) are the supreme occasion to save nature and to maintain the ecosystem of the environment. It is the most celebrated event for this tribe. In the summer , when the mangoes are about to ripen, the priest (pujari) is invied to perform a 'Puja' (religious activity) before whichv one is permitted to pluck the mangoes. After the puja is over everyone shares the fruits. Thus dalit theology is an attempt to appreciate the fact that the identity the tribals is so integrally linked to their immediate environment, land and forests which is the way for Dalit theology to be an ecological theology. Aruna Gnanadason quotes a song by Daya Pawar, a dalit woman in Maharastra, which captures the plight of the dalit women in India—

> As I build this dam
> I bury my life ...
> ....
> The dam is ready
> It feeds their sugar-cane fields
> Making the crop lush and juicy
> But I walk miles through forests
> In search of drops of drinking water
> I water the vegetation with drops of my sweat
> As dry leaves fall and fill my parched yard.

Dalit theology can and must widen its theological and hermeneutical horizons, linking the social concerns of the Dalits with their ecological issues. But dalit theology has still 'miles and miles to go' before it can be considered an integral eco-dalit theology. In the poem "Sunlight" of Monoharmouli Biswas translated by Anandalal he expresses:

> We know how to swim inside the dark room
> We know how to till the field and to thresh
> We know how to stay alive inside this
> Ancient dark room, sniffing the smell of sweat.
> Now look, the window in the east room is open
> O sunlight, tell me when you'll come.

We are also feasted with the same vision as expressed in Jhuma Mandal's "We have also the sun" (translated by me) published in *Chathurtha Dunia*.

But we have also the sun
That sun has its power of rays
It rifts the stony skin
That sun has its dazzling sunshine
It demands with own confidence.

So dalit ecology and theology go hand in hand being integrally link to their immediate environment, land and forest which opens the way to ecological balance and theological affirmation. By worshiping nature they are linking their life with nature and purifying their mind being aware of land, forest, air, water, sky. This harmony between nature and man has to be protected and promoted from generation to generation to save the gifts of God.

Works Cited

Berry, Thomas. *The Dream of the Earth.* San Francisco: Sierra Club, 1988.

Bouma-Prediger, Steven. *For the Beauty of the Earth: A Christian Vision for Creation Care.* Grand Rapids, Mich.: Erdmans, 2001.

Calvin, John. *Institutes of the Christian Religion* (1559). Philadelphia: Westminster Press, 1960.

Cobb, John B., Jr. *Is It Too Late? A Theology of Ecology,* rev. edition. Denten, Text.: Environmental Ethics Books, 1995.

Fox, Matthew. *The Coming of the Cosmic Christ: The Healing of Mother Earth and the Birth of a Global Renaissance.* New York: Harper, 1988.

French, William. "Subject-Centered and Creation-Centered Paradigms in Recent Catholic Thought." *Journal of Religion* 70 (1990): 48–72.

Gregorios, Paulos Mar. *The Human Presence: An Orthodox View of Nature.* Geneva, Switzerland: World Council of Churches, 1978. McFague, Sallie. *The Body of God: An Ecological Theology.* Minneapolis, Minn.: Fortress Press, 1993.

Moltmann, Jürgen. *God in Creation: A New Theology ofCreation and the Spirit of God,* trans. Margaret Kohl. San Francisco: Harper, 1985.

M.E. Prabhakar,"The search for a dalit theology". In A.P. Nirmal ed. A reader in dalit theology, James A. *Loving Nature: Ecological Integrity and Christian Responsibility.* Nashville, Tenn.: Abingdon Press, 1991.

Roderick Frazier. *The Rights of Nature: A History of Environmental Ethics.* Madison: University of Wisconsin Press, 1989.

Ruether, Rosemary Radford. *Gaia and God: An Ecofeminist Theology of Earth Healing.* San Francisco: Harper, 1992.

Santmire, H. Paul. *Nature Reborn: The Ecological and Cosmic Promise of Christian Theology.* Minneapolis, Minn.: Fortress Press, 2000.

Simkins, Ronald A. *Creator and Creation: Nature in the Worldview of Ancient Israel.* Peabody, Mass.: Hendrickson, 1994.

Teilhard de Chardin, Pierre. *The Hymn of the Universe,* trans. Simon Bartholomew. New York: Harper, 1965.

Thomas, Keith. *Man and the Natural World: A History of the Modern Sensibility.* New York: Pantheon, 1983.

Tillich, Paul. "Nature and Sacrament." In *The Protestant Era,* trans. James Luther Adams. Chicago: University of Chicago Press, 1957.

Watling, Tony (2009), *Ecological Imaginations in the World Religions: An Ethnographic Analysis,* London and New York: Continuum International Publishers.

White, L. Jr. (1971). "The Historical Roots of our Ecologic Crisis." Reprinted in A.E. Lugo & S.C. Snedaker, (Eds.) *Readings on Ecological Systems: Their Function and Relation to Man.* New York: MSS Educational Publishing.

20

Dalit Life Narratives: From Silence to Articulation

Arpita Chattaraj (Mukhopadhyay)

Dalit literature has emerged from historical, sociological, cultural, economic as well as political inequity, which largely contributes to its counter-canonical implications. The unique nature of dalit literature lies in the fact that it possesses an ironical propensity of subverting the essentializing approach of the privileged/ bourgeoisie/higher caste/class discourse. Dalit literature is therefore predisposed towards opposition, revolt, rejection, ethnic re-discovery as well as a process of aesthetic re-creation. Dalit literature exposes most intensely the sufferings of dalit existence, the presentation of the suffering is authentic since it is exclusive/ subjective to the dalits.

The agony that is manifest in dalit literature is not imagined, but a 'lived' experience - the expression of this experienced pain becomes a quest for construction of dalit selfhood or identity. But to merely restrict dalit literature to 'narrative of suffering' (to use Sisir Kumar Das's terminology) would be a delimiting perception of the issue and belittling its importance. The celebrated dalit writer Baburao Bagul points out the fundamental spirit of this literature when he says, "... it is dalit Literature, which has the revolutionary power to accept new science and technology and bring about a total transformation. 'Dalit' is the name of total revolution; it is revolution incarnate"(289). The bitterness that is consequent upon a continued, inexorable cycle of discrimination, determines dalit experience to be conveyed in the idiom/language of revolt and resistance directed against the manuistic, brahminical ,social order of subjugation and abuse. Dalit literature thus entails a process of 'negation' by which it debunks/rejects the brahminical, hegemonic ideological framework that colonizes /enslaves their consciousness.

The project of ethnic re-discovery as a manifest agenda in dalit literature is further complicated by the fact that the inhumanity that is exposed is not due to a lost homeland (like the African Americans) but being the 'other', peripheral in their own country and silenced by a discriminatory cultural heritage. As Arjun Dangle asserts in his essay "Dalit Literature: Past, Present and Future", this literature is marked by the simultaneity of the processes of 'demolition' and 'reconstruction'. Dalit Literature is directed towards destroying hegemonic social and cultural order and foregrounding an aspired for social reality based on freedom, dignity and equality. As an agency of protest and resistance against discrimination and inequity, Dalit Literature is therefore largely humanist in its attitude. Tarachandra Khandekar a Dalit writer underscores this: " Man is the centrifugal force in the philosophy of Dalit literature. Man is supreme. He is above all God, sacred books and science. It is man who can make and unmake anything. ...it (Dalit literature) proclaims that nothing is true which is not applicable for man's sublime freedom, nothing is good if it is not useful for man's welfare, nothing is beautiful which is not useful for beautification of mankind."(147)

Life narratives or 'Atmakathan' forms a major part of dalit literature. Unlike conventional autobiographies, dalit life narratives do not reveal the individual's tendency toward self-glorification or even self-indulgence; on the contrary, these Life narratives reveal the plight of the individuals caught in the maelstrom of caste-based oppression and discrimination. The dalit life narrative emerges as a form that seeks to mediate the position of a 'dalit' vis-à-vis his society thus transforming the journey of the 'I'. (It is central to autobiographical Phillippe Lejeune, in his famous essay "The Autobiography Pact" which refers to four key ingredients of an autobiography; it is narrative in prose, it is about an individual life, the author is the narrator and it is retrospective in point of view). The act of writing an autobiography is a conscious one, by which the author/narrator documents his/her life mediated through memory. What needs to be taken into account, however, is that the identity/self/ 'auto' which are being written will be influenced by the specificity or context of the individual's life or 'bio'. When a dalit writes his/her own life, it will be a definite political act, since the life that is being narrated/ written is predominantly about oppression and marginalization. Therefore, the autobiographical centre which is the individual self is not realized in the same manner in dalit life narratives; The life narrative in this case challenge official forgetting of histories of oppression and manifest resistance and identity formation. They are distinct from the bourgeoisie genre of autobiography by being predicated on the interface between self and society and the dialectic between the two.

Dalits writing personal narratives have often been compared to digging out stench from hateful bins of the past. But Arun Prabha Mukherjee a translator of such narratives asserts that the life narratives are not 'sob stories' but stories of anger against injustice. Gopal Guru also points out that life narratives are " sociologically illuminating, politically subversive and aesthetically interesting." These narratives not only traces individual journey but collective journeys, they indicate a movement from dalit individual to dalit community. They can be treated as signifiers of historically and culturally specific understanding of memory, experience and identity.

Hazari's *Untouchable: The Autobiography of an Indian Outcaste* narrates the life of a dalit during the colonial period and has an interesting publishing history, it was first published in US by the Bannisdale Press and then in 1969 by Praeger Publishers. The life narrative does not give the narrator's original name, he belongs to the scavenging community and he reveals in the process of narrating his life story his conversion to Islam. He was born in a village in the district of Moradabad, in erstwhile United Provinces which is present day Uttar Pradesh. Hazari does not give any definite dates regarding his life history but intertwines it with various events of pre-independent India, with references to Congress Party and Muslim League. Hazari refers to the idea of 'karma', which ensures an ethics of submission and indoctrination of certain ideas that facilitates the complicity of the Dalit in his own degradation. As he says: "our philosophy of life was that God has created us and that he would provide for our needs according to His will. Our fortunes, good or bad, were the will of god, and we were always taught to think that our lot was better that that of most people." After several trials and tribulations, Hazari sets for France for higher education, sponsored by one Mr Newman, with which the narrative ends. The emotional turmoil that Hazari communicates through his narrative reflects not only his own context but also a larger frame of a caste-ridden society.

Laxman Mane's *Upara* narrates a life of deprivation and torture. Born into Kaikadi community, which is landless and nomadic, Mane observes the inherent social oppression firsthand. Especially poignant is the section in which he describes their haste for collecting leftovers after an upper-caste feast: "Then we would be on the lookout to find out when the guests were going to get up. They would get up together at the same time. There would be a pile of plates made of jackfruit tree leaves with the leftovers. We would rush and pounce upon the. Whatever eatable came to our hand we wou;d grab it and put it in a piece of cloth. We had to finish our job before these plates were licked clean by the treet dogs. Then, tying our 'loot' in a piece of cloth and abusing each other, we would return home." (94)

Dalit women employing the strategy of narrating personal lives for articulating against and refuting this 'invisibility' is comparable to the slave women's narrating their lives- slavery is manifest in the latter as a legally sanctioned institution, but the fundamental paradigm of economic exploitation, chattel serfdom, sexual violation and trampling of personhood are applicable in the case of the former. When the narrating voice is that of the woman it adds further significance since concerns of specifity of gender oppression enters into the rubric of investigation. As Sharmila Rege points out in her *Writing Caste/Writing Gender* "Dalit women's testimonios, offered counter narratives that challenged the selective memory and univocal history both of the dalit and the women's movement"(75). A dalit woman is a dalit among dalits. Exploration of specifities of dalit women in India reveal that they constitute a lower segment in Indian society and suffer from dual disadvantages of being dalit, that is, from the socio-economic and cultural marginalization and being women, that is from gender-based inequalities and subordination. Dalit feminists have formulated the position of the three-way oppression of dalit women:

i) As subject to caste oppression at the hands of the upper castes

ii) As labourers subject to the class- based oppression, also mainly at the hands of the upper and middle castes

iii) As women who experience patriarchal oppression at the hands of all men, including men of their own caste.[1]

Traditioanlly dalit women have been kept under servitude, their voices silenced, their dignity and personhood trampled upon. Thus articulation of the trauma and anger by dalit women in their writing has definite political dimension. Dalit feminism operates on the interface between gender and caste. Writing caste/ writing gender underscores the inseparability of caste and gender inequalities. Prof Gopal Guru describes the stand of the dalit feminism which contributed to the formation of National Federation of Dalit Women (NFDW) as "politics of difference".

This difference was essential in understanding the specifity of Dalit woman's subjugation, characterized by their experience of two distinct patriarchal structures: as identified by Anupama Rao in her "Caste, Gender and Indian Feminism" Dalit women are subjected to a brahminical form of patriarchy that deeply stigmatized dalit women because of their caste status, as well as the more intimate forms of control by dalit men over the sexual and economic labour of their women.[2] The dalit woman's position subvert the Indian feminism's hegemonic impulse to represent 'Indian' women as a unitary, homogeneous phenomenon as well as the proliferation of patriarchal norms within dalit communities.

Kumud Pawade's *Antasphot* (Thoughtful Outburst) insists that her outburst should not be construed as an 'emotional' one, rather her attempt is to analyse the interface between the experiences of individuals and communities. Dalit women, she underlines are the victims of double exploitation: "When a culture based on hierarchy as in the case of Indian society literally bites the flesh off the minds of individuals and communities and wounds them, then how do I see my life and that of my wounded community as human beings? This question keeps eating at my brain. Because of this, I begin to feel as if my brain will burst and when this state expresses itself in words – the thoughtful outburst happens.This is my position on *Antasphot*" (4). She asserts that *Antasphot* is not an 'autobiography' but a critical narrative of her experiences. In fact she feels that all dalit life stories are critical narratives and not autobiographies. Janabai Kachru Girhe is the first woman teacher and the first woman of Gopal community, a nomadic set, to write her *testimonio*. In the Preface she says, "Wherever there is a village there is a 'pala' (groups of nomadic families who set up temporary camps on open grounds outside village boundaries), wherever there is water, there is pala. The sky as the roof and earth as the floor, food to assuage the immediate hunger – this is the way of life." Janabai's book is dedicated to her parents and to all brothers and sisters of the nomadic communities. She writes:

> To them who begged from door to door
> Who cared for me, through sun, rain and bitter cold and storm
> Did more than they did fir their own lives,
> Who crossed mountains of hard labour to put a pen in
> my hands rather than the customary begging bowl,
> I dedicate this book at the wounded and tired feet
> of my parents and sisters, who move from field
> to field, forest to forest leading thorny lives. (7)

Marankala as Janabai calls her *testimonio* foregrounds the fact that being born a girl in her community is a 'deathly pain' or *marankala*, but it is not unrelieved suffering , since death consists seeds of new birth.

Faustina Bama whose *Karukku* was first translated in French before it was translated into English asserts that caste, class and gender are important markers for social exclusion. In a colloquium organized by Women's Word India, a free speech network of feminist writers addressing issues of gender-based censorship Bama vehemently voiced her opinion which perhaps sums up the ethos of all literatures of suffering and resistance: "I am a Dalit woman writer. The challenge for a writer is to remain rooted. To have experienced pain, hunger - and contempt. My story is my people's story... . Through my writing, I allow the militancy of the victimized persons to emerge. I believe the life experiences of people can be conveyed only in their own language. My writing has been called bawdy and immoral. It has broken a lot of taboos. I did not write for publication; my first book, I write for my own healing... . I feel satisfaction when ripple of consciousness surface in my community due to my writing. Writing has helped me break down a thousand barriers."(*The Hindu*)

References

1. Chakravarti, Uma. *Gendering Caste: Through a Feminist Lens* Kolkata: Stree, 2004.
2. Rao, Anupama ed. *Gender and Caste.* New Delhi: Kali for Women, 2003.

21

Bengali Dalit Literature and Culture: A Dignity Discourse

Manohar Mouli Biswas

Historicity

Dalits in Bengal are found resistive in nature. In the interest of own community development, they have shown their character sometimes as of pro-establishment and sometimes as of anti-establishment. For reference I shall mention two incidences from history. The first one is of pro-establishment and the second one is of the anti-establishment.

It's a known history to all that British in India had divided Bengal (the then Bengal was a very big state having Assam, Orissa and some portion of Bihar in its boundary) in 1905 into two parts for administrative reasons. This division had given birth to a vigorous Swadeshi movement in the state of Bengal. Protests were found in an organised way from every corners. Politicians such as Surendra Nath Banerjee etc. of INC, poets such as Rabindranath Tagore etc. from the field of art, literature and aesthetics, spiritualists such as Aurovindo Ghosh etc. of Anushilan Samity of passive resistance; and revolutionists such as Kshudiram Bose etc. from the field of violence and activism took part in the then all-out Swadeshi movement. Their sentiments were totally passionate to keep the Bengal nation undivided. On the other hand the dalits from the fields of have-nots and social neglects had shown an opposite sentiment to play. They were unquestioningly in search of their material gains of social uplift. They remained away from the main stream thought.

While Ambika Charan Majumdar, a close associate of Suredra Nath Banerjee and the Faridpur District Congress president approached to have the dalit support for Swadeshi movement, their leader Shri Shri Guruchand Thakur declined in a straightforward argument: It's unwise for us to go against the British government who are, and have been honestly trying long to improve the condition of the untouchables.[1] They had been doing it through the different missionary activities. In a reply to the letter of Surendra Nath Banerjee what Guruchand said the same we may get quoted from Mahananda Halder's poetic verse:

> Unity can be had while equality is amongst us.
> No ally can singing the tune on an uneven fuss.
> Poor penniless while we're into a working hard.
> Why shall we take part against our ruling Lord.[2]

On scrutinising this statement of a renowned dalit poet it becomes conspicuous to us that the untouchables during that period had been by the side of the establishment. Perhaps, they believed the British more than the Swadeshiwalas in respect of their community development.

The second one is an incident of anti-establishment in character. In the second half of the nineteenth century there was a call of 'General Strike' in the year 1872-73. At that time the conception to launch protest against the establishment through a 'Call of General Strike' was not a natural phenomenon. The call was given by the Namasudras of a greater part of rural East Bengal.[3] Particularly, in the district of Faridpur. Khulna and Barishal. It was against the government establishment. The bottommost layer of government were none other than the upper caste Hindus serving in the government sectors. Whenever any incident of theft or dacoity was happening in anywhere in village the policemen were putting the untouchables behind the bar without proper proof or investigation. On the basis of guess only. In the jail these people were being forcefully used for cleansing dirties of the jail. At that time the peons of the post offices were not going to the untouchable villages to deliver letters. The sanitation people were not sanctioning the tubewells for pure drinking water in the untouchable locality. All these were happening due to the caste neglects and social hatred. This call of non-cooperation movement of the Bengal peasants continued for about a month. Then they had to surrender to the people against whom they had given their call. The Govt. machinery in the district level authority of Faridpur and Khulna such as the District Magistrate as well as the Superintendent of Police had noted the incident in their official records.[4] The cultural, sociological and professional aspect of the Dalits had got its sensational focus in their deliberations.

Post-independence Situation

The people, revolted against the partition of Bengal in 1905 had sponsored the partition of 1947; and in a reverse manner we note, the dalits from the zones of have-nots of Bengal who welcomed or favoured the division of Bengal in 1905 for their own benefits as a protagonist to the government had demanded independence of an integrated and undivided Bengal in 1947; a bulging of the mind and thought of Jogendranath Mondal, the then prominent Dalit leader.[5] But what was an eventuality to note, the independence from the hands of the British ultimately came through partition, a cruel truth in the life of common people of Bengal. This division had put both dalits and non-dalits in an equal sufferings, and as a matter fact, the dalits were found little more meagre to overcome the situation.

In afterward times of the post-independence, while the spread of literacy in the country along with progress in higher and professional education, the pace of urbanisation, the development of means of communication and transport etc had taken place, it became the instrumental in loosening somewhat the rigidity and hangover of caste system, particularly, in the urban areas; then, at the same time on the other side what is noticed, in contrary to this positive development, caste has come to be used blatantly and indiscriminately for political ends. It has sharpened caste and sub-caste identities and resulted in caste alliances of different types in different regions for the sole purpose of wildering political power.[6] As a resultant, at this time some provinces are found to have undergone the political manoeuvre by dalits though the communists and socialists have considered the caste as superstructure of society. But what is in reality in India it has always been undoubtedly the basic structure; and nobody can ignore, if anyone has studied the marriage advertisement pages of a Bengali Daily, particularly, the Sunday supplement which is having wide circulation in the market.

Cultural Fascism

Then to tell what is now another reality. The dominant castes either in numerical strength or in terms of economic clouts are struggling to retain their monopoly over power and thus the marginal castes who are operating on periphery of power structures seen to have arousing their caste consciousness for uplift in political, social, literary and cultural arenas. In support to this fact we can refer to a prognostication of M.N.Roy, an internationally known radical humanist of India. He said of the Indian fascism. Indian fascism though not violent in nature but is of centuries old. Working is of different manners in the different areas. In the field of art, literature and culture it is of the characteristics to nourish superior caste monopoly. Prior to independence he told in a seminar in Kolkata on 30 January, 1947, "when political power is concentrated in the hands of small community you may have a facade of a parliamentary democracy, but for all political purposes it will be dictatorship even it may be paternal and benevolent."[7] In the coming over to power, every time, by the minority dominant castes, in the inner sense what we trace out, we may, perhaps, smell of fascism sounds like 'negation of the negation' which was long back told by Hegel.

Scope of Identity

Identity glorifies the inner strength. It is linked to self development. The dalit literature and culture in Bengal has come out in the form of a movement through the understanding and exercise of identity question in the post independence era. They desire to go beyond caste system in ideological reconciliation with Buddhism. They are in search of recognition. They are in search of equivalence. For this, they have to be protestant against caste hatred and neglect. They are to come forward for establishing the sense of sameness. The question of identity is sometimes problematic and sometimes unproblematic. It becomes problematic when the narrower thought of separatism is attached with. And when the idea of acquiring the proposition of 'one equal to one' becomes motto, it is then blessed with the qualitative improvement.

Dalit identity means the lifelong struggle. Is there any sense of aggravation? No and not at all. Any one sensible should have his own right to know, what he is and where he is. Whenever anyone is born of dalit identity he is to perform a long journey through his own experiences entrust enthusiasm in him to build up a new form of literature, I mean, dalit literature comes into existence. He worships his own matrix of life. He is to suffer hoaxes of new dimension. He is to cut the edges, a war between man and machine.

To understand the question of identity in an easy manner, let us assume, two medicinal pills of life. One blue and the other one red. Men in blue one, live without knowing truth of life who they actually are and men in red one discover the truth of life and can figure out the reality of their own position in societal panorama. That is the reason, why all of dalits, whosoever they be, aren't and can't become capable of creating dalit literature and anyone of non-dalits, whosoever he be, similarly doesn't and can't qualify in the field.

The mainstream thinkers of Bengal shall not fall in line with me; because of the fact that they think, any one of the mainstream can share the sufferings and hatred of the dalits. I personally feel that this type of sharing comes out of the sympathy for them. A dalit, while he is writing his own experiences is a depicter of something born out of the empathy, and not out of sympathy; and that is the reason why the dalit literature produces a neo-reality, now the modern Indian literature is dealing with.

Two Decades of Movement in Bengal

In the last two decades the dalits in Bengal have shown their presence in creative and non-creative writings in a larger extent in view of their sufferings and deprivations. Both creative and non-creative writings are of the nature of resistive index. Non-creative writers have gathered the weapons in hand to fight out the cause which has every time ushered new thoughts in creative field. It's they who have set up the backbone of argument. It is not as such as the common people think of. We know the case of self immolation of Chuni Kotal, a tribal girl whose death, a sanguine example of caste oppression in Bengal, is a major tragic occurrence had penetrated into the movement from 1992.[8] Prior to that, the mass killings of dalits in Marichjhappi in 1969 had opened the eyes. Anna's fight against the monetary corruption is as necessary as we talk of the socio-religious corruption of the country. The non-creative writers have searched out their history through the comparative studies.

Dr. B.R. Ambedkar from Maharastra has implanted his excellence nationally and internationally. He had put forward the arguments strongly. It has encouraged the other parts of India. Bengal has accumulated energy and courage from him. A number of scholars have come forward to delve out into the history of their own sufferings and deprivations. Some of them are academicians and some of them are from government offices.

Socio-Religious Indictment

Dalit literature is anti-canonical in character. Unlike the mainstream writers they have opened new door to swim into the water of a dire chill strait. Civil society people are very much conscious about the interest of the upper caste educated middle class and in West Bengal they do not differ much from the rest of India. Very recently, we have noticed with the saddest eyes that they had never expensed a word any time to maintain the 'Reservation Policy' properly in educational institution or government service sector though the 'Constitution' has taken good care of them by safeguarding and guaranteeing 'Right of Reservation' for scheduled castes, scheduled tribes and other backward communities to uplift them on an even-surface, as equal as to the other superior castes. The places where there is no reservation there is no place for them. Even in the places where there is reservation, the same is not exercised to the extent fullest to their benefits. They do not find a man from dalits to be a representative of any committee constituted. They do not find to have suited any of the unimportant literary award for their writers. Even during last six decades of our independence not a single one from them has been nominated to represent the Rajya Sabha from Paschim Banga. We, the writers are naturally of the different views.

About the unto-death-movement of Anna Hazare, a Gandhivadi from hair to toe, is a man of civil society much bothered about monetary corruption and not about socio-religious corruption of the country, though both are equally hindering the progress of nation at the bottom most layer of the society. Let we people, the writers should have a mind, Anna should take the issues of dalits to stop caste discrimination, deeply routed into the blood of society.

Jan Lokpal Bill, a weapon sponsored by Anna to fight monetary corruption, needs be termed as 'Bahujan Lokpal', a weapon to fight discriminatory societal corruption which has been undermining the nation for a long time.

Researchers' Argument

The people who have, so far, been a subjective of writing by the litterateurs in-general are, now, seen to have risen to the occasion the place of writer-in-themselves. This has given a total change in the parameters of literature. It has brought about a new paradigm. Unforgettable contributions have been had from the thinkers the personages such as Dr. Anil Ranjan Biswas, Prof. Sripada Das, Prof. Achintya Biswas, Dr. U.N. Biswas, Sunil Kumar Das, Prof. Jagabandhu Biswas, Thakur Panchanan Barman, Sadhu Ramchand Murmu, Jagadish Chandra Mondal, Dr.Pashupati Prasad Mahato, Shanti Ranjan Biswas, Dr. Sunil Kumar Mondal, Dhurjati Naskar, Dr. Atul Krishna Biswas, Sukata Mondal, Dr. Birat Bairagya, Tulsi Charan Mondal, Dr. Nanda Dulal Mohanta, Manohar Mouli Biswas, Prof. Dilip Halder, Shyamal Kumar Pramanik, Dr. Gunadhar Barman, Sukriti Ranjan Biswas, Satya Ranjan Talukdar, Swapan Kumar Biswas, Narottam Halder, Promode Baran Biswas, Prof. Sanat Kumar Naskar, Dr. Suranjan Midde, etc. Most of the researchers have tried to project Dalit-entity culminating in divergent horizons. New hopes and aspirations are set up in Bengal as well as throughout India.

Researchers are seen to have overcome the trajectories thrown upon them by the Hindu religious traits. Learning the arguments to ignore miseries of life, whatever be of centuries old and pushing back them inhumanely, they are, now, in a mood to corner them all out. Their fights are, perhaps, of the populous strength of the populace. They are now not to care hindrances anymore.

Category of Dalit Writings

The dalit writings is a broader field can be branched out into the categories such as (i) Autobiography, (ii) Novel, (iii) Short Story, (iv) Drama, (v) Poetry and (vi) Critique. Dalit writings are different from the traditional literature which believes in the Hindu mythological teachings and patrons the caste divided societal values. The former one can be and may be clearly distinguished as and when any of the autobiography is gone through. *Rang Beranger Dinguli* of Dr. Anil Ranjan Biswas (1916-2005), *Prof. Sripada Das: Son of a Street Cobbler* of Prof. Sripada Das (b. 1938) , *Ekjan Daliter Atmakatha* of Dr. Manoranjan Sarkar (b.1934), *Deener Atmakahini Ba Satya Pariksha* of Rai Charan Sardar (1875-1941), *Abor Belay Paari* of Banamali Goswami (1894-1976), *Itibritte Chandal Jibon* of Manoranjan Byapari (b. 1951), *Shekar Chera Jiban* of Jatin Bala (b.1949) and finally do I mention of my own autobiography, i.e., *Prishnika* (Hyacinth) of Manohar Mouli Biswas (b.1943).

Novel as Detailers

Novels are the descriptive narratives, and to form classic giving an elaborate clan studies. Wherein the mannerism of day-to-day life and hardship they suffer becomes picturesque to enjoy. They are petulant, resilient and defiant. Focus on particular clan, caste or community. Highlighting their struggles in profession such as fishing, cleaning, foresting, boating, cultivating, canning, gardening, mowing, polishing, skinning, laddering, mopping, planting, husking, spading, fencing, shaving, watering etc. They inherit them. The knowledge is acquired from the time when a child is born to parents. Life is under categorical apprenticeship. Profile differs from one sub-caste to another sub-caste. The particular professionalism is seen to run on through generations. Some of the items attains to the world heritage setting where people are found striving to survive against the serious odds of life. Some of the novelists have depicted the injustice or slandering flung upon them by the ruling machinery. A powerful narrative writer Nakul Mallick has donated a fact finding one about the mass killing of dalits in Marichjhapi of Sundarban. Of the novelists, Adwita Malla Barman in his novel *Titash Ekti Nadir Naam*, Mohitosh Biswas in his novel *Maati Ek Maya Jaane*, Kapil Krishna Thakur in his nevel *Ujantalir Upakatha*, Anil Ghorai in his novel *Mukuler Gandha* and Samarendra Baidya in his novel *Pitrigan* have shown the hardship, attire, exigency and struggle in their ancestral low profile professions.

Short Story as Depicters

When we talk about short stories we shall have to name the names of Manohar Mouli Biswas, Anil Gharai, Brajen Mallick, Gobinda Shounda, Goutam Aali, Bimalendu Halder, Sarajit Kumar Mondal, Manoranjan Byapari, Harendra nath Bhakta, Utpalendu Mondal, Kishore Biswas, so on and so forth. Different kinds of hurdles in dalit life are in scanned picturesque focused in the story. Caste identity certificate to prove their societal status, needed to get a govt. job or an admission to the institution are mostly found denied by the issuing authority on some pretext or rather. People with the caste identity found to be looked down upon in premises of school or college or university or in various service sectors. Just few days back I have gone through a story of Sunil Kumar Das based on his own personal experience where he shown how a higher caste fellow of Kolkata showed him impatience for being a member of scheduled caste family. In respect of drama writing Raju Das, Smriti Kana Howlader, Pran Gobinda Biswas etc. are in prominence.

Poetry as Foretellers

Bengali dalit poetry have taken the situation of oppression and sufferings such as mass-killing in Marichjhapi, uprooting in Singur and political infightings in Nandigram etc. into their accounts. Poets are seen intolerant and insurgent more in comparison with others. In Marichjhapi, the loss of kith and kin are the memories unforgettable. In June 1977 while the Left government came to power, surprisingly, no follow-up of the promises so far they made to were sufficed.[9] This u-turn taken by the Lefts ushered into the marginalised section the sentiment the killing of ethics. And one poet has thus voiced: "One thousand children/ Stretched out their eternal bed/ Into saline water and mud of island Marichjhapi/ We are in wait:/When shall they rise up from sleep." Another poet has taken the case of Marchjhapi as a tragic historical murder: "Division of Bengal has severed heart and life to death/ Marichjhapi brings humanity to an end/ Marichjhapi a historical slay in the time and space/ Tears adding salts to the food we take."

One poet has expressed; she is undone and impatient of the sequentials of Singur, Nandigram and Marichjhapi. She utters in the poetic verse: "Singur villagers, Nandigram villagers/ The deceased of Marichjhapi being of ours/ Can't I but to shed a silent tear/ Of sad soliloquy on the pillows under head."

The poets are lot in numbers. Of them, to mention the names of prominences are Kalyani Thakur, Manju Bala, Kiran Talukdar, Bina Roy Sarkar, Chuni Kotal, Lily Halder, Jhuma Mondal Sujata Biswas, Sonalisa Das, Lakshmi Mandi, Sushama Moitra Sarkar and Sritikana Howladar as women poets. While talking of powerful poets we can remember the names of Raicharan Biswas, Anil SarKar, Mahananda Halder, Basanta Kumar Mondal, Ramchand Murmu, Manohar Mouli Biswas, Marshal Hembram, Anil Krishna Mallick, Rajit Kumar Sikdar, Sudhir Mallick, Amar Biswas, Amar Halder, Samar Roy, Bimal Biswas Kalidas Bala, Debashis Mondal, Hrishikesh Halder, Gopal Biswas etc..

Aesthetics of Resistivity

Beautification of 'nothing' is everything to understand— to the people outside the domain as well as within the domain. What is told of, the case may be as of nothing or zero, whatever you say, poses to be out in the universe, *I mean to tell of,* incomputer world, a zero shares a half of the whole. Hence, philosophy of 'zero', virtually, neither can be denied nor can be vanquished. People once were to grow the fodder food are seen now into a greenery, the sea of a creative impasse, literary journey to reach a new zenith of their own.

The question of triadic concept of traditional aesthetics, 'Satyam' (the true), 'Shivam' (the secres) and 'Sundaram' (the beautiful) is considered implanted aesthetics; one from the Sanskrit classification, founded on Hindu religious traits; may have turned to a new aesthetics procrastinated by Bengali Dalit writings. Belief of what is truth of life is the beauty of life. The 'Shivam' does not come in between. The untouchable life in India is, of course, grounded on the professional hardship, prescribed by the deeds of previous life, a cruel and undignified reality seen resulted into a separate kind of beauty, a beauty of neo-reality.

It is, now, in a pursuit to disbelieve the sympathy from others, which, of course, gives birth to a dependence as well as a kind of roundabout subjugation; needs be thrown out, through the creativity of their own. I mean to say, a creativity, meaningfully, a terminal of the progeny the old dominating factors; to set up own empathy, highlights the lifelong beauty in experience.

Known to them their critical position of the colonial and postcolonial status, shabby and insignificant in society, have put an urge on them to write and make a social equilibrium mongering on balance, harmony, proportion and symmetry. Which have automatically cut a nice figure to overreaching. It is now found as an emerging trend in Indian literary scene. Given by the facts of overreaching preoccupation, number of arenas or literary zones, whatsoever, seen, got the shape of creation, with locating selves in Hindu caste-based indignant society, and their struggle for dignity, justice and equality, this literature becomes, by nature oppositional and non-canonical, creating new aesthetics and values. With growing popularity through translation of their works, that is the works of Bengali dalit writers in Hindi, Gujarati and English it has now got the pan-Indian presence and popularity.

References

1. Acharja Mahananda Halder, Sri Sri Guruchand Chartit, Matua Mahasangha, Dist 24 Parganas (North), W.B, 4th ed. 2003, pp. 312 (Note: During the period of Swadesi Movements the dalits and particularly the Namasudras of eastern part of Bengal were very much organised for their self-development and their leaders asserted themselves to be pro-policies of the Government.) In Bengali: *Prabhu jabe kare rag, Andolan kare tyaag, Rajbhakta hoilo proman.*
2. Ibid., pp173 and Dr. A.K. Biswas, *The Namasudras of Bengal*, Blumoon Books, New Delhi, 1st ed.2000, pp25. (Note: Namasudras are poor people. They do not indulge in luxury nor do they know of it. The only foreign goods they use are cheap imported clothes. It is the high castes who are wont to use imported goods. This agitation [boycott], therefore, should remain confined inclusively amongst themselves.)
3. Dr. U.N. Biswas, *The Strike* (Earliest Movement For Dignity & Equality Before Law 1873), NCMB Memorial Trust, CG, 22 Salt Lake City, Kolkata 700 091, 1st ed. 2004 pp. 48.
4. The report of C.A. Kelly, ICS, District Magistrate, Faridpur in this regard discloses the fact: In the early part of this year (1973), the Chandals made a general strike (emphasis made) in the district resolving not to serve anybody of the upper class, in whatever capacity, unless a better position among the Hindu castes than what they at presentoccupy was given to them). *Letter of W.L. Owen*, SP, No.66, dt.18th March 1873.
5. Nakul Mallick, Division of Bengal & Jogendra Nath (Banga Bhanga o Jogendranath), *Chaturtha Dunia Patrika*, Stall 22 Bhabani Dutta Lane, Kolkata 700 073, Special Issue, 2003. (Note: In view of the Hindu-Muslim communal riots the decision for division of Bengal is totally unwise. This animosity between the two is a momentary. This temporary we shall overcome it. What we want we want the independence of undivided Bengal. Press conference by Jogendranath Mandal, a dalit leader of Bengal on 21.04.1947 in Delhi.)
6. Dr. Balachandra Mungekar, former V.C., University of Mumbai, *Frontline*, Volume 28, Issue 15, July 2011.

7. R.M.Pal, Gandhi, Democracy, and Days of Struggle: Political Scientists Views on M.N.Roy, *Mainstream*, Vol. XLV, no 35.
8. M.M.Biswas & S.K.Pramanik (edited), *Shatobarsher Bangla* Dalit Sahitya, Chaturtha Dunia, Stall 22 Bhabani Dutta Lane, Kolkata 700 073 1st ed. 2011, preface designated as 'Parjyaonukramonika'. (This compilation has accommodated about 83 Dalit writers' in 1911-2010)
9. Prof. Dilip Halder, *Atrocities on Dalits since the Partition of Bengal*, Mittal Publication, New Delhi 110002, 1st ed. 2008 pp. 31. (This book is an endeavour to make out a case for Human Rights Commission and Human Rights activists highlighting the situation of Dalits in West Bengal.)

22

Venomous *Touch*: Meena Kandasamy's Poetics of Resistance

Abin Chakraborty

In the last few years, the study of Indian English literature has grown more responsive to various articulations of dalit voices in different generic forms. However, within the realm of Indian English poetry, violence and discrimination based on caste-identities has long remained an unheard, unnamed, excluded area of Indian experience.

The poetry of Meena Kandasamy is of path-breaking and pioneering significance in this regard as it polemically highlights the entrenched ruptures in Indian society, along the lines of caste, because of which thousands of individuals belonging to scheduled castes still continue to lead a subalternized existence. While on the one hand, they are subjected to various forms of casteist violence and are forced to endure severe material disadvantages, leading to miserable living conditions, on the other hand, they also face a critical identity crisis on account of the preponderant hegemonic authority of that brahminical culture which justifies casteist discrimination and subjects various expressions of dalit culture to systematic erasure. Therefore, as Kancha Illaih states "the condemned must learn to condemn the others" and that "unless the culture and consciousness of the oppressed is put forward visibly in public debate, unless this culture is prepared to clash with the culture and consciousness of the enemy in public, a society of equals will remain an illusion" (Illaih 169, 168). The polemical thrust of his arguments is justified in advance by his declaration that "The dalitbahujan experience – a long experience of 3000 years at that—tells us that no abuser stops abusing unless there is retaliation. An atmosphere of calm, an atmosphere of respect for another is never possible unless the abuser is abused as a matter of shock." (Illaih 168-69)

The poetics of Meena Kandasamy operates along similar lines and her poetry, especially in *Touch* (2006), is filled with relentless militant assaults on those structures, customs and conventions which have persistently been used to justify and then gloss over dalit subjugation of various kinds. For example, even though brahminical scriptures abound with references to how the touch or even the shadow of an untouchable can be contaminating, the same scriptures arealso fraught, on the other hand, with innumerable indictments of physical, corporeal existence which is bound to be decayed and the concomitant privileging of man's spiritual being, away from all tactile considerations.

It is this hypocritical contradiction within the entire discourse of brahminical Hindu philosophy which Kandasamy scrupulously highlights as she states:

> You will have known almost
> every knowledgeable thing about
> the charms and the temptations
> that touch could hold.
> But, you will never have known
> that touch—the taboo
> to your transcendence,
> when crystallized in caste
> was a paraphernalia of
> undeserving hate.
>
> (Kandasamy 2006, 36)

The male brahmin addressee is thus made aware of the fact that despite all his persistent attempt to transcend touch, it remains the undeniable everyday reality for thousands of people who are humiliated, discriminated against and violently subjugated precisely by those brahminically encoded hierarchies of caste that make 'touch' indeed a matter of life and death. Kandasamy therefore mordantly scoffs at the vaunted Hindu philosophy of non-dualism, revered by people around the world, by emphasizing that foundational binary or duality, between the touchable and the untouchable, between the upper castes and the outcastes which the ancient texts codified and naturalized:

> One More
> Final Question
> Can My
> Untouchable Atman
> And Your
> Brahmin Atman
> Ever Be
> One ?
> (Kandasamy 2006, 37)

The sarcasm directed at such scriptural texts is an integral element of a counter-discourse that seeks to displace altogether the supposed glory of ancient Hindu religion and the associated cultural framework because it is these discursive frameworks that also provide the basis of the various massacres and atrocities that keep occurring in the name of caste, as exemplified by either the familiar legend of Ekalavya or the Karamchedu massacre that Kandasamy herself writes about:

> Liquid Tragedy: Karamchedu 1985
> Buffalo Baths. Urine. Bullshit
> Drinking Water for the Dalits
> The very same Pond.
> Practice for eons.
> A bold Dalit lady
> dares to question injustice.

> Hits forth with her pot. Her indignation
> is avenged. Fury let loose. Violence. Rapes.
>
> (Kandasamy 2006, 52)

What exactly had happened at Karamchedu in 1985? As Kathi Padma Rao, a former leader of Dalit Mahasabha, explains:

> Two Kamma (upper caste) youth, Potina Seenu and Rayineedu Prasad, took their buffaloes to the drinking water tank in Madigapalle. They fed the buffaloes with washings of rice in buckets. While they were washing the dirty buckets in the tank, Katti Chandraiah, a Dalit boy, objected to it. His courage angered Seenu and Prasad. They were about to beat up Chandraiah when Munnangi Suvaartha, a Madiga woman, came to the tank to collect water. She tried to protect the boy from the attack of Kamma youths. Seenu and Prasad threw hunters at her. She lifted her vessel and warded off the hunters. Suvaartha's lifting of vessel in self-defence became a pretext for Kammas, who were itching for a fresh quarrel with Madigas after the election clash... . They raided every Dalit's house, drove Madigas into fields. The blood thirsty Kammas beat Madigas, stabbed them and axed them. They raped Dalit women... . The murder and mayhem had no parallel in the Indian subcontinent.
>
> (Rao, para 4)

These axed Madigas as well as the assaulted or raped men and women of Karamchedu operate as those silenced subalterns of post-independence Indian history whose anguish seeps into the poetics of Meena Kandasamy and provokes that militant rhetoric which prompts her to revise the myth of Eklavya and carve a militant out of him:

> You can do a lot of things
> With your left hand.
> Besides, fascist Dronacharyas warrant
> Left-handed treatment.
> Also,
> You don't need your right thumb,
> To pull a trigger or hurl a bomb.
>
> (Kandasamy 2006, 44)

Of course she does not only stop at revision but systematically denigrates the vaunted glory of some of the Brahmanical gods and goddesses. Therefore, not only are the gods verbally abused as "indifferent bastards" (Kandasamy 46), the poet even mocks their actual inability to intervene in any way by referring to roadside walls, adorned with images of divinities, which however are also covered with layers of urine:

> And yet, the Gods are covered with
> layers of smelly urine—they don't retaliate.
> Tolerance is a very holy concept.
> Or like someone said,
> the Caste Gods deserve
> the treatment they get.
>
> (Kandasamy 2006, 72)

The same rhetoric is also used elsewhere where she either scoffs at Brahmma as "villain who willed our deaths/...four-faced, dour-faced father figure/ who fucked up our lives" (Kandasamy 2010, 43) or uses the myth of Indra splintering the fetus of Diti, the mother of gods, into 49 pieces, in order to lash out at the brahminical violence, ingrained in vaunted scriptural texts of ancient India, by identifying Indra as being a worse psychopath that Herod or Hitler. The nature of her condemnation is further illustrated on other occasions when she hurls her vitriolic invectives at some of the other gods and goddesses of the Hindu pantheon, who, however, have no presence in dalit beliefs and whose processions never enter the dalit localities:

> We understand
> why upper caste Gods
> and their 'good-girl' much-married, father-fucked,
> virgin, vegetarian oh-so-pure Goddesses
> borne in their golden chariots
> don't come to our streets.
>
> (Kandasamy 2006, 53)

Her ire is particularly directed at the figure of Saraswati about whose origins there remains a lot of ambivalence in the puranas. While on the one hand she is supposed to be the daughter of Brahma, on the other hand she is also presented as one of the wives of Brahma. As a dalit, what makes such contradictions all the more sickening is the fact that dalit women have been vilified for generations as women of 'loose morals' and have been subjected to the sexual gratification of upper caste men occupying several positions of social or political authority. Furthermore, while such scriptural protestations of purity have become a part of dominant, mainstream culture, there has also continued a relentless process of sexual violence against dalit women, as evident from the increasing number of rapes recorded in the data of the National Crime Research Bureau. It is in acknowledgement of this particular crisis that she scoffingly states:

> "Dalit Girl Raped"
> is much too commonplace.
> Humiliation gnaws
> the sixteen year old.
> Gory scars on a wrecked body,
> serve as constant reminders
> of disgrace, helplessness.
>
> (Kandasamy 2006, 58)

What makes such blatant injustices all the more brutal is the fact that the offenders are often able to go scot-free as various arms of the administration collude to ensure their safety on account of their upper-caste status. As Kandasamy explains:

> ...the criminals have
> already mainstreamed—
> Their caste is a classic shield. (Ibid.)

The history of the recently concluded Vachathi case may be cited as one example of the obstacles dalits generally face in securing justice as the caste-identity of the perpetrators enabled them to manipulate the judicial and administrative system in various ways. One of the rape-victims of that atrocity later recalled:

> I was just 13 then when they dragged me by the hair, abused me in foul language and raped me on the bund of a lake...When I pleaded that I was a small girl studying eighth standard, the men in khaki responded saying 'Being a girl is enough.
>
> (Palaniappan, para 2-3)

This is precisely the kind of double-subordination that dalit women generally face and this is further amplified through the phenomenon of witch-hunting which operates on the basis of a nexus between casteism and patriarchy and ends up humiliating, assaulting or even killing dalit women identified as witches by upper-caste members of the society, especially those who are defiant and rebellious. As Kandasamy herself explains in an article:

> It is no surprise that almost all the 'witches' have been Dalit or Adivasi women. Nowhere else in Indian history can we see such an explicit tie-up between patriarchal oppression and casteist subjugation. Witch-hunting is a powerful tool in the hands of caste-Hindu men who want to persecute assertive Dalit and Adivasi women who might directly challenge caste hegemony, or indirectly subvert local power equations... . A Dalit woman, Badam Bai was beaten to death by four men at Bhunein village in Sultanpur in Kota district. Lajwanti Harijan of Kamolar village in the same district met with a similar fate. When a Dalit woman in Tarra village in Raipur district claimed rights to her dead husband's land, she was killed after being branded a witch by her brother-in-law. Memki Bai Bhajaat of Varlipahada village and Sakri Bai Meena of Sailana village of Udaipur district were branded witches because of property disputes... . An Adivasi woman panchayat president in Udaipur district in Rajasthan was declared a witch by caste-Hindu villagers who wanted to settle political scores.
>
> (Kandasamy 2008a, para 5)

This is precisely why Kandasamy herself assumes the role of the witch in order to launch a scathing attack both against the individuals who perpetrate these crimes and the system that allows them to do so with impunity:

> I fancy myself being a witch.
> Broomstick borne and black as pitch.
> Thin, stark-naked and with fire for eyes.
> Killing men whom I despise...
> Haunting oppressors to shave their heads.
> Cutting all their holy threads.
> Experiencing joy as they bleed.
> Dance, rejoice my black black deed.
>
> (Kandasamy 2006, 49)

These wrathful remarks are poetic cannonades against casteism which ends up claiming the lives of hundreds of dalit women who are not even supposed to love members of other castes:

> . . . Our passionate love,
> Once transcended caste.
> Let it now
> Transcend mortality. . .
> Fear not beloved,
> In Love—
> Life is not compulsory.
>
> (Kandasamy 2006, 51)

Such statements allude to the continuing orthodox reaction against inter-caste marriages which even lead to death of the lovers, as evident from the recent spate of 'khap killings' across a large area of northern India where casteist prejudices still remain entrenched. These silenced individuals represent what Ranajit Guha calls the "small voice of history" (Guha 1-12) which is exactly what Kandsamy tries to recuperate as she excavates the violent ruptures of both our historical past and our everyday present:

> poured poison and pesticide through the ears-nose-mouth/
> or hanged them in public/because a man and a woman
> dared to love
> and you wanted/ to teach/ other boys and other girls/ the
> lessons of/ how to/ whom to/ when to/ where to/ continue
> their caste lines.
>
> (Kandasamy 2006, 60)

It is precisely this matrix of pervasive subjugation that leads to her anguished cries and interrogations such as "India, what is the caste of sperm?/ India, what is the cost of life?" (Kandasamy 2006, 62). Such interrogations pierce through the heart of the narrative of the nation and highlight a foundational crisis in imagining the nation – a nation that finds its most hegemonic icon in the image of Mahatma Gandhi. Gandhi did consciously attempt to resolve the problem of caste and at the same time he also did not wish to abolish the caste system as a whole which is exactly what irked Ambedkar the most. And despite using Gandhi's name, image and ideas to legitimize itself, the nation-state continues to unleash violence of one kind or another against the new subalterns, including casteist violence, implemented on the basis of upper-caste nexus across social institutions, administrative machinery and the political establishment. It is in acknowledgment of this hypocrisy and farce that Kandasamy explosively exclaims "Bapu, bapu, you big fraud, we hate you", and adds:

> That trash is long overdue.
> You need a thorough review.
> Your tax-free salt stimulated our wounds
> We gonna sue you, the Congress shoe…
>
> You knew, you bloody well knew,
> Caste won't go, they wouldn't let it go.
> It haunts us now, the way you do
> with a spooky stick, a eerie laugh or two.
>
> (Kandasamy 2006, 54-55)

However shocking such statements may seem, they are quite natural from an ardent, self-confessed follower of Ambedkar as Ambedkar himself had consistently castigated both Congress and Gandhi through such texts as *What Congress and Gandhi have done to The Untouchables,* where he went on to declare

> The social ideal of Gandhism is either caste or *Varna.* Though it may be difficult to say which, there can be no doubt that the social ideal of Gandhism is not democracy. For whether one takes for comparison caste or *Varna* both are fundamentally opposed to democracy. It would have been something if the defence of caste system which Gandhism offers was strong and honest. But his defence of the caste system is the most insensible piece of rhetoric one can think of. Examine Mr. Gandhi's arguments in support of caste and it will be found that every one of them is specious if not puerile.
>
> (Ambedkar, para 25)

Kandasamy's critique is only a poetic version of this long-standing critique of both Gandhi and the kind of Gandhi-centric nationalist narrative that has acquired dominance in post-independence India where the prevalent brahminical discourse still holds sway, as already illustrated by the various examples. And herein lies the relevance of Kandasamy's poetry as she assumes the role of a 'consciously political' poet, who is aware of her 'historical responsibility'. As Adrienne Rich explains:

> Historical responsibility has, after all, to do with action – where we place the weight of our existence on the line, cast our lot with others, move from an individual consciousness to a collective one.
>
> (Rich 145)

It is in acknowledgment of this historical responsibility that Kandasamy declares, in an undated interview for Orupaper.com:

> The annihilation of caste is a historic necessity, and at the same time, it is a historic inevitability as well. So, I am sure that it is a

> dream that I share with thousands of others. I think that such a change can come about only through a social revolution…And I think it is in the hands of writers to make people think about it. Writers have the power of the written word, and they can plead with people to unite for change.
>
> (Kandasamy 3-4)

Kandasamy has cast her lot decisively with dalits and she places the whole weight of her individual and collective existence as a dalit on her poetry. As the self-confessed 'Ms. Militancy' she authors a poetic discourse that not only castigates the prevalent modes of subjugation but also resolutely strives towards futures that are yet to be born:

> We will learn/ how to fight/ with the substantial
> spontaneity/ with which we first learnt/ how to love.
> So/ now/ upon a future time/
> there will be a revolution.
>
> (Kandasamy 2006, 61)

Works Cited

Ambedkar. B.R. *What Congress and Gandhi have done to the Untouchables. <http://www.ambedkar.org/ambcd/41L.What%20Congress%20and%20Gandhi%20CHAPTER%20XI.htm>*, accessed on 20 October, 2011.

Guha, Ranajit. "The Small Voice of History". *Subaltern Studies IX: Writings on South Asian History and Society*. Eds. Shahid Amin and Dipesh Chakrabarty. New Delhi: Oxford UP, 1996. 1-12.

Illaih, Kancha. "Productive Labour, Consciousness and History: The Dalitbahujan Alternative". *Subaltern Studies IX: Writings on South Asian History and Society*. Eds. Shahid Amin and Dipesh Chakrabarty. New Delhi: Oxford UP, 1996. pp.165-200.

Kandasamy, Meena. *Touch*. Mumbai: Peacock, 2006.

_______. "Dangerous Dalit Women and Witch-Hunters". April 14, 2008. *<http://ultraviolet.in/2008/04/14/dangerous-dalit-women-and-witch-hunters/>* Accessed on 28/10/2011.

_______. Interview with Oru Paper. *<http://www.meenakandasamy.com/mk/Press_files/interview%20to%20orupaper.pdf>*. Accessed on 28/10/2011.

_______. *Ms Militancy*. New Delhi: Navayana, 2010.

Palaniappan, V.S. "A long agonising wait for justice ends". *The Hindu*, 30 September 2011. *<http://www.thehindu.com/todays-paper/tp-national/tp-tamilnadu/article2499078.ece>*. Accessed on 28 October, 2011.

Rao, Kathi Padma. "*History of Karamchedu and what actually happened?*" Thursday, 21 July 2011 15:23. *<http://roundtableindia.co.in/index.php?option=com_content&view=article&id=3450:history-of-karamchedu-and-what-actually-happened-&catid=118:thought&Itemid=131>*. Accessed on 29 August 2011.

Rich, Adrienne. *Blood Bread and Poetry: Selected Prose 1979-1985*. New York: W.W. Norton and Company, 1986.

23

Emergence of Dalit Literature and Gujarati Dalit Novels

Harish Mangalam

The movement of dalit literature can be divided into four phases. Reformative activities carried outby establishing 'Brahmo Samaj' in 1828. The iconoclastic thoughts i.e. equal respect to all religions, apungent protest against *satipratha* (chastity custom), *Balvivah* (child marriage), and an encouragement of inter-caste marriage. In 1867, Raja Rammohan Roy established 'Prathana Samaj' with the high rated motto of world brotherhood under an oath of slogan "Service to the dalits is service to God." Thereafter, Atmaram Dadobha Tarkhadker and Bhasker Dadoba Tarkadker, started the school for the untouchables. In 1875, Swami Dayanand Saraswati established 'Arya Samaj' and voiced against untouchability. Gopal Ganesh Agarker was a staunch supporter of freedom and social equality. He was also against untouchability prevailing in the society. Swami Vivekananda strongly believed in equal rights and he had full credence in socialism. He was of the firm opinion that, "untouchables are in sheer need of education rather than brahmins. If, where there is requirement of one lecturer for teaching brahmins, then there is requirement of ten lecturers for teaching untouchable."

Mahatma Jotiba Phule was rebellious reformist. In 1848, he started the school for girls. He got trained his wife Savitribai Phule and made her a teacher and joined in social work. In 1852, he started the school exclusively for untouchable girls. He kept his cistern open for making available the potable water to the untouchables.

In 1920, Dr. Babasaheb Ambedkar started *Muknayak* magazine with a view to found platform for the dalit cause. Then he established *Akhil Bahishkrit Hitkarini Sabha'. 'Chavdar lake Satyagrah of Mahad* (*a real struggle for Truth*), he set *Manusmruti* on fire in Mahad, 'Entry in Kalaram Temple of Nasik in 1930,' Pune Pact in 1932,' 'Formation of Labour Party in 1936' and he declared conversion of religion in 1935 which was followed by in Mahar Conference in 1936 where Ambedkar declared:

> Religion is for man, man is not for religion
> If you want to gain self-respect, change your religion
> If you want to create a co-operative society, change your religion
> If you want power, change your religion
> If you want equality, change your religion
> If you want independence, change your religion
> If you want to make the world in you live happy change your religion

So, in 1956 he took Diksha in Nagpur. The conversion movement gave new changed identity, as Pro. Gangadhar Pantawane stated, "*Bhimrao has placed us in the lap of a life giving religion and so has awakened psycholigical independence. This is the religion of Gautam, who with love won the world, and the spine of this religion is humanity.*" In this regard, Namdev Dhasal said, "*Conversion to Buddhism, freed the scheduled castes from mental and psychological enslavement. Religion has an attraction for the common man and it was not easy to change his attitude towards it. The Buddhists have liberated themselves from old ideas of Karma and destiny and from worship of Hindu Gods. To some extent this facilitated their adopting rational attitudes to their conditions in society, the chance of their actively striving to change their conditions for better.*" (Pradeep K. Sharma, *Dalit Politics and Literature*, P. 68).

Thus, B.R. Ambedkar, is the great champion in the Dalit history. He awakened self-respect in the whole Dalit Society. He made the poor-naked people rebellious against inhuman treatment, insult, agony, attrocity, all kinds of their exploitation and any kind of injustice caused to them. By organising so many meetings, conferences, assemblies, gatherings, satyagrahs he fastened his battle for the self-consciousness and existence of dalits. He continued the constant struggle by his social journalism,his speeches and writings, his life and work, his *Dhamma* (not *Dharma*) and law-policy, his struggle for the social justice to the people of our nation during the post-independence period. At this juncture, the dalit literature emerged.

Namdev Dhasal and Raja Dhale established an organisation *'Dalit Panther'*. The Dalit Panther Movement indirectly inspired the dalit youth in neighbour state Gujarat. At that time, Gujarati dalit magazines, i.e., *Aartanad* (1972), *Dalitbandhu* (1973), were published. *Panther* (1975) and *Aakrosh* (14-4-1978) were brought out in which poetry of dalit poets were published. One irregular magazine, *KaloSuraj* by Dalpat Chauhan was initiated in 1979. Before publication of these magazines, some dalit poets had written plaintive poems at the time of sudden death of Dr. B.R. Ambedkar. But literary point of view, poetry was of the primary level and recognisition to this poetry was yet to be awaited. For the social awareness, dalit poets, writers, activists, journalists, intellectuals played active role. The dalit poets and writers issued pamphlets and published dalit literature to protest dalits rights. Thus, dalit literature emerged abundantly and a boost to it. And since the last 15 years we have been publishing *Hayati* magazine and run *Gujarati Dalit Sahitya Academy* for various dalit literary activities. Till today, we have published near about 60 books of Gujarati dalit literature in Hindi, Gujarati and English Languages.

In Gujarat, 1981 and 1985 were the cursed years. During this period, under the guise of anti-reservation stirs, a civil war was raged and cruel, merciless attacks were started against dalits. This opened the closed eyes of the dalit whole society and then they initiated united protest and for their constitutional rights they all came under one umbrella.

In 1987, a collection of Gujarati dalit short stories *Gujarati Dalit Varta* edited by Harish Mangalam with Mohan Parmar was published which collection proved to be the best collection of dalit short story and which received eulogy from the all corners of the Gujarati literature. If someone goes through this collection, he will be enthralled by the realistic delineation and variety of social subjects. This collection of Gujarati dalit short stories includes 15 dalit stories. They have got vide publicity accoss the milieu of Gujarati literature and created a halo which scourged many non-dalit writers. The said collection was selected and included in the syllabus of the Gujarat University, Mumbai University and Hemchandracharya University of North Gujarat and at present again in Gujarat University it has been selected in the curriculum. During this period one may demarcate the line of dalit literary movement stimulation and the wings have now been spread out in their trajectory with a high flight in the boundless sky of literature. At present more than 100 writers are very active for animating all the forms and genres of literature, i.e., poetry, novel, novella, short story, drama, essay, sketch, et al.

Today I would like to assess and focus on some of the Gujarati dalit novels of the authors those who are writing with full commitment, because there is time constraint. In Gujarat, some non-dalit writers have also generated novels depicting the miserable condition of untouchables in the fourfold social structure of our society. The non-dalit writers have not self-experiences of the agony of untouchables and they have cultivated on the basis of their self-imagination.They are not also directly the sufferers of the discrimintion prevails in the Hindu society. Among all these novels are - *Kalpvruksha* (Divine Tree), by Ishwar Petalikar, *Varal* (Vapour) by Ramchandra Patel, *Mashari* by

Kishorsinh Solanki, *Pralambpanth*-Long-way by Pinakin Dave, *Aansubhino Ujas* (Lightofwetted Tears) by Dileep Ranpura, *Ichhavar* (Desired Thing) by Raghuveer Chaudhary, *Kalo Angrej* (Black Britisher) by Chinu Modi, *Andharu* (Darkness) by Manilal Patel, *Kotarni Dhar Par* (On the edge of ravine) by Kanji Patel, *Prayc.'it* (Repentance) by Sopan, *Samudi* by Yogesh Joshi, *Ganthchhutyanivela* (A moment of releasing of a not) by Varsha Adalja, *Chhoot-Achhoot* (Touchable-Untouchable) by Sarang Barot et cetara. The dalit novels written by the dalit authors are - *Aangaliyat* (stepchild), 1986, by Joseph Mecwan, won the Central Academy Award, *Mari Parnetar* (My wife) 1988, *Aa-janma* (Severe test of Laxman) 1997, *Amar Chandlo* (Immortal mark of red colour on the forehead) 2002, *Dariya* (Sea) 2002, are also written by Joseph Mecwan, *Tirad* (Crack), *Chowki* and *Aganzal* (Flame) by Harish Mangalam written in the year of 1989 but published in the year of 1992. *Aganzal* was published in 2007, *Malak* (Region) 1991, *Gidh* (Vulture) 1999 and *Bhalbhankhalu* (Dawn) 2004 by Dalpat Chauhan, *Neliyu* (narrowpath) 1992, *Priyatama* (Lover) 1995, *Daya Pashani Wadi* (Field of Daya Pasha) by Mohan Parmar, *Shul* (Thorn) 1995, *Moolane Dhul* (Root and Dust) by B. Kesharshivam, *Astitva* (Existence) 2000, by Ganesh Acharya, *Shosh* (Thirst) 2003, 'Savitri' 2008 by Daksha Damodara, *Kidiae Khankharo Khadho* (The Ant roared like a lion) 2005, *GebiTimbo* (The mysterious Hillock) 2006, by Kantilal Parmar, *Diwalina Diwaso* (Days of Diwali) 2004 by Pragjibhai Bhambhi, and *Sangharsh* (struggle) by Harishkumar T. Solanki etc.

Joseph Mecwan's *Aangaliyat* (*stepchild*) is the first Gujarati novel. The author has depicted vitality of awakening of the dalits during the period of pre-independent and post-independent Gujarat. This novel has created maelstorms in the literature milieu. "Not only an uncommon novel is emerged in the fiction of Gujarati literature-flow, but a broad minded sympathetic and sensible man wandering here and there who has made our fate to see him amongst the speakers of our language but has brought pacification to our hearts." Very well-known personality and great writer *Umashankar Joshi* who was also Vice-Chancellor of Shantiniketan has uttered these words and welcomed the novel with his ardent feeling. *Dr. Dhaval Mehta* a very reputed educationist and thinker has established this novel as a *Forth-wave* of Gujarati literature. It is the first novel of the Gujarati literature delineating the struggle of dalit community against so-called 'upper-castes' inhumanity treatment to the dalits. The dalit characters are agitating for their identity and existence.

In Dalpat Chauhan's novel *Malak* (Region), instead of any particular protagonist, the whole dalit society is in the centre of the realistic story of the novel. The story is completely based on the self-experiences of Dalit ghetto. There is not at all imagination but only and only realisation of real life being lived by dalits. The author has interwoven socio-cultural conducts and created an atmosphere of naked truth of rural India. In the novel he has used colloquial language of the north Gujarat region.

In the centre of the story is intercaste relationship between a dalit young man Bhago and youthful Santok, a daughter of Hatha Chaudhari. Here, Santok is antagonist and belongs to the so-called upper caste and Bhago is the protagonist who belongs to the dalit community. Santok invites dalit Bhago and uses many tactics to tie sexual relationship with Bhago, and for fulfilment of her lust she chases Bhago. She becomes so enarounded with Bhago that she desires to have him at any cost and she spreads her strong arms. Bhago, knowing and anticipating the terrible result of such a type of relationship, is frightened. At last, Santok has sexual enjoyment with Bhago and as a result becomes the mother of a child. From the figure of the child's face, the shrewd villagers are easily able to compare the face of the child with the face of Bhago. Thus, the seeds of enmity are sowed and the so-called sa*Varna* people's mind starts seething. The whole the village is gripped in the flames of revenged fire. The situation for the dalits to survive and exist in the village is very crucial and next to impossible. Some of them starts to agitate and over come the situation but before the majority of the uppercastes they are helpless and disappointed with the turbulent situation. At last, all the dalits of the ghetto decide to emigrate at midnight's darkness to save their lives. It is the first time that the author has painted and created realistic characters and an adolescence Santok belongs to the uppercaste and chases a dalit young man like Bhago in a sexual relationship. What is likely to happen is not beyond one's imagination. It happens in rural India. This is very common and happens frequently and casually with no surprise. We are mute spectators. We know that silence is the powerful enemy of social justice and we should give dismissal to silent acceptance and dumb approval, but we being intelligent persons always remain silent sound and such evils remain unerased!

My novels are, *Tirad* (crack), *Chowki*, and *Aganzal* (Flame). One cannot justify one's novels because they are one's progenies and in the whole creation, a mother has always an exceptional affection to her children. But I must mention that many Gujarati critics have praised *Tirad Chowki* and *Aganzal* and are compacted novels. In both the novels, socio-cultural manners of uppercastes and dalits have been woven in a colloquial language using colloquial idioms, proverbs, words, and subtly portrayed the various characters realistically. I have narrated the patriarchal tradition and hegemony of the uppercastes which has oppressed, suppressed and exploited dalit women from their womb to the tomb in our society. Over and above I have described the real picture of the life of the dalits in rural India. In where, most of all the dalits are landless labourers who remain fully dependent upon landlords. They have to labour very hard in their fields to make both ends meet. They have not only to suffer from rigorous extreme till the end of their life, but they also have to suffer from the uppercastes, 'attrocity, inhuman treatment, discrimination and untouchability'.

In *Tirad* the main character is a dalit woman named Joiti. Around this character, all these points have been drawn. Being a dalit woman she has to suffer more than other women because over and above patriarchal suppression, she is being oppressed as an untouchable.

In *Chowki*, Akhusinh of the uppercaste is a chowkidar of dalit mohalla. Instead of protecting the mohalla and the dalits, he adopts various bad tactics during his round at midnight and snatches some ornaments from the bodies of dalit women sleeping outside their houses in hot summer days. As a contract Protector chowkidar he becomes the main burglar though he misguides the dalits and raises doubts in their mind regarding the thief. Sometime he irritates and plays mischiefs with the bodies of the dalit women when they are in sound sleep. I have snapped such moments which are very pleasant and jocular. Akhusinh is a lecherous person. To pacify his lasciviousness, one day he elopes with Shanta, a daughter of Patel, and whole society, is agitated. A terrible atmosphere is created. The caste-conflict started bubbling. The central theme of both the stories is caste-discrimination, exploitation of dalits by uppercaste people, implementation of untouchability, etc. While assessing both the novels a very well-known writer, Pushkar Chandavarkar has explicitly evaluated, "...with which incident the story of *Chowki* is initiated and with that incident of burglary it has ended." Thus, a complete circle is formed and in that circle how many long lines have been drawn! Out of them one line is of the best prose-writer, the second is of the best story-writer, the third is of the best revolutionary mind and the last of the naked truth. With my transparent knowledge and sharp study of dalit society. I have adorned these creations. I have also made a deep and thorough study to produce novels thematically.

My novel *Aganzal* (Flame) is an autobiographical novel. I have created this novel realistically and depicted my struggle completely based on self-experiences of my rural life. The central theme of the novel is based on the path of ideology of Dr. Babasaheb Ambedkar. Dr. M.B. Gaijan, a social thinker and critic has categorically assessed in his article 'Gujarati Dalit Novel: A Thematic study to build 21st Century India' that "The novel presents the picture how the protagonist, Veeru, has emerged from all the obstacles.... Thus he struggles hard to come out from the adverse situation. He continues his study in the light of deevo (*self hand-made lantern of inkpot*). He knows that with the help of educatioon, darkness disappears. So he follows that path. During his highschool days, he starts library to awaken them for their human rights...." The writer has presented the worst conditions of dalits during the anti-reservation stirs, an unpleasant dark chapter in the history of Gujarat. During these stirs, dalits were mercilessly treated by the uppercastes. Veeru took active part to protest cruelty of uppercastes' fury but all dalits 'united-protest stops the uppercastes' cruelty. He also tried a lot to provide electricity to the dalit ghetto under Jyotigram scheme of the Government. The uppercastes do not want that there should be an electric pole near the dalit's ghetto. At last they cannot prevent the facility of the electricity. The truth is accepted, "Get education, get more and more knowledge and leave villages and settle in the cities, our progress is posible there..." (p. 178). Thus the novel presents how dalits struggles a lot and Veenu emerges as the model person for the dalit community.

Daxa Damodara's novels *Shosh* (Thirst) and *Savitri* are outstanding novels in Gujarati literature. *Dr. M.B. Gaijan* has clearly stated that, "Daxa Damodara's novel *Shosh* set new identity in mainstream Gujarati literature as well as in Gujarati dalit literature, because of aesthetic values of the novel. The writer was awarded the *Sister Nivedita First Prize* by *Gujarati Shitya Parishad* in 2003. The novel is a multi-thematic work. One important appealing aspect of the novel is human excellence of the Dalits." (Article on Gujarati Dalit Novel: A Thematic Study to build 21st Century India). *Savitri* is a biographical novel on *Savitribai Phule*, wife of Jotiba Phule. She devoted her whole life to mankind and struggled for the rights of the dalits. Dr. Gaijan categorically remarked that, "Daxa Damodara's recently published Savitri is a landmark novel... The writer has goal and vision to bring unnoticed, a dedicated couple from the downtrodden community before the world community." (ibid.).

Two novels by B. Kesharshivam are *Shul* (Pain, Thorn) and *Mooland Dhul* (RootandDust). Both the novels narrate the real picture of rural dalits suffering from the caste system. These novels depict the very strange experiences that are highlighted and a reader comes to know the worst situation of the dalits during the time of stirs of anti-reservation, when they went directly attacked. Another novel by Anil Vaghela is *Gnatyjantu* (An insect of caste) is also a very important dalit novel.

Due to time constraint, this is merely an overview of some of the important dalit novels written by the committed dalit authors. So, I would like to conclude with the famous quotation of Victor Hugo, "No power on earth can stop an idea whose time has come !" And this is the time of dalit literary age, i.e. Dalit Sahitya Yug.

24

Interview with Harish Mangalam

Jaydeep Sarangi

Harish Mangalam is a leading Gujrati writer and the Editor of 'Hayati'.

Dr. Jaydeep Sarangi is a bilingual poet-academic, editor, administrator, and translator who teaches English at Jogesh Chandra Chaudhuri College (Calcutta University). He is an expert on dalit studies. He is the Vice-President, GIEWEC.

J.S. Hello ! Would you please tell us about your childhood?

H.M. I was born in an obscure village Falu in Mehasana district in North Gujarat on February 15, 1952. I have had experiences of poverty and agonies of the dalits and social discrimination in my childhood and young age. Those were the days of starvation. The whole ghetto was suffering from have-nots. As if the ghetto was like a boiling cauldron and in it my kindred, my brethren were blazing. The witch of untouchability was behind the dalits which still prevails just as it was in the fourfold stratified society, and there is not at all any noticeable change in rotten mentality.

J.S. Your education?

H.M. After striving very hard, primary school days passed away very pathetically. My father named Jethabhai was weaving a day and night on a handloom and my mother named Divaben was assisting my father in making skein and another supplementary work pertaining to yarn. The income was not sufficient to make both ends meet for such a big family in which there were thirteen members! There was no money available even to purchase notebooks and school uniform. I was compelled to go to the fields to do agrarian work on Sundays, holidays and durings vacations. During summer vacations, I used to go to far-flung areas to collect gum of scattered babul trees and in ravine land of Sabarmati river. I was storing this collected gum in an earthen vessel (in Gujarati called *Matlu*) and at the end of the season, gum was sold to the shopkeeper. I have had experiences of labour work carrying heavy bags containing tobacco, construction work material, weeding in fields, mango plucking, production of cement-pipe et.al. Thus, I was able to bear the expenditure of notebooks and uniform (particularly cloth hand-woven by my father). I passed my Old SSC in first class in the year 1971 and on the basis of merit, I got a job in central government office. At that juncture, my illiterate parents' hearts were throbbing joyously which is indescribable. Thereafter, I completed my B.A., LL.B. and English Shorthand.

J.S. Who are the writers inspired you in your formative days?

H.M. I had started to write at the early stage of thirteen years when I was a schoolgoing boy. One of my friends, Manilal N. Patel 'Jagatmitra', who is a very good writer and one of the rarest of human beings one may ever meet, guided me in the whole creative process of poems and criticized my poems. At that time, I had written nearly two hundred poems in meter, and really it proved to be a good exercise which gave me newer insights into poetics. I was very much involved during my schooldays in the multifarious activities, such as drawing, drama, editing of school magazine Sadhna, participation in sports (particularly volleyball and kho kho which were my favourite), and was coordinator of Falu centre of *Kalasadhna* (main centre in Nutan School of Visnagar in Mehasana district.) We had then started a small library for the dalit students. My close friends Shiva Devabhai

Chamar and Raman Laljibhai Pandya and I converted to Sikhism in 1967-68 carrying the very deep impression that nobody dared even to touch or stare at the aggressive and furious Sikh community. Thereafter in 1971, I came to Ahmedabad City for further study at the collegiate level. In Ahmedabad, many intellectuals were shocked due to two caste-wars under the guise of anti-reservation stir in 1981 and 1985, and that was the time when I started writing for the downtrodden community with a full sense of commitment. A renowned poet Mandhukant Kalpit, started a Literary Study Forum. We also started to publish *Akshay* (imperishable) a cyclostyled magazine. We founded Dalit Sahitya Sangharsh Sangh and Dalit Sahitya Sangh etc. During my formative days, I used to read Gujarati writers, i.e., Ramanlal V. Desai, Kanaiyalal Munshi, Dhumketu, R.V. Pathak, Zaverchand Meghani, Pannalal Patel, Umashankar Joshi, Dr. Suresh Joshi etc. But I have faith in perspiration rather than inspiration.

J.S. Do you consider dalit writing as the corpus of pain and suffering?

H.M. I consider dalit writing as the corpus of pain and suffering but not only of pain and suffering because it is the main weapon to awake the people against injustice. Dalit literature is fully based on the ideology of the great social revolutionary reformist, Dr. Babasaheb Ambedkar. Dalit literature depicts and speaks about the values of humanity, liberty and brotherhood, which are the basic virtues for the unity of the people and a bulwark on which a nation-state can stand. A nation can neither be built on a shaky foundation nor be built without the above-mentioned three basic and inevitable virtues of the people. Dalit literature promotes all the three ideals. Thus, dalit literature is positive and constructive about the entire process of nation-building.

J.S. Who are the leading dalit writers in your state?

H.M. The late Mr. Joseph Macwan, Praveen Gadhvi, Dalpat Chauhan, B. Kesharshivam. Dr. Pathik Parmar, Madhukant Kalpit, Arvind Vegda, Sahil Parmar, Kantilal Katil, Daksha

Damodara, Dr. Mansukh Gaijan, Annil Vaghela, Dr. Raman Madhav, Chandraben Shrimali, Priyanka Kalpit, Kantilal Parmar, Dinu Bhadresariya, Satyam Barot, Dr. Kanti Malsatar, Dr. Ratilal Rohit, Dr. Bharat Mehta, Raghavji Madhad, Dharmabhai Shrimali, Pro. K.M. Makwana,Bharat Vala, Dr. Girish Rohit, Dr. Maheshchandra Pandya, B.N. Vankar, Dr. K.K. Vaishnav, Mavji Maheshwari, Samant Solanki, Neerav Patel, Raju Solanki, Chandu Maheriya, Sanjay Chauhan and Amrit Makwana are the leading dalit writers in Gujarat state. Approximately, 100 poets, 20 novelists, 15 short story writers are active in cultivating Gujarati dalit literature.

J.S. Why did you start writing?

H.M. During my school days, I met Manilal N. Patel 'Jagatmitra' and Hasmukh Kantilal Raval 'Nayan' (my classmate) and we started to write 'lalit' poems in meter and short stories. Thereafter, there were two casteist attacks on dalits in the name of anti-reservation stirs, in the years of 1981 and 1985. At that time I was terribly forced and compellted to write dalit literature only. Being born in the dalit community, I had a frightening past filled with atrocities, untouchability, discrimination of high-low caste system, varnashrama (fourfold stratification of caste-system), exploitation of labourers by the farmers, injustice, inhuman treatment, dependency, a ban on education etc. All these forces caused a measure shifting and I made up my mind to write literature for the upliftment and awakening of the downtrodden people whose existence has since ages been denied by the so-called *Manuvadis* (people who believe in *varnashrama* created by Manu in *Manusmriti).*At present I am writing only dalit literature committedly adhering to the ideology of Mahatma Jyotiba Phule and Dr. Babasaheb Ambedkar.

J.S. Would you please mention your works?

H.M. Prakamp (poetry, 1991), *Talap* (short story collection, 2001), translated into Hindi as *Talab* by Dr. Fulchand Gupta and into English as *Light of Darkness* by Dr. Rupalee Burke, 2012, *Tirad* (novel, 1992, 2nd edition, 2001), translated into Hindi as *Darar* by Dr. Hasmukh Barot, *Chowky* (novel, 1992, 2nd edition 1995, 3rd edition, 2012), translated into Hindi as *Chowky* by Surendra Doshi and Harshad Rana, *Aganzaal* (autobiographical novel, part-I, 2008), *Samvitti* (criticism, 1987), *Vidit* (criti. 1989), *Panachh* (*kavyaswad* 2001), *Ekvachan* (criti. 2006), *Pratidhwani* (criti. 2006) translated into Hindi as *Pratidhwani* by Dr. Girish Rohit,

Compilations: *Bungiyo Vage*, 1984, *Gujarati Dalit Varta* (1st edition 1987 and 2nd edition 2010, *Gujarati Pratinidhi Dalit Varta*, 1996, *Ghar* (short stories, 1996), *Dundhubhi* (with others), *Gujarati Dalit Sahitya Swadhyay ane Samiksha* (with other), *Dalit Geetane Gazal*, 2006 with Dr. Pathik Parmar, *Dalitvani* (poems of Praveen Gadhvi), *Pristine Land*, 2009 with Dr. M.B. Gaijan, *Gujarati Dalit Katha*, 2006 in Marathi translated by Aruna Joshi, *Gujarati Dalit Ekankiyan* translated in to Hindi by Ramgopalsinh Jadaun, 2010, *Vartalok* (short stories compiled with others, 2010, *Dalit Sahityanu Saundarya Shastra* translated into Gujarati from Hindi with Dr. Kanti Malsatar, 2010, *Samarth Sarjak Joseph Macwan* (with others, 2010), and other five books in Hindi translated from Gujarati are under pipeline and shortly to be published by Yash Publisher Delhi.

J.S. Your autobiography?

H.M. I have written an autobiographical novel titled *Aganzaal* (eternal flame) which is in the real sense my *autobiography*. A renowned critic, Dr. Silas Pateliya, has written four articles from the point of various angles of dalit literature and highly rated it in his criticism. This is *part-I,* and *part-II* is yet to be published. Veeru is the protagonist and throughout his life, since childhood till today, fights against injustice and existing social pollution to uplift and awaken the downtrodden people. This virtue to fight against injustice has percolated from his father named Hirabha.

Hirabha is also very aggressive against sub-human treatment by an antagonistic classes. Seeds of revolutionary actions are sown in *Aganzaal.*

J.S. Are you familiar with Bengali dalit writers?

H.M. My dear Jaydeepji, upon organization of National Seminar on 'Writing as Resistance: Bengali and Other Dalit Writings in english' on 29 & 30 November 2011, I came to know the names of Bengali dalit writers. Before that I had heard but was not so familiar with Bengali dalit writers. I came to know Kiran Talukdar, Badal Hembram, Manohar Mauli Biswas, Jatin Bala, Kalyani Thakur, Manju Bala, Manoranjan Byapari, Namita Das, Nakul Mallik and so many other dalit writers for which credit goes to you and to the department of English of Jogesh Chandra Chaudhari College, Kolkata for bridging the gap and bringing Bengali dalit literature onto the national platform. It was your foresightedness to organize such a well-planned national seminar with enriched paper presentation on various subjects.

J.S. You run a popular journal, *Hayati,* Why did you start it?

H.M. *Hayati* is a mouthorgan of our organization Gujarati Dalit Sahitya Academy, Ahmedabad. Jaydeepji, dalit literature is not a cosmetic commodity, written only for the sake of entertainment. Dalit literature in the real sense is the weapon of social movement. It is a movement to awaken the society against atrocities, injustices, agonies and inhuman treatment. It has its own objects and subjects. It is being created purposefully. Dalit movement cannot be related to the mainstream literature. To make dalit literature widespread to lead the downtrodden people on the path of Mahatma Jyotiba Phule and Dr. Babasaheb Ambedkar, one must have one's own weapon. One must not be dependent on others, therefore, we have started a journal *Hayati* to achieve the goal without any unnecessary obstacles.

J.S. Are you satisfied with the critics of the dalit corpus?

H.M. Dalit writers should never bother about criticism of dalit corpus. They should keep in mind the ideology of Mahatma Jyotiba Phule and Dr. Babasaheb Amberkar, and continued on write with commitment and make available the dalit literature in abundance. One day the critics will come on the right path and proceed in the appropriate direction.

J.S. Do you attend seminars on dalit writings?

H.M. Yes, Jaydeepji. I very much like to attend seminars on dalit writings. I attended the national seminar on 29 & 30 November 2011, well organized by you and the department of English of Jogesh Chandra Chaudhary College, Kolkatta, and presented the paper on "Emergence of Gujarati Dalit Literature and Gujarati Dalit Novels", and convened one session too. Over and above, I focused on valedictory session. Before that my team members and I had attended International Seminar in Chennai (organized by Writers club internationalIndia Intercontinental Cultural Association, Chandigarh, India). We recited dalit poetry and presented the papers on dalit literature too. There after, on 16, 17 & 18 February, 2012, I attended National Seminar, organized by the department of English, Delhi University and presented the paper on Gujarati dalit literature titled "Evolutionary consciousness in Gujarati Dalit Literature". On 28 & 29 February 2012. I attended the National Conference organized by the department Gujarati, Mumbai University and presented the paper on "Bengali novels of 19th Century".

J.S. Dalit literature is militant in texture. Do you subscribe to this view?

H.M. Yes, I would like to justify the view stated by you, that dalit literature is militant in texture. Dalit literature is a weapon of the dalit movement. And a weapon should be pungent. Because, all around are untouchability, discrimination, inequality, atrocity, fourfold castesystem of high-low and inhuman treatment. The stench of ghettoization is all over the place. The fragrance of humanity is missing—it seems to be a hollow word, burdened with feelings of emptiness and absences. Incidents triggered by burning issues of existence and tormenting survival rend my heart and make me cry. I find it difficult to breathe, difficult to bear. In such dreadful circumstances, one should not carry a blunt weapon which has ultimately no meaning except foolishness. So, militancy in dalit movement is the first and foremost object.

J.S. Who are dalits?

H.M. They are the downtrodden, apart from castes and creeds inclusive of females and adivasis.

J.S. Can it be branded as marginal literature from the margin?

H.M. It can be branded as marginal literature too. There is no harm at all. Because, the contents of dalit literature is much more important rather than any type of brand name. I think, any word carrying the same meaning may be replaced but objects and subjects of the contents ought to be as per the ideology, and there should be no slip-up.

J.S. What is the main theme(s) in your writing?

H.M. The main themes in my writing: to strive to eliminate superstitions found abundantly in canonical literature, to rise up against bigots, pundits and inequality, inhuman treatment, to aim at the welfare of common man and a society which is casteless and classless; to voice the sufferings of the oppressed people.

J.S. Do you write for a select reader?

H.M. Jaydeepji, when I write, I write with great consciousness keeping in mind the ideology of Mahatma Jyotiba Phule and Dr. Babasaheb Ambedkar only and nothing else. I write for the common man.

J.S. What is the future of dalit literature in India?

H.M. All over India there is a trend of dalit literature. An ideology of the dalit literature has now gained stability with its pace of consistency. The dalit literature is inclusive of dalitism, feminism, Marxism, progression etc. Thus, larger areas have been covered leaving very small room for the 'dalit' literature. So, this is an era of dalit literature age because postmodernism terminology is an imported one. I have no faith in astronomy but logically based on my micro-observation, I can firmly assess the present situation and make the tatement that now onwards, in the whole world, two 'D's will survive: One *'D'* for *Dollar* and another '*D*' for *Dalit Literature.*

J.S. Is there a message in your works?

H.M. Yes, Jaydeepji, there always a message in my works because my works are not pieces of entertainment, but there there is no direct message. There is an indirect message of humanity, liberty, equality, rationality and to eradicate untouchability.

J.S. How do you find my edited book *Writing as Resistance: Litgerature of Emancipation* (Gnosis: New Delhi, 2011) which contains articles by many established writers and critics?

H.M. It is indeed a very valuable work for understanding dalit literature in a better way. In this book you have included scholars' well-studied papers from major parts of India. I especially appreciate your work because you have included three papers from Gujarati dalit writings by Dr. M.B. Gaijan. In Gujarat we have been working since the mid-70s. In Gandhi's Gujarat injustice and cruelty on Dalits are still going on. In this book, you have included dalit writers' interviews, Jai Prakash Kardam, Manohar Mouli Biswas and Kalyani Thakur. The interviews have a high significance, "Why they write this". I also like Prof. Bajarang Korde's paper "Dalit Literature in Marathi as a part of Indian Literature: A Brief Survey," G.A. Ghanashyam's paper "I Was

Ever a Fighter, So – One Fight More", Khusi Pattanayak's paper "Liberate me If you Can" and Premila Bhaskar's "The Supressed of the Oppressed". All the papers are scholarly prepared and are highly useful for understanding twenty-first century dalits' writing as a resistance against injustice and cruelty. The book presents the unpleasant reality of unaccepted Indians, dalits. Through their writings they try to get emancipation from their upper caste exploited world. I highly appreciate your book and congratulate you for this profound work.

J.S. Any immediate wish?

H.M. My immediate whish is to eradicate *varnashrama* (fourfold caste-system) and untouchability immediately.

Index